Jack Benny

AN INTIMATE BIOGRAPHY

Jack Benny

AN INTIMATE BIOGRAPHY

Irving A. Fein

Introduction by GEORGE BURNS

G. P. PUTNAM'S SONS
NEW YORK

SBN: 399–11640–0
Library of Congress Cataloging in Publication Data

Fein, Irving, 1911–
  Jack Benny: an intimate biography.

  Includes index.
  1. Benny, Jack, 1894–1974.
PN2287.B4325F4   791.4'092'4   [B]   75–30975

For my wife
Marion
who helped

ACKNOWLEDGMENTS

After spending twenty eight years in intimate association with Jack Benny, I thought he had told me every detail of his life and every anecdote he could remember. In addition, I sat in on literally thousands of press interviews and heard every possible question asked of him about his past, present, and future. I thought I had it all down pat. That is, until I spoke with many of his close friends and associates who provided an immeasurable contribution to this manuscript with dates, facts, and wonderful stories. Some of the people to whom I am indebted are Johnny Carson, Bob Hope, Danny Kaye, George Burns, Phil Silvers, John Green, Benny Rubin, Ralph Levy, Hugh Wedlock, Steve Allen, Milton Berle, Al Gordon, Hal Goldman, Buddy Arnold, Taft Schreiber, Mervyn Le Roy, Arthur Phillips, Joan Blumofe, Arthur Marx, Edgar Bergen, Candy Bergen, Norman Krasna, Ben Landis, Jack Carter, Buddy Hackett, Fred De Cordova, Harry Tugend, Dr. Charles Pincus, Phil Harris, Mel Blanc, Jesse Block, Seymour Berns, Isaac Stern, Eddie Villery, Dorothy Ohman, Helen Remley, Ned Miller, Barry Mirkin, Larry Adler, David Tebet, Billy Wilder, Hank Grant, Sam and Jo Ehre, Jerry Lavin, Rand Smith, Arthur Wilde . . . and so many others whose names will come to me after this book has gone to press. To them, my apologies and most sincere appreciation.

If you can talk with crowds and
        keep your virtue,
Or walk with Kings— nor lose the common touch. . . .

—RUDYARD KIPLING

Introduction

I'M George Burns, this is a book about Jack Benny, and it was written by Irving Fein. Now a few of you may have heard of me and Jack, but I'm sure that everybody knows who Irving Fein is. But for the handful of people who never heard of him, let me explain what an Irving Fein is.

He was Jack Benny's personal manager and producer for twenty-eight years. Jack often told me how valuable Irving was to his career, so about five months before he died, I went to Jack and said, "Jack, I know you're not working as much as you used to, and I'm sitting around waiting for vaudeville to come back, and since Irving has time on his hands and my vocal cords are getting rusty, would you mind if he represented me, too?" Jack said, "George, I'd be happy to share Irving with you; which part of him do you want?"

Now that I've explained the author of this book, let me recall a few fond memories of my close friendship with Jack Benny.

We knew each other for about fifty-five years, and he was the warmest, the most gentle, the nicest human being I ever met in my life. I really feel fortunate to have had him as a friend for that many years. Jack and I laughed together, we played together, we worked together, we ate together, and in the entire fifty-five years I never walked out on Jack when he played the violin, and he never walked out on me when I sang a song. Now that's really putting friendship to the test.

Even though Jack was one of the biggest stars in show business for most of his life, and rubbed elbows with presidents and royalty, it was the little things in life that were important to him. For example, a few years ago, he signed a contract for a couple of million dollars, and he had to go to downtown Los Angeles to sign it. I was at the Hillcrest Country Club

11

when he came back, and when we sat down to have lunch, Jack seemed very excited. I knew he had just signed this million-dollar contract, so I said to him, "Jack, I know how thrilled you must be."

He said, "Oh, I am. I just found out that when you drive up Wilshire Boulevard at exactly twenty-eight miles an hour, you miss every red light!"

I just sat there and looked at him. Then I said, "Jack, I hate to bring this up, but didn't you just sign a two-million-dollar contract?"

He said, "Oh, sure, if it wasn't for that, I wouldn't have driven up Wilshire Boulevard."

That was Jack Benny.

Another time at the club he stopped me and said, "George, I've just had the coldest glass of water I've ever had in my life!"

What do you say to a remark like that? I just looked at him and said, "Jack, I'm glad you told me, I'm going to ask the chef to please let me take some of that water home." Well, that line broke him up. He laughed; he hit the table; he kept laughing. So I went into the cardroom, played two rubbers of bridge, and when I came back, he was still laughing.

But I loved making Jack laugh. I remember once I had a little dinner party at Chasen's for about seven or eight people, and Jack was having dinner in the other room. He came over to say hello, and I said, "Sit down, Jack, and join the party. Would you like a little salt?"

Now I don't think that's the funniest line I ever said, and I'm sure nobody's going to steal it, but Jack became unglued. He laughed so hard I had to help him back to his table.

But that wasn't the end of it. Jack told everybody in town that I was one of the funniest men in show business, and then he'd quote that line. He'd say, "What do you think George Burns said to me at Chasen's! He said, 'Would you like a little salt?'" Then Jack would laugh and fall down, and people didn't know what he was talking about. And besides, everybody thought I was an idiot. I finally said to Jack, "Jack, when you tell that hilarious joke about the salt again, would you mind telling people that Milton Berle said it?"

Being so close to Jack I knew what tickled his funny bone, and I took advantage of it. One night at a party at Norman

Krasna's house there must have been about eighty people. During the evening Jack got up and went over to the mantel-piece and picked up a match and cigarette. Just as he was about to light it, I said, "Hold it, everybody, Jack Benny is now going to do his famous match bit." Everybody stopped and looked at him, and Jack didn't know what to do. So he lit the cigarette, and I said, "Oh, a new finish."

I didn't think it was possible, but that even topped the line about the salt.

I'm not the only one—practically everybody in show busi-ness made Jack Benny laugh. His laughter was so sincere and honest it made them feel good, too. The only reason Jack laughed more at me was that I knew him longer.

But once I made a horrible mistake. You couldn't plan to make Jack Benny laugh. It just had to happen. There was one night I invited Jack and Mary to our house and told them to wear their dinner clothes. When they came in, Gra-cie and I were in our dinner clothes, and I had a four-piece orchestra, a little dance floor, and had hired an extra butler. The four of us sat down and had a drink and some hors d'oeuvres. At eight thirty the butler came in and formally announced, "Dinner is being served."

Gracie and I both looked at Jack, expecting him to fall down. But he just looked at Mary, and Mary looked at him, and he looked at us . . . there was a lot of looking going on. Then in his slowest delivery Jack said, "Where . . . are . . . the . . . rest . . . of . . . the . . . guests?"

And in my funniest delivery I said, "This is it. After dinner you can dance with Mary, I'll dance with Gracie, then you can dance with Gracie, and I'll dance with Mary . . . we'll have a wonderful time because there's nobody here to bump into us."

I waited . . . nothing!

Jack just gave me one of his longest looks—I would say it lasted about a minute and a half—then he said, "George, you're out of your mind. But as long as we're dressed, let's all go to the Bistro and have dinner," which we silently did.

There you are . . . I spent $600 to try to make him laugh, and I didn't get a snicker, but "Would you like a little salt?" was a sensation.

Jack Benny was a beautiful man to the whole world, but to

me he was something special. It's hard for me to believe that he's gone, but the wonderful memories I have of Jack will be with me forever.

Sure, I'm going to stay in show business, and I know the show must go on. The show will go on, but it will never be the same without him.

—GEORGE BURNS

1

THE weatherman had predicted a 50 percent chance of rain, but the day dawned clear, cold and sunny. It was Sunday, December 29, 1974, and Jack Benny was to be laid to rest at the Hillside Memorial Cemetery in Culver City, California.

The funeral had been announced for noon, but the fans started to arrive at sunrise, and all morning they came to pay their last respects to a man who had brought laughter into their lives for fifty years. These were the people who had followed him loyally through all his years on radio and television. In the 1930's and 1940's they listened to him every Sunday night at 7 P.M. Eastern Standard Time, the half hour that NBC had deeded to him. On a warm Sunday evening in May one could walk through any residential area in the United States and listen to the entire Benny program as it filtered through the windows of every home.

Even though the Los Angeles Rams were playing the Minnesota Vikings in a televised championship match that very noontime, the people came by the hundreds. They came in old cars, motorcycles, bicycles, and buses.

By 10 A.M. that Sunday a thousand people were gathered on the green sloping lawns surrounding the chapel of the cemetery. Despite the size of the crowd, the mood was quiet, somber, and waiting.

A California highway patrol helicopter was flying overhead, and extra motorcycle officers were on hand to aid the traffic flow on the freeways which adjoined the cemetery. Special police had been assigned to the cemetery to handle any emergencies, but the fans were silent and polite in their sadness.

15

The small glass-walled chapel could seat only 375 people. In anticipation of a large crowd, 500 additional seats had been placed outside under a huge canvas awning, which had been erected in case of the predicted rain. Loudspeakers had been installed so that the service would be heard outdoors as well as inside. Unfortunately, with all the extra seating, there was still only enough space to accommodate the close friends, fellow workers, and celebrities.

Finally, through the crowd a walkway to the chapel was cleared, and the mourners who were fortunate enough to have seats entered. They came—Jack Lemmon, Walter Matthau, Cesar Romero, Henry Fonda, Raymond Massey, Irene Dunne, Goldie Hawn, James Stewart, Edgar and Candy Bergen, Andy Griffith, Rosalind Russell, Merle Oberon, Dinah Shore, Governor Ronald Reagan, Senator John Tunney, ex-Senator George Murphy. Fellow comedians who made Jack laugh came—Johnny Carson, Danny Thomas, Groucho Marx, Morey Amsterdam, Jack Carter, George Jessel.

There were the Sunday night regulars from the radio and TV gang—Phil Harris, Dennis Day, Don Wilson, Rochester, the Sportsmen Quartet, the voice of the Maxwell, Mel Blanc, the tout, Sheldon Leonard, the original tout, Benny Rubin, the hilarious telephone operator, Sandy Burns.

Benny Rubin was with his former wife, Mary O'Brian. They had married in March, 1927, just two months after their good freinds Jack Benny and Mary Livingstone had married. The four were inseparable, and when the Rubins had their first child in 1929, Jack and Mary were the godparents. Then, in 1934, the Rubins were divorced and hadn't seen each other in the forty years that passed. The day before the funeral Mary O'Brian telephoned Benny and said, "We were there at the beginning; let's be there together at the end."

One of the last mourners to arrive was Robert Stack. Jack used to remind Bob that they were the last two actors still living from the cast of Ernst Lubitsch's motion-picture classic *To Be or Not to Be*. And now Robert Stack was the sole survivor.

By eleven forty-five the crowd had swollen to an estimated 3,000 people; one show business veteran said, "Jack's got a

16

great house for his last performance." The family arrived in two cars. With Mary Benny rode her daughter, Joan, and Joan's four children; Jack's sister, Florence Fenchel, who had come from Chicago; Mary's sister, Babe, and her brother, Hilliard, who had been one of Jack's writers. In the first row of the chapel the ten pallbearers were seated: Frank Sinatra, Gregory Peck, Milton Berle, Billy Wilder, Fred De Cordova, Leonard Gersh, Armand Deutsch, Hilliard Marks, Mervyn Le Roy, and me. Behind them sat the close friends and honorary pallbearers, many of whom were leading executives of the motion-picture and television industry and friends of the concert and theater world.

At noon sharp the chapel doors were closed, and Rabbi Edgar F. Magnin walked to the rostrum to begin the short but moving service with the Twenty-third Psalm. He left the final farewells to Jack's two closest friends, George Burns and Bob Hope. George had not been sure that he would be able to overcome his grief enough to speak aloud what was in his heart, but he walked slowly to the rostrum and, in a tear-choked, barely audible voice, said, "I don't know whether I'll be able to do this. I told Mary I might not be able to do it, but she said, 'Do it, George, you've got to do it.' So I'm going to try but it won't be easy. You're all Jack's friends, but he was something special to me. He was my closest friend. I knew him for fifty-five years, and I can't imagine my life without Jack Benny. . . . I'll miss him very much. . . ."

Then George walked slowly back to the family room, and Bob Hope strode briskly out and spoke:

"It is said that a memorial service is for those who are left behind, for those who mourn the loss of a loved one. If this is the case, then this service is for the world, because last Thursday night the world lost somebody it loved a lot. As President Gerald R. Ford wired Mrs. Benny, 'My family and I were deeply saddened to learn of the passing of your devoted husband. For the past half century Jack Benny brought joy and laughter not only to us but to millions of other Americans. Jack's service to his country, his charitable works, and his genuine enjoyment of the humor of others are accolades that he wore with modesty, grace, and charm. If laughter is the music of the soul, Jack and his violin and his good humor

17

have made life better for all men. We will remember you in our family prayers.'

"When Benny Kubelsky was born, who would have imagined that eighty years later at the event of his passing, every television program, every radio show would stop . . . and that every magazine and newspaper would headline it on their front pages. The millions of people who had never met him, who had only seen him or heard him, would feel the pain of a very personal loss.

"The void that is left with us at Jack's passing is quickly filled with the happy memories that we have of him. That's the way Jack would like it to be. He wants us to remember the happiness we shared with him rather than the sadness of losing him. Any path that Jack Benny crossed was left with more laughter, not less.

"How do you say good-bye to a man who is not just a good friend, but a national treasure? It's hard to say no man is indispensable. But it is true just the same that some are irreplaceable. No one has come along to replace Jolson or Bogart or Gable or Will Rogers or Chevalier. I think it's a safe bet that no one will ever replace Jack Benny. Jack had that rare magic—that indefinable something called genius. Picasso had it. Gershwin had it. And Jack was blessed with it. He didn't just stand on the stage . . . he *owned* it.

"For a man who was the undisputed master of comedy timing, you'd have to say that this was the only time when Jack's timing was all wrong. He left us much too soon. He was stingy to the end. He only gave us eighty years, and it wasn't enough.

"And it's an amusing footnote that the penny-pinching cheapskate we all knew and loved was portrayed by a man who gave so much to all of us. Though the idol of millions, he remained modest. Though the homes of the great were open to him, he remained a simple man. Though blessed with a sharp wit, he never used it to injure or belittle.

"Admired by presidents and royalty, he never lost the humble, down-to-earth quality of Benny Kubelsky from Waukegan. Kings and porters, they were all the same to Jack. He was getting ready to do a picture called *The Sunshine Boys*. But then Jack was always getting ready to do something, whether a concert, a TV show, or a benefit, and all his life he was a sunshine boy. He brought more sunshine to this world than Easter morning.

"Jack Benny long ago ceased to be merely a personality and became an institution. If there is a Mount Rushmore for humanitarians, that first stone face might easily resemble him. And if stone could talk it would say . . . 'Well!'

"Jack was one of the richest men I knew. He was happy with who he was. He was happy with what he was. He was happy with where he was. Few are as rich as that.

"Jack Benny, a gentle man, crossed all barriers, all boundaries, all countries, all races, all creeds. I'll never forget in 1958 when I made my first trip to Moscow and it was announced in the papers that America's leading comedian was visiting. That night I went to Ambassador Thompson's house, and Mrs. Thompson met me at the door and said, 'How wonderful that you could come. Did you bring your violin?'

"His first love was the violin, which proves once again, as Jack used to say, you always hurt the one you love. And yet, with that violin, Jack raised more money and benefited more worthwhile causes and charities than a dozen violin virtuosos. His technique wasn't much, but God sure loved his tone.

"It is a cliché to say that in time of darkness, Jack Benny brought light with his gift of laughter, made us forget our troubles. For Jack was more than an escape from life. He was life. A life that enriched his profession, his friends, his millions of fans, his family, his country.

"Perhaps what made Jack Benny such a great laugh maker was that he himself loved to laugh. He was the greatest audience a comedian could ever want . . . and all of us would play jokes on him just to break him up and hear him laugh. I know it might sound corny, but there will be times from now on when the lightning will crackle with a special kind of sound or thunder will peal with a special roar, and I'll think to myself that Cantor or Fields or Fred Allen must have told Jack a joke.

"Jack had another quality that's become as rare as nickel candy bars—taste. When Jack was on the tube, you didn't have to chase the kids out of the room. And he was a perfectionist, a meticulous craftsman. His radio show was a classic, a masterpiece of ensemble playing.

"How many generations grew up to the sound of Jack Benny? To the names of Mary Livingstone, Don Wilson, Dennis Day, Rochester, Phil Harris, Anaheim, Azusa, Cucamonga? For over forty years, first on radio, then on television, Jack was a pioneer, ever extending the frontiers of humor. He was one of the first, if not the first, to have great film stars on his show, playing themselves and getting big laughs. The Ronald Colmans, the Jimmy Stewarts, the Gregory Pecks— they went on for Jack because they trusted him and his sense of what was exactly right.

"Jack knew that the best laughs were the ones you worked the hardest for. He and Mary felt the same way about friends. They both cultivated lasting friendships because they were friends in return. This is the kind of love that surrounds Mary now and will surround her as long as people remember Jack Benny and Mary Livingstone.

"When a man can leave as much of himself as Jack Benny left, then he never can be truly gone. He has to be immortal. . . .

"Jack had a great talent . . . and he learned somehow to use the whole of it. In his beautiful, full lifetime, Jack succeeded . . . gloriously. Jack found a great joy in the joy he brought to others. I cannot say it better than these words:

> His life was gentle
> And the elements so mixed in him
> That nature might stand up and say to all
>   the world
> This was a man!

"God keep him. Enjoy him. We did for eighty years."

As Rabbi Magnin closed the service with the Kaddish, which is a prayer for the dead, many of the mourners remembered a fall day in 1951 when this same cemetery was first opened and dedicated with an Al Jolson Memorial Service. That day, some twenty-three years earlier, the touching eulogy for Al Jolson was delivered by Jack Benny.

As the crowd filed past the closed casket which was draped

with a beautiful blanket of white gardenias, the curtain descended the last time for Jack Benny, aged thirty-nine.

2

BEFORE the turn of the century people came through Ellis Island in New York from all the countries of Europe. One day in 1890 a young man named Meyer Kubelsky arrived in New York from a small Russian town near the Polish border. Seeking a new life in the United States, he eventually chose Chicago for his home. In time he amassed a horse, a wagon, and a load of pots and pans and rode through the towns of Illinois and Wisconsin near Chicago selling his wares. It was a lonesome life for Meyer Kubelsky, but before too long a marriage broker arranged a meeting with a young lady in Chicago named Emma Sachs, who had also emigrated from a small Russian village.

Emma's parents had arrived in the Windy City some years earlier and had accumulated modest wealth. Meyer became very interested in this pretty young girl, and soon after they met, they were married in 1893. With some financial help from Mr. Sachs, Meyer Kubelsky bought a saloon in the toughest part of Waukegan, a small city forty-five minutes by train from Chicago.

Soon the young Mrs. Kubelsky became pregnant, and on February 13, 1894, when she felt the time was close, Meyer bundled up his bride and took her to her parents' home in Chicago so that she would be near the hospital. The next day, February 14, a son, Benjamin, was born at Mercy Hospital in Chicago.

Lest the suspense be too great, Benjamin Kubelsky eventually adopted the name of Jack Benny. And to set the record straight, Jack always maintained that although he was actually born in a hospital in Chicago, he could claim that Waukegan was his birthplace since his mother carried him around there for nine months. And to clarify further any misunderstandings, Jack claimed that he was born on February 14 and years later it was named Valentine's Day!

In his Las Vegas and theater routines, Jack always said, "I was born in Waukegan a long, long, *long* time ago. As a matter of fact, our rabbi was an Indian . . . he used a tomahawk . . . I was eight days old . . . what did I know? . . . I'd like to meet him now. . . . So would Mary."

The Kubelsky family lived in a small apartment on Glendon Street over a butcher shop. Life was dull for little Benny the first few years. The biggest happening was a drunk in the saloon who hit Meyer Kubelsky over the head with a pool cue after an argument, cracking his head open and injuring him badly. Emma, who had never approved of her husband's means of making a living, took that opportunity to convince him to sell the saloon. He opened a dry goods store, and when that didn't do well, he opened a men's haberdashery shop, a business he continued until his retirement.

Jack remembered, "I always had very little in common with my folks and was very bored every night at dinner, when the entire conversation was about the day's receipts, the credit difficulties, or the inventory in the store." The only thing that was at all interesting to little Benny was that his mother played the piano, and he found that he liked to listen to that.

Then, just before his sixth birthday, there was a little excitement in the family when his sister, Florence, was born. In later years when he remained thirty-nine years old, he would joke, "She used to be my younger sister, Florence. Now she's my older sister, Florence."

There was hidden understanding in Meyer Kubelsky because he had noticed Benny's enjoyment of music, and on his son's sixth birthday, he gave him a half-size violin which cost $50. Benny was ecstatic, and Meyer and Emma promptly enrolled him in violin lessons.

"My first violin teacher was a big old bald-headed man named Professor Harlow, who charged fifty cents a lesson. I took two a week, which showed that my father was really serious about me and the fiddle," Jack recalled many years ago.

After a year or two with Professor Harlow the violin student started to take a weekly lesson at the Chicago Musical College from Dr. Hugo Kortschak, who had a respected reputation in the music world even in those days. Later Dr. Kortschak became a professor of music at Yale and subsequently founded the Berkshire String Quartet. Jack studied with Dr. Kortschak for years and thereafter talked about him in many magazine and newspaper interviews. Jack then heard that he had retired to Honolulu and, in 1953, while on vacation there, went to visit him.

Bob Krause, a reporter on the Honolulu *Advertiser,* brought the violin professor and his wife over to the Royal Hawaiian Hotel to meet his former pupil. Krause reported that on the way to the hotel Mrs. Kortschak asked some questions so she wouldn't embarrass Mr. Benny by knowing so little of his work.

"What does he do?" she asked.

"Have you listened to him on the radio?" questioned Bob Krause.

"Yes. I believe I heard him once, but I didn't know it was he because he was talking. Doesn't he play the violin anymore?"

"Well, his program is mostly talking now," he answered.

"What sort of program is it?" she asked.

"It's a comedy program."

"For children?"

"No, it's supposed to be for adults."

Actually, Dr. Kortschak had lost track of his former pupil completely until just before he met him again in Honolulu. The truth of the matter was that he had no idea a radio, movie, and TV comedian named Jack Benny had once studied under him.

Although Meyer and Emma had their hearts set on their son becoming a great concert violinist, Benny hated to practice. He liked to perform and did so for all his friends and relatives in their living rooms. The highlight of his grandmother Sachs' visit to Waukegan was Benny setting up the chairs in the living room for her, his folks, his sister, and anyone else he could entice into the room and playing a few selections for them. He had no desire at that time to become a comedian. Instead, he pictured himself in a snappy suit and straw hat, doing serious poems and speeches, interspersed with a few violin numbers. His father had tried to get him interested in the haberdashery business, but Jack did not ap-

23

pear to like that or anything else except playing the fiddle—without practicing.

Meyer Kubelsky was a religious man and a highly respected member of the only Jewish Orthodox synagogue in Waukegan. Little Benny very rarely went with him to attend the services, much to Meyer's unhappiness, but the cardinal rule was that on Yom Kippur, the most sacred of all the religious holidays, Benny had to sit with his father in the synagogue all day. Jack recalled that one Yom Kippur when he was about twelve years old, he arrived very late at the synagogue.

"When I came in and sat down next to my father, everyone else had been there for hours. My father felt that I had embarrassed him before all his fellow Jews on this most holy of days. He became so angry that he picked up the first thing at hand which was his siddur and struck me across the face with it before the entire congregation. He didn't look at me the rest of the day and didn't say a word all the way home. I went to my room and waited for supper. After a while he came in and in a very hesitant voice said, 'You know, Benny, it's a mitzvah [blessing] to be hit by a siddur on Yom Kippur.' That was the only way he knew how to apologize."

As a boy Benny wasn't a problem to his parents because he never got into scrapes. Perhaps, as Jack used to say, "I couldn't lick anybody, so I never fought anyone." He never was much of an athlete and didn't participate in any of the sports with the other kids. He did enjoy baseball, however, although he wasn't a natural player by any means. The other kids made fun of him because he threw the ball like a girl. Later, when Jack became a star, everyone teased him about his walking like a girl, too. Once when we got off a train and Jack was walking ahead, Phil Harris asked everyone to watch Jack walk. "You know," commented Phil, "you could put a dress on Jack and take him anywhere."

The arguments continued at the Kubelsky household about Benny's lack of practicing, but in spite of that, he managed to play the violin fairly well and eventually his father bought him a genuine imitation Amati for $75 to play at the grammar school graduation exercises. He played in a trio with Leo Sackman, clarinetist, and Mary Harris at the piano. They opened their recital rather ambitiously with "La Serenata" by Gaetano Braga and closed the evening with "Health and Flowers" by Tobani. Meyer and Emma were happy in their belief that Benny's concert career was starting.

After he was graduated from grammar school, he started to play in stores and at parties and bar mitzvahs with a children's orchestra. Jack charged $1.50 an engagement, and although he was kept quite busy with that, he also played with an orchestra managed by a friend named Hapke in Libertyville. For going to Libertyville, he charged $2 a night, and eventually he raised his fee to $3.

When he started his first year at Central High School, much to the distress of Meyer and Emma, he got a job playing the violin in the pit of the Barrison Theater, which was owned by Joe E. Howard, who wrote the hit song "I Wonder Who's Kissing Her Now." Benny played the evening performances at the vaudeville theater and doubled as an usher as well from time to time. He loved every minute of it, which was more than he could say about his studies at Central High School. He was constantly in trouble with his teachers and parents for skipping school on matinee days. Finally, when he failed every examination, the principal requested him to take his leave, which was a great heartbreak to Emma and Meyer. Now they recognized not only that their son was not a student, but that he was playing the music of a cheap vaudeville theater and would never be the concert violinist they dreamed about.

Although his mother died from cancer when Jack was twenty-three years old and unhappily never saw him amount to much, his father lived to see him achieve the fame and success of later years. When Jack became a wealthy star, he sent his father to Miami Beach to retire. Meyer was so proud of his son that he would stop people in the streets or on the beach and hand them pictures of Jack whether they wanted them or not. Meyer Kubelsky never stopped speaking English with a pronounced European accent. Jack used to say that his father also wrote letters to him with the words spelled exactly as he pronounced them, syllable for syllable. Once Jack received a letter from Miami which read, "I *findly* found a man who didn't know you. But what did he know— he was just an old Jew."

The Kubelsky family was living on Genesee Street when

25

Jack left Central High School. Meyer had to find a worth-while business for his son since playing in a pit orchestra was not a job a man could make into a life's work. First he tried to make Jack a salesman-assistant in the haberdashery store, but one day when he found Benny asleep on a table while four pairs of pants had been stolen by a customer, he fired him. Then Meyer enrolled Benny in the Waukegan Business College, but the boy was so completely uninterested that Meyer gave up and reluctantly allowed him to continue to play for the Barrison, where his salary had risen to $8 per week. Benny did a good job and learned all the tricks of accompanying the other acts so well that once when the Marx Brothers played the theater Minnie Marx, their mother and manager, offered Benny the job of being their musical direc-tor. But Meyer put his foot down and would not allow little Benny to go on the road.

His real start in show business came when Jack was sixteen and the Barrison Theater closed down. Cora Salisbury, the pianist in the orchestra and a mature woman, decided to go back into vaudeville. She recognized Benny's ability and sug-gested that they form a partnership act. And so "Salisbury and Benny—From Grand Opera to Ragtime"—was born.

3

THE act, Salisbury and Benny, was paid $50 a week, of which Miss Salisbury pocketed $35 and young Benny kept $15. Their first booking was in Gary, Indiana, which was not only his first vaudeville job but his first bit of traveling. Jack Benny recalled this trip in an article he wrote many years ago:

> In order to get to Gary, we had to take the train to Chica-go which I had done many times before, but this was differ-ent. Practically the whole town came to see us off, including my father, mother and my sister, Florence.

After about an hour of advice, especially about keeping warm and what foods to eat, we left. After reaching Chicago, we transferred to another train that went to Gary and from then on it was all new and exciting. Somehow, the passing scenery was completely different from anything I had seen before. The grass was greener and the trees seemed taller. In those days it took about two hours to get to Gary because there were some short stops on the way. When the porter took my bag down, I gave him two of my hard-earned dollars. When Miss Salisbury, who was like a mother to me, heard about it, she bawled me out for being such a big spender and told me that fifty cents would have been enough. This was the beginning of my thrifty image.

From the train, we went directly to a theatrical boarding house, and I was given a room that vaudeville comedians used to make jokes about, like . . . my hotel room is so small, the mice have to be midgets to get in.

After I washed up, we went down to my first boarding house dinner. I took my mother's advice and ate everything. In fact, I ate so much I was sick all night and barely made it to our rehearsal the next day.

After a few days at the boarding house and the theater, I felt like an old timer at the business of being away from home.

I've taken thousands of trips since and have been all over the world, but I think I can remember every detail of my first trip to Gary, Indiana, a long, long, long time ago.

The Salisbury and Benny act opened with a big rendition of the *Poet and Peasant Overture*, and then they played a medley of ragtime tunes that included "Everybody's Doing It, Now."

"My big solo was 'The Rosary,' which I played under a purple spotlight," Jack recalled, "and then we'd play another popular number of the day with a little humor in it and I'd flirt with the girls in the box, which was the first time I felt that girls were really attracted to me."

They played three days in Gary, and the act went over very well. From then on his career advanced steadily. When Jack talked in later years about writing his autobiography, he wondered whether it would be successful since there was no great drama in his life, no rags-to-riches story, no real set-backs. His friend, the late producer William Goetz, suggested that if he wrote his autobiography, he should entitle it *I Always Had Shoes.*

Salisbury and Benny played all over the Midwest, and gradually they learned audience-pleasing tricks to keep improving. Occasionally they would run into difficulties. Recently, the Storm Lake Iowa *Register* reported that Salisbury and Benny arrived there in 1911 in the midst of a snowstorm to discover the theater was in the final stages of construction. There were no dressing rooms; some sheets were strung up on stage for privacy, and heat was provided with a hastily set-up oil stove. It was 10 degrees below zero outdoors and not much warmer inside.

They presented their first show in the afternoon, but after the second show that night the irate manager, on his first job in the theater, paid them a visit.

"Say," he told the two, "you folks gave the same show tonight that you gave this afternoon. You done the same act and played the same durn tunes."

When he learned they were going to do the same show twice a day for the three-day engagement, he thought that the city slickers were trying to put something over on him.

So he took their oil stove away.

Salisbury. and Benny worked together until 1913, when her mother became ill and Miss Salisbury decided to leave the act and return to Waukegan to care for her. Luckily, in Chicago Jack found a young pianist named Lyman Woods who was to become his partner for the next several years.

By now the nineteen-year-old Benny felt he was a show business veteran, and he named the new act Benny and Woods. Jack kept the "From Grand Opera to Ragtime" billing, and they started with the same routines he had done with Cora Salisbury, gradually changing the numbers as the years went on.

Soon they were earning $200 a week. Even though Benny and Woods split the money evenly, Jack managed to save some each week. He still didn't have much rapport with his parents and continued to turn to his friends for understanding and companionship. One such friend was Julius Synikan, a Waukegan department store salesman, who was five years older than Jack. Each week Jack sent money to Julius to bank for him. He followed this practice for many years, and even after Jack became a star, he and Julius remained close friends. In 1958 *Life* magazine assigned Shana Alexander, who was then a young reporter, and photographer Leonard McCombe, to do a feature picture-and-text story on a concert Jack Benny gave with the Chicago Symphony Orchestra to benefit the City of Hope. Jack invited his old pal Julius, who was by then a little elderly man, to spend four days with him at the Ambassador East Hotel. The *Life* photo of Jack and Julius in adjoining twin beds having breakfast in bed was probably one of the highlights of the late Julius Synikan's life.

Benny and Woods were finally booked into the Palace in New York. Although they were in the number two spot, right after the acrobats, it was a great honor to play the leading vaudeville theater in the United States. The headliners on the bill were Smith and Dale and the Avon Comedy Four, one of the most hilarious acts in vaudeville. Fifty-six years later Neil Simon was to write the hit Broadway play *The Sunshine Boys,* patterned after Smith and Dale, and fifty-seven years later, just before his death, Jack Benny was cast to play one of the two leads with Walter Matthau in the MGM motion picture based on the play.

Variety reviewed the eleven-minute act of Benny and Woods at the Palace:

> Two young men, a pianist and violinist, opened with syncopated duet, piano solo medley with the player travestying the long-haired musician type. 'Poor Butterfly' duet exaggeratedly rhapsodized, etc. Both with violins for encore laughs, the pianist though holding the fiddle awkwardly. Pleasing turn for an early spot.

The act kept improving and life was good. Then came the day in November, 1917, when Jack was called home by his dying mother. Her death deeply affected him because he had failed in his promise to her to do something toward a serious violin career. From that time to the day of his death her dying of cancer implanted in him a terrible fear of this disease.

The last professional engagement of Benny and Woods

before Jack enlisted in the Navy at the Great Lakes Training Station was at the Majestic Theater in Milwaukee early in 1918. Jack couldn't recall ever seeing Lyman Woods again, but George Jessel, who had seen the act once, used to ask Jack how Woods was every time they met. And each time Jack fell down with laughter at the ridiculousness of the question. For Jack's birthday a number of years ago, Jessel presented him with a set of gold cuff links with "Benny" on one link and "Woods" on the other.

Our young violinist had been on the vaudeville stage for seven years and had yet to utter his first words.

4

MANY years ago Jack Benny was the mystery guest on *What's My Line?* When John Daly asked him how it felt to be the man who made Waukegan famous, Jack answered: "It was just the reverse. Waukegan made me what I am today because if I hadn't been born there I wouldn't have enlisted in the Navy at Great Lakes and gone into the *Great Lakes Review*, where I did my first comedy lines."

After Jack enlisted at Great Lakes early in 1918, he immediately applied for the theatrical company that was being prepared to present shows in the Midwest for Navy Relief. He teamed with a fine piano player named Elzear "Zez" Confrey, and they formed an act similar to Benny and Woods, except that Confrey did some cute things on the piano for laughs and Jack did more eye rolling and other jazzy stunts on the fiddle that contributed to the comedy. The author and director of the show, Dave Wolf, brought the boys in for an important spot on the show.

During rehearsal Dave Wolf announced, "I need someone to read two comedy lines as the part of an orderly."

"Now, I knew nothing about comedy at the time . . . or at least I thought I didn't," Jack reminisced later, "but I tried it and evidently he liked my reading because I won the part of Izzy There, the Admiral's Disorderly."

He delivered the two lines in a flat voice, and the contrast with the other fellows who were would-be actors and were hamming it up was so great that the rehearsal audiences roared. Wolf kept giving him more lines, and by the time the *Great Lakes Review* opened Jack had won the comedy lead of the show.

Jack and Zez decided that when the war ended, they would form an act. But when Jack was discharged first and it looked as if it might be a long time before Confrey would get out of the service, Jack decided that while he waited for Zez he'd go out on his own as a fiddle-playing comedian.

He called his first single act "Ben Benny—Fiddleology and Fun," and it consisted of a lot of violin playing, eye rolling to the ragtime tunes, jokes after each number which he picked up from the humor magazines of the day, and two vocal numbers: "After the Country Goes Dry, Goodbye Wild Women, Goodbye" and "I Used to Call Her Baby but Now She's a Mother to Me."

He did not stop the show, but the act was passable enough to keep him employed fairly regularly in small-town vaudeville circuits. In time he changed his act title to "Ben Benny—Aristocrat of Humor" and continued with the same mediocre success.

When Zez was finally discharged, he began writing songs. After a few piano solo hits like "Kitten on the Keys," he was on the road to success as a composer, and that helped Jack make up his mind to continue performing as a single.

"I was either going to be a comedian or get out of show business."

Now that his mind was made up, a classier title was in order, so his new act, with more jokes, was "A Few Minutes with Ben Benny." But as Jack became more popular, Ben Bernie, the bandleader and comedian, felt that Jack was trying to cash in on his reputation, which was much bigger at the time than Jack's. So again he changed his name, and this time the act became "A Few Minutes with Jack Benny." More than forty years later he brought a revue to the Ziegfeld Theater in New York for a six-week engagement, and after a little thought, Jack came up with the title he wanted: *An Hour and Sixty Minutes with Jack Benny*, which was what he called his one-man show for the rest of his career.

Even though he called himself Jack Benny, none of his

friends called him by his new name. He was still Ben to his old pals. The first time he was important enough to see "Jack Benny" in lights on a marquee, he said, "I got the strangest feelings . . . as if this wasn't me and I was an impostor and someday the audience would find me out."

Despite his insecurity, which was to plague him all his life, Jack's act kept improving, especially when he stopped singing. He gradually did more and more comedy until he became a comedian who used a fiddle as a prop. He would start to play, but before the first note he would think of a line and say it and then continue talking until the finish of his act. Originally he did ten minutes, but as he improved, he went to fourteen, and by the time he was in the next-to-closing spot on the bill, the star position in vaudeville, he got seventeen minutes.

George Burns says, "You'd determine the status of an act in those days by the amount of time they were given. You'd meet a vaudevillian on the street and ask him how he was doing, and he'd answer 'seventeen minutes' if he were a top act."

Jack Benny always claimed about an act, "It's how you start that's important. Once you get rolling and get the attention of the audience, it's not important how you finish. You'll be a hit. You can always get off a stage—there are two exits! It's what you do when you get *on* that counts." He practiced that theory all through his theatrical career and would spend hours and hours on his opening line for every dinner he spoke at, for all the theater and nightclub dates, for all opening monologues for his TV shows. On his opening television show in 1950 his first line was: "I'd give a million dollars to know what I look like." Through the years he developed many good openings for theater and club dates, but one of the best was: "The last time I was here in 19—— was twenty-two years ago when I did a benefit for the ——. Fortunately, I've had other work in between. Now, my being here twenty-two years later may mean nothing to you, but the American Republic Life Insurance Company is thrilled! I'm not going to tell you how much life insurance I carry, but when I go, they go."

At charity dinners he often started out by commenting in his usual low-key manner, "I had my choice tonight of buy-

ing a hundred-dollar ticket or being up here on the dais
. . . so, good evening, ladies and gentlemen."

Somehow, even early in his career, he always seemed to
have an instinctive sense of comedy. After World War I,
when he started as a single act, his opening found him standing with his back to the audience, playing scales on the violin,
as the curtain went up. He'd turn and say, "Oh, I guess I'm
on," and then play a number as the audience gave a little
opening laugh. As the years progressed, he'd walk out to the
center of stage at the opening of his act and say to the orchestra leader, "How's the show going up till now?" "Fine," the
answer would come back. "Well, I'll fix that," would start the
laughs rolling.

From the start of his comedy career, Jack was different
from most of the comedians of that time. Vaudeville comics
were generally loud and raucous, coming onstage in funny
outfits. Jack was always quiet and slow, never rushing into
the punch line. Instead of doing "jokes," he tried to build his
humor around events of the day so that it sounded ad-libbed
and current. He'd talk about new one-way streets, flappers,
his troubles trying to get a date and keep a girl, about
"cheap" things he did, which he took from Scotsman stories
that were then in vogue.

His quiet, relatively sophisticated humor didn't always suc-
ceed. Often audiences, especially at matinees, consisted of
unemployed hoods or salesmen goofing off. If they didn't
like what they saw and heard onstage, they would boo, yell,
throw things on stage and generally make life miserable for
the performer. One matinee at the Academy of Music Theater on Fourteenth Street in New York, famed for being one
of the toughest vaude houses in the city, Jack walked quietly
on stage as his opening music cued him, and, advancing to
center stage as the music died down, he said, "Hello, folks."

A loud roar rose, laced with boos, and a few tomatoes were
pelted toward him. Jack simply kept walking past the center
stage until he reached the other side and said, "Good-bye,
folks," and walked out of the theater, never to return.

Jack's subdued manner and conservative clothes were unusual in many theaters in which he appeared. When he first
played the Palladium Theater in London in the early thirties,
English audiences were attuned to comedians who came out

in crazy outfits, baggy pants, short trousers, rube clothing, and the like. One critic reviewed the act: "Jack Benny came on looking like a Harley Street physician."

The first time he played in Chicago after he was a full-fledged comedian, he invited Meyer Kubelsky to spend the weekend with him and see the show. Later in the dressing room, Meyer said sadly, "Benny, you carry the violin out on the stage, but you don't play?"

"Well, no. You see, Papa, my act has changed. I tell jokes."

Meyer thought for a moment. "Then why do you carry the violin?"

"It's a prop, Papa. It gets laughs."

"The violin is funny?" Jack remembered him staring at him incredulously. Then Meyer laughed apologetically. "I'm sorry, Benny, I couldn't laugh."

5

IN 1921 a historic meeting took place which was to create a close friendship which would last more than fifty years. Jack Benny met George Burns. At that time Jack was interested in a beautiful young actress named Mary Kelly who was living at the Coolidge Hotel on Forty-seventh Street in New York. Mary Kelly's roommates were two other actresses named Renee Arnold and Gracie Allen. George Burns was seeing Gracie and doing his best to persuade her to team up with him. The two young comics liked each other from the start, and the story of their friendship will be told later.

The Coolidge Hotel was largely occupied by entertainers. It was one block away from the Palace Theater which was *the* theater every actor dreamed of headlining. Those who were second-rate on the billing were reminded constantly of their goal of stardom, for all they had to do was look out the window and up the block to see the Palace marquee.

Jack's career at that time was progressing slowly. At best his success could be called mediocre, and he had many layoffs. This gave him time to write funny parodies to popular songs. He was very accomplished at this, and it was a talent he used for the rest of his life, often singing or reciting his famous poems in parody about a guest of honor or host or hostess of a party. During a layoff while he was living at the Coolidge Hotel, he wrote this poem:

THAT LITTLE OLD COOLIDGE HOTEL

I've laid off all season
I don't know the reason
In that little old Coolidge Hotel
Many tears have I shed
On my old-fashioned bed
In that little old Coolidge Hotel
The bellhops are out
The clerk's in a trance
To get me on the phone
You're just taking a chance
Yet, my poor heart would ache
If I'd ever forsake
That little old Coolidge Hotel

I sit here and grieve
Though I know I won't leave
That little old Coolidge Hotel
I wait an hour—or later
For the old elevator
In that little old Coolidge Hotel
My room is a morgue
But I stay here and groan
All the sunshine I get
Is when Blanchy and Joan
Knock on the door of a cell I call home
In that little old Coolidge Hotel

Now I know what you'll say
Perhaps I can't pay
My bills in the Coolidge Hotel
But I want you to know
Not a cent do I owe
To that little old Coolidge Hotel
I cannot explain it

The fault is all mine
It's just that I know
If I leave for a time
Like a murderer returns
To the scene of his crime
I'll come back to the Coolidge Hotel

Oh, I've threatened to go
I'd pack up and start
When everyone else was asleep
With my shoes in my hand
From the room I would dart
Down the rickety steps I'd creep
And when I'd get to the lobby
Oh God, how I'd try
To reach the glass door
And then—I would spy
The little old clerk—with a tear in his eye
And I'm stuck in the Coolidge Hotel

But now I'm rehearsing
A new act I'm nursing
In my room at the Coolidge Hotel
And with my smart little skit
I hope that I'll hit
Just a block from the Coolidge Hotel
And if ever I'm famous
And fortune I'll meet
Do you think I'll forget
The old joint on this street
Say, if it burns to the floor
I'll be living next door
To that little old Coolidge Hotel.

As Jack's single act matured and his unique style of dig-
nified, sophisticated humor developed, he became dedicated
to refining his monology. He studied the great monologuists
of the day, and he noticed that they worked without props of
any kind—they just got up and talked. So he decided to omit
the fiddle. George Burns recalls the first time Jack worked
without the violin:

"We were in Wilkes-Barre, Pennsylvania, where the coal
miners used to come into the theater with lights still on their

hats. It was impossible to tell where the footlights ended and the audience began. I was on the bill with Jack, and I knew he had been thinking about dropping the fiddle for a long time. I gave him the extra push and made him leave the violin at his hotel just to be sure he wouldn't change his mind. He came on, told his first joke, and the coal miners were still adjusting the lights on their hats. No laugh. He didn't know what to do with his hands. He tried two more jokes, and, then shaking with perspiration, he leaned over the orchestra pit and asked the conductor, 'Could you lend me a fiddle?' As soon as it was passed up to him, he clutched it like a drowning child and went on with his act."

He still wanted to get rid of the fiddle and eventually managed to do it when a fellow performer bet him that he couldn't do his act without it. With the money as an incentive, he went on one night without his prop and was a big hit. From then on he only used the violin when he wanted to do a gag number.

At this time in his career he started to do jokes with a "cheap" angle which was the forerunner of the character he would assume on radio many years later.

"I took my girl to dinner, and she laughed so hard at one of my jokes that she dropped her tray." Another of his lines was: "I was going to buy my girl a Packard car for Christmas, but it took too long to deliver, so I bought her some handkerchiefs." This gag was revived many years later on a radio show with Mary Livingstone as the "girl." Another laugh was: "I took my girl to the movies and there was a sign on the marquee—'The Woman Pays.' So my girl bought the tickets."

The act continued to improve. He worked more and more regularly and was usually fairly successful. Jack said about those early days, "When I was a hit, the hotel or rooming house was always great, the food in town was sensational, the people were the nicest. But when the act bombed and no one laughed at my jokes, the hotel was a dump, the meals were inedible, and the people had no taste."

In the days before radio, music publishers resorted to all sorts of ruses to get their songs plugged around the country. One of their methods was to offer a singer to a vaudeville act free if the act would let the vocalist sing a song or two for the audience. Jack was offered such a deal by Leo Feist in Chicago, and knowing a good thing when he saw one and being lonesome traveling alone anyway, he created a spot in his act in 1922 for Ned Miller.

Ned was a nice-looking twenty-one-year-old song plugger with a sweet soprano voice. In later years he was to write many hit songs, including "Why Should I Cry Over You" but in 1922 he was a naïve young man who was impressed with Jack Benny, the vaudeville pro who had already traveled all over the United States many times.

"Jack dreamed up a great bit in order to work me in," Ned remembered. "He'd save me for his encore and then say to the audience, 'I've got my kid brother backstage, and if you give him enough applause, he'll come out and sing a wonderful song he wrote.' I'd come out wearing knickers, a sweater, and holding a cap. Jack would take the cap away from me and I started to sing, and I wouldn't know what to do with my hands. Just before the big B-flat finish, when it looked as if I wouldn't be able to make it, Jack would hand me back the cap so I could hold it with my two hands, and then I'd hit the note with a big finish. It always stopped the show."

When Jack got tired of the kid brother act, he'd put Ned into a theater box and Ned would keep standing up and interrupting the monologue until Jack would say, "Okay, okay . . . if you want to entertain, go ahead." The audience wouldn't expect a good singing voice, but when Ned would go into his song, they were always amazed, and he always got a big hand.

One Yom Kippur, Ned, who was religious, went to temple for the whole day but forgot to tell Jack. When Jack came to the interruption sequence, he kept throwing the cues, but nothing came back. He was frozen for a moment; then he borrowed a fiddle from the orchestra leader and went into a violin solo finish.

"In those days Jack was the most handsome guy you'd ever seen," Ned recalled. "The women were always sending him notes backstage or calling our hotel for him, and I found myself acting as his secretary for the ladies. Once he made a blind date with a girl who sounded sensational on the phone and agreed to meet her at the drugstore. I went with him, and we hid in a store across the street until we saw the girl waiting. She must have weighed at least three hundred pounds, and so he sent me over to tell her that he was sick and couldn't make it."

After two seasons on the road Ned went back to Chicago to get married and write songs, and for many years he saw Jack only on his occasional visits. But in 1958, when Ned moved to California, he went to work as Jack's stand-in on the TV shows and also did various bit roles for Jack. One year when circumstances caused one of the Benny shows to be taped on Yom Kippur, Jack remembered that other Yom Kippur so many years before and told Ned to take the day off, that he would stand in for himself that day.

Like George Burns, Ned Miller remained a close friend from that day in 1922 until Jack's death.

Although he had no writers and could not afford to hire any, Jack had developed a basic comedic sense which he implemented by watching all the comedians and monologists of that time. He continued to polish his act by studying performers like Willie Collier, Frank Fay, and Julius Tannen, all great monologuists. He realized that he had to adapt his routines to the various theaters, cities, and seasons. He saw one comedian who did the same routine every show. Even when there was a two-foot snowfall that day, he would still say, "When I was playing golf this morning with a fellow. . . ." He watched others who did jokes about their uncle in Connecticut who was so so stupid that . . . and follow with a line about a parade down Fifth Avenue.

He watched, listened, and learned. He was finally able to build a routine where every joke followed another in proper sequence, making sense as a narrative, as if he were telling true stories that had happened to him.

When he was finally booked into the great Palace Theater in New York as a single, the *Variety* reviewer disposed of his act: "Jack Benny has evidently seen Julius Tannen . . . but not often enough."

6

SOMEONE once said "If you have one truly good friend, you are a wealthy man," and if this be the case, Jack Benny was very wealthy, for he had many friends. But his closest friend for almost fifty-five years was George Burns. In all that time they never had an argument that amounted to anything, and they always supported each other in their private lives as well as in their careers. They both were good listeners, and when one was troubled or had any problem, no matter how intimate, he could count on the other to lend an ear and give honest advice.

Many people could make Jack laugh, but he laughed longest and hardest at everything his best friend, Burns, said and did. And the irony of it was that the number one comedian, Jack Benny, who made millions of people laugh every week, couldn't make George Burns laugh no matter how hard he tried.

George reminisced: "It all started right after we met. I was struggling to put an act together with Gracie Allen, who liked another fellow. Jack seemed to like me and started to pal around with me, even though he was in a higher spot on the bill and was making a lot more money than I." One night George telephoned Jack, and right in the middle of the call they were disconnected. Jack thought George did it on purpose and thought it was hilarious. When he told George how funny he thought it was, that started things. From then on George always hung up on Jack in the middle of a sentence. This gag went on year after year, and Jack never seemed to tire of it while George kept adding little touches.

In 1948 Jack played the Palladium Theatre in London. It was customary on the night before every opening for Val Parnell, the Palladium's managing director, to give a party at his apartment for the star attraction. During the party Jack was summoned to the phone for a transatlantic call. It turned out to be George Burns, calling from their golf club in Beverly Hills, Hillcrest.

"Can you imagine that Burns?" screamed Jack as he laughed his way back into the room and fell to the floor, pounding it in his characteristic fashion. "He called all the way from Beverly Hills, eight thousand miles, to wish me luck and right in the middle of a sentence, he hung up on me."

In their fifty-five-year friendship, Jack rarely, if ever, stumped Burns. But the year following Jack's appearance at the Palladium he played a great return joke on George, even though it was a costly one.

Burns and Allen were headlining the London Palladium in 1949, and George had asked Jack to come to England for their opening. Jack said that he'd be busy at that time but then decided to surprise George. He called Lew Grade, who was then a London variety agent who had handled Jack's engagement the previous year. He wanted Lew to help him set up a gag. Lew Grade in more recent years has become Sir Lew Grade, England's leading entertainment tycoon.

Accompanied by Charles Pincus, his friend and dentist, Jack arranged to arrive in London late in the afternoon of the night Val Parnell was giving his party for Burns and Allen. Lew met them at the airport, sneaked them into a suite at the Savoy Hotel, where they hid until all the guests were assembled at Parnell's party. Then Lew and Val brought Jack up the service elevator and into a back bedroom. Academy Award-winning actress Jane Wyman was at the party, and she was let in on the gag, brought into the bedroom, and put on an extension telephone. Then Val Parnell walked into the living room and told Burns that there was an overseas call for him.

"I bet that's Jack Benny calling from Hillcrest," George announced to the crowd as he went into the den to take the call.

"Mr. George Burns?" Jane Wyman asked in a stilted English voice. "This is the transatlantic operator. I have a call for you from Beverly Hills." Then she gave the phone to Jack.

"George, this is Jack, and I just called to wish you and Gracie luck for tomorrow night. And let me tell you something, George—" and Jack hung up.

George walked back into the living room and announced to everyone that Jack had just called from Hillcrest in Beverly Hills, and as he was explaining the call, Jack walked into the room and just stood there. There was stunned silence for a few moments from everyone in the room, particularly from George. Then Jack fell down on the floor and started pounding it and screaming at the thought of the great joke he had finally pulled on his pal. For once George couldn't think of a topper.

"Jack was the greatest audience in the world, and that was

why everyone loved to be funny when they were around him," George says. "He would laugh so heartily and so long that we all thought we were the greatest comedians living. We would spend our time trying to think of funny things to do and say to Jack because he was such a bolster for the ego.

"Once in a while," George continued, "Jack would try to do a funny thing to get a laugh from us, but it usually backfired, or we would gang up on him and intentionally not laugh, which again would strike him funny and send him off into gales of laughter. One of the things he would do was stick a piece of toilet paper on each eyelid, push his hair down over his forehead, push his coat back off his shoulders, and pretend he was reeling drunk. He thought he looked very funny, but it was really corny. Once he was expecting a girl up to his room and quickly did the toilet paper bit and pushed his hair down. There was a knock on the door, and when he opened it, there was a couple at the wrong door. They saw this strange man, let out a shriek, and ran. He didn't do the toilet paper stunt for a long time after that."

When Jack Benny and Burns and Allen all started to do a little better and make more money, they moved into one of the better actors' hotels, the Forrest, on West Forty-ninth Street. There Jack blossomed out and bought a suit of white tie and tails which was the evening dress of the elegant people in New York at the time. It was about then that he met a beautiful Chinese opera star who was playing the Palace, and they began to see one another frequently. Jack told his friend all about his new girl. One night Jack had a date to take her to the theater and to supper later. She was dressed in a lovely evening gown, and he was in his tails. Since she lived uptown, she suggested picking him up at the Forrest. As they left Jack's room and entered the elevator in all their formal splendor, George came running down the hall and threw a bundle of laundry into the elevator, and as the elevator doors were closing, he yelled, "No starch, and have it back by Wednesday." As embarrassed as Jack was, he couldn't help breaking up. Fortunately, his beautiful girlfriend had a good sense of humor.

About this time Jack met Jesse Block, who was teamed with

42

his wife, Eve Sully, in a boy-girl act. Jesse was younger than Jack and admired the handsome comedian. He remembers vividly their first meeting.

"George Burns, whom I had known, took me to the Forrest Hotel to meet Jack. He left me in Jack's dressing room because he had to rush off to a meeting with Gracie. While Jack was dressing, I told him how wonderful I thought he was and how I had studied his whole routine and knew it by heart. He was impressed with me and enjoyed all my praise, and when he finished dressing, he absentmindedly walked out the door and locked it from the outside. As I heard the lock turn, I was so amazed that I was tongue-tied. Then, I was too embarrassed to call down to the desk to tell them my predicament. I sat there until two A.M. when Jack came home from his date. When he opened the door and saw me, he was so shocked at what he had thoughtlessly done that he simply looked at me for a second and then roared. From then on we became fast friends and were close the rest of his life."

The only interest of Jack and his friends was show business, and all their thoughts and conversation revolved around vaudeville. Since Burns and Allen and Block and Sully were married by this time and their rooms were always decorated with drying lingerie, they usually gathered in bachelor Benny's room, where, with Jack's girl, Mary Kelly, included, the boys would put on a show when they weren't actually working in a theater. Sometimes others like Blossom Seeley and her piano-playing partner, Benny Fields, would join the group. A sheet would be stretched across part of the room, and the girls would take seats in the two chairs and the bed on one side of the sheet. The boys would go behind the sheet to plan the show. Invariably, George would peek out from behind the "curtain," look at the same three or four girls, and say, "Hey, fellows, looks like a good house tonight." And as many times as Jack heard that line, he would fall down, laughing uproariously.

The agent for most of their acts was Tom Fitzpatrick. Not only was he a good agent and an honest ten-percenter, but he was a kindly man who hated to tell anyone that there was no job. When a client would come to his office, often he would stall instead of telling them the truth, and he would pretend that he was searching for an important offer as he busily rifled through his desk drawers. One day George came down from Fitzpatrick's office and ran into Jack on the street.

"I guess I'm laying off, Jack. Tom Fitzpatrick's looking through his desk drawers."

Jack fell on the sidewalk in hysterics and couldn't stop laughing, and George kept stopping people asking them if the man was crazy and why was he laughing like that. George stopped so many people that finally there was a small crowd gathered. As Jack saw what George was doing to him, he kept laughing harder until George picked him up and walked him away.

The first time Burns and Allen played the Palace they were on the bill third and Jack was on the same bill fifth. The boys worked up a small bit in which George would interrupt Jack in the middle of his act, asking, "What happened to you in the upper berth on the train last night?" Jack would have a funny answer that led to a few jokes between the two of them. One night, for no reason, George came on the stage for the usual interruption, but instead of talking, he merely looked at Jack and didn't say a word. Jack waited for the line, and when it didn't come, he started to laugh so hard that he couldn't speak. Finally he had to push George offstage so that he could continue his act.

Another time, when they worked on the same bill at the Fifth Avenue Theater in New York, the show ended with a minstrel show as the grand finale. Jack was the interlocuter with George as one end man and Harry Morton of Kramer and Morton as the other end man. The end men had to put on blackface in true minstrel fashion, but at each performance, George kept making his mouth bigger and bigger until he was practically all mouth. Jack started to laugh each time as George progressed with his makeup job until finally, when George was all white except for a black line around the edge of his face, Jack couldn't control himself any longer and almost ruined the finish. Eventually the theater manager put his foot down and made George go back to full minstrel makeup, whereupon George would take his bows and pull his gloves down to show his hands were white—which made Jack just as hysterical.

7

THE story that Jack Benny told about George Burns on hundreds of stages throughout the world and the one that seemed to tickle him most went like this:

"I was living at the Radisson Hotel in Minneapolis and George Burns was following me into the theater there. He closed in Chicago a day early, and one Saturday morning, my closing day, he arrived at the hotel and phoned up from the lobby. Now George could always make me laugh, and I could never make him laugh, so I wracked my brains trying to think of something funny to do. I took off my pajamas and stood on top of the bed absolutely nude . . . and I put a book on top of my head, held a glass of water in one outstretched hand and a rose in the other. Now, wouldn't you think that would make a funny picture and George would have to laugh? Well, he must have suspected something because when I heard a knock on the door and said, 'Come in,' . . . he sent the maid in! Now, how do you tell a maid that you're waiting for George Burns? Until I opened my mouth she thought I was a lamp . . . an Italian lamp . . . an old Italian lamp. . . ."

George always frustrated his best friend. One time Jack spent hours composing a funny 300-word telegram to George. George wired back: DON'T WORRY JACK I WON'T SHOW YOUR WIRE TO ANYONE.

When the Jack Benny show and the Burns and Allen show became leading radio programs, the four stars moved to Hollywood, where they could star in motion pictures at the same time. They quickly became a part of the Hollywood social set and were invited to all the leading parties. Even there George always played his little pranks on his friend. One time they were at a party given by Louis B. Mayer, the head of MGM studios. After dinner the guests were told to come to the music room, where chairs had been set up and MGM's singing star, Jeanette MacDonald, was to perform. As they entered the room, George whispered to Jack, "Now remember, Jack, when Jeanette MacDonald starts to sing, it would be very impolite if you were to laugh." Jack started to bite his lip to keep the giggles from escaping. As Miss MacDonald approached the piano, George continued to mouth his admonition while staring directly at Jack, and at the first note there was a loud roar from Jack, who rushed out of the room followed by George, who also collapsed in the hallway.

In 1961 he did it again. Jack and George flew to England for a command performance which was attended by the queen mother. The stars were to meet the royal family after the performance, and as they lined up for the presentation, George leaned over to Jack and whispered, "Now when you meet the queen mother, be sure you don't laugh when you shake her hand."

As the queen mother walked down the row of stars, Jack tried his best to look away from George's riveted look, but those fixed eyes were like a magnet, and poor Jack started to bite his lip as the royal lady approached. She extended her hand to Jack and said, "I enjoyed your performance very much, Mr. Benny," and miracle of miracles, Jack didn't laugh. He was so intent on biting his lip that he couldn't even thank her for the compliment.

During this trip in 1961, I was taking a walk through the London streets one day with Jack and George. George and I were walking ahead, while Jack dawdled behind. "Watch this," said George, and he proceeded to stop at every stoop and look down into the basements. As he kept doing this, we saw Jack doing the same, looking down the stoops, too. Finally, George stopped and asked, "What are you looking down into those basements for, Jack?"

Jack answered, "I don't want to miss anything."

When George told him that there was nothing, we practically had to carry him back to the Dorchester Hotel. Incidentally, the Dorchester Hotel had the biggest, heaviest room keys, and one day George called for a bellboy while Jack was in the room with him.

"What do you want a bellboy for?" asked Jack.

"To carry my keys down to the desk," snapped George. That was good for a ten-minute scream.

In 1953 Burns and Allen and Jack and his wife, Mary Livingstone, decided to spend a week in Honolulu. The boys took the *Lurline,* a luxury liner that sailed between the mainland and the Islands. Gracie and Mary planned to fly over to meet them a few days after they would arrive.

On the second day out a fellow from Grand Rapids, Michigan, came over to their table to speak to them, and after he left, George told Jack that he thought Jack was rather rude to the man.

"After dinner," George remembers, "Jack went over to the man's table to apologize, and that was the last I saw of him on that boat trip. He spent every minute with the fellow, his wife and aunt."

They stayed at the Royal Hawaiian Hotel. Their first night was a Saturday, when it was customary for the men to wear white dinner jackets and the women to dress in evening dresses. Jack and George, in their best resort dinner clothes, were dining at a table for two when in the middle of their meal, a nice-looking gentleman came to their table and spoke to Jack.

"I'm sorry to disturb you, Mr. Benny, but I'm here with my grandmother who is celebrating her ninety-fourth birthday. You have always been her favorite entertainer, and I can't think of a nicer birthday present than if you would say hello to her."

"Of course," said Jack, jumping to his feet.

"Please, Mr. Benny," the man said. "You're in the middle of your dinner, and we've already finished. You stay here, and I'll bring my grandmother over to you."

In a little while the man came back to their table with a beautiful little white-haired old lady, hobbling on a cane. In a frail voice she said to Jack, "Mr. Benny, this is the happiest day of my life and meeting you makes this the best birthday I've ever had. You've been my idol since your early vaudeville days, and I never missed a radio or television show you ever did. I've followed your career from the beginning, and I really love you."

Jack was embarrassed and was trying to think of what to say to this sweet old lady when she whispered to him, "May I kiss you, Mr. Benny?"

And she moved to him, and as he leaned toward her, she kissed him lightly on the cheek. As she hobbled away, leaning on her nephew's arm, George said, "Well, Jack, I guess you're all set for tonight," and the last thing the old lady heard was a mighty yell that seemed to come from near where Jack Benny was pounding the floor.

One time Jack and George went to New York together to attend a dinner. They shared a two-bedroom suite at the Plaza Hotel. On their first night in town Jack was sound asleep when he was awakened suddenly at 4 A.M. by George, who thrust a deck of cards under Jack's nose and said, "Pick a card."

Sleepily, Jack picked a card.

"Put it back in the deck," insisted George, and then he promptly went back to his room and to sleep, leaving Jack up the rest of the night to figure out just what had happened.

Jack loved to tell theater audiences about the time he had been on the road for three months and finally came back to Beverly Hills.

"I saw George sitting in his car across the street, and he honked his horn at me and motioned for me to come over. I was so delighted to see him after all that time that I rushed across the busy intersection, but just as I got near him, he rolled up his window and drove away. And to let you know what kind of jerk I am, that was the third time he did that to me!"

One evening at a Beverly Hills restaurant, George noticed a white thread on the lapel of Jack's navy blue jacket. As he plucked the thread from the lapel, George said, "That's a darling thread . . . so becoming. Would you mind if I borrow it to wear to a party tomorrow night?"

Two days later a special messenger arrived with a small, beautifully wrapped gift box for Jack. The accompanying card read: "Thanks so much for loaning me your thread. Everyone at the party just loved it. George." When Jack opened the box, neatly perched on a small black velvet cushion, was a white thread. A half hour later and with the help of two servants, Mary Benny was still trying to pick her husband up from the floor.

One of the last things George did to Jack was at Chasen's Restaurant in Beverly Hills one night when the two were dining alone.

"Listen, Jack," said George, "I've got a great gag to play on Dave Chasen. Now, we're both pretty good customers here, so when the check comes, we'll call Dave Chasen over and you say, 'I want to pay this check, and if you let George Burns pay the check, I'll never come in here again,' and I'll say, 'Look, Dave, if you let Jack pay this check, I'll never come in here again,' so Chasen will have to grab the check himself because he won't want to lose us as customers."

Jack thought that was a terrific idea, and so they called Dave Chasen to the table.

"Listen here, Dave," Jack said holding up the check, "I'm going to pay this, and if you let George Burns pay the check, I'll never come in here again."

George sat there silently, never saying one word, while Jack waited for his protest. Nothing. Dave looked from one to the other and then said, "Okay, Jack, if that's the way you want it, it's okay with me," and he moved to another table.

8

VAUDEVILLE was Jack Benny's whole world, and the ultimate a performer could achieve, in his opinion, was to headline a season on a top vaudeville circuit and eventually to attain star billing at the Palace Theater in New York. Jack always said about those days, "All I knew was, 'Two Jews got on a streetcar,'" which really was all he knew or was interested in then. Politics, business, world problems were of very little importance to him. Instead, he spent most of his waking hours talking and thinking vaudeville.

The performers spent hours and hours discussing the merits of Fink's Mules as a strong opening act as compared with a Japanese juggling troupe. They talked about the singers, about the strength of one opening song over another. And then the comedy routines. How to build a joke, how to segue from one line to another, how long to pause before the punch line of a joke. It was in this area that Jack spent more time than the others in thinking out his own routines and changing a sentence or sometimes even only one word to make the difference between a mild joke and a big laugh.

Jack's career was coming along very well; he was getting

more than his share of laughs, as audiences started to appreciate his quiet, elegant brand of comedy, until one tour when he was booked to follow the Four Marx Brothers. It was the first time Jack had seen them since he played for them in the pit at the Barrison Theater in Waukegan, and by now the four, Groucho, Harpo, Chico, and the youngest brother, Zeppo, all were well known.

The Marx Brothers were one of the greatest acts ever to play vaudeville, and their riotous comedy so overwhelmed their audiences that it was almost impossible to follow them successfully. When a quiet, sophisticated act like Jack Benny followed, the silence was deafening. After his first performance that engagement Jack was very despondent, and when he found himself getting the same subdued response from the audience at each show, he was ready to quit the tour; but Minnie Marx, who was not only the mother, but the manager of the Marx Brothers, persuaded him to stay on, convincing Jack that it wasn't that he was not a good performer, but that no one had ever been able to follow the Marx boys' crazy act. Jack then started to relax and found his confidence returning as he began to get a few more laughs until soon he actually began to enjoy the tour.

When the troupe reached Vancouver, Zeppo met a girl named Babe Marks, who invited him to her home for dinner. Zeppo told her he wanted to bring his friend Jack Benny over one night, and Babe said she had a kid sister at home, so bring Jack Benny along. Zeppo told Jack all about the terrific date he had arranged for him, and off they went to the Marks' home. When Jack saw his "date," twelve-year-old Sadie (she eventually became Mary Livingstone) all dressed up in her older sister's clothes and high-heeled shoes for the event, he was so disappointed that he completely ignored her for the entire dinner and could hardly wait until the meal was ended so he could make his exit. Sadie was both angry and mortified and decided to get even with this big-time actor. The next day she rounded up about a dozen of her friends and took them to the theater for the matinee. They took up the entire first row and proceeded to heckle Jack all through his act so that he didn't even bother to do his encore. When he came off stage, he told everyone that it had been one of the worst audiences he had ever played to, never real-

izing that his young date from the night before had perpe-
trated the plot.

By 1926 Jack had developed into a well-established comedian on the vaudeville circuit. If his rise was not sudden or
his success made overnight, one could hardly call his career
checkered. It was marked throughout by a slow but steady
increase in recognition. He was now making $450 a week,
which was enough to enable him to "buy" some jokes from
professional writers. One of the writers Jack liked best then
was Al Boasberg, who eventually became the top vaudeville
writer in the business, even writing for the Marx Brothers
for many of their Hollywood films. Boasberg started as a jewelry salesman who hung around backstage trying to sell items
to the actors. He found that he was quick with good ad-libs,
and soon he was selling a joke here and there until finally he
was selling more jokes than jewelry and ended up trading
one business for the other. The first joke he sold to Jack was:
"I was on the Staten Island ferry this morning, and I saw an
old Jewish man selling candy. He was yelling, 'Candy
. . . two cents apiece,' and not selling very much. He passed
a woman who said, 'He looks Turkish,' and the man then
started yelling, 'Turkish candy . . . two cents apiece.'"

About this time he found himself on the same bill with
Nora Bayes, one of the great singing headliners of vaudeville. Miss Bayes not only admired the talent of Jack Benny,
but had a keen romantic interest in the handsome thirty-
year-old comedian. Her personal interest in Jack led her to
arrange for him to be on the same bill with her for an entire
tour of the Orpheum circuit. Not only did he do his own act,
but he came on for the finale of her act and did a short comedy routine with her which ended with them sitting on a
bench, hugging and kissing as the curtain went down. As the
curtain was raised for bows, they were still hugging and kissing, an innovative comedy switch for those days. Jack was to
use similar closing gags for the rest of his career, onstage and
for television.

Forty years later I was on a theater tour with Jack. It had
become his habit to ask me to hold his money—usually a roll
of bills—each night before he went onstage because he never
liked anything in his pockets to detract from the excellent
tailoring of his suit.

51

One morning at breakfast, he was reminiscing about his romance with Nora Bayes. He told me about an overnight train trip they had made where he had had an upper berth and she had had a drawing room in the next car. He said that after he had undressed, he slipped a dressing gown on over his pajamas and went into Nora's drawing room to have a drink. He did not return to his berth until the next morning, and there to his dismay he found that someone, probably the porter, had stolen $300 from his pants pocket. That was a sizable sum of money to him in those days, but there was nothing he could do about it because he dared not reveal where he had spent the night.

After listening to his story, I said, "Jack, it was your own fault, you should have let me hold the money for you." The ridiculousness of the remark about a forty-year-old happening sent Jack to pounding the floor, and every time after that when he would hand me the money as he was about to go on-stage, he'd have a big laugh.

When that same tour reached the Orpheum Theater in Los Angeles, one night Nora Bayes made a date with some old friends and did not include Jack. That evening, dining alone, he ran into Babe Marks from Vancouver. She was by then married to Al Bernovici, a fiddle-playing vaudevillian who worked under the name of Count Bernovici. Babe was very happy to see Jack, and she immediately suggested that she could get her pretty sister and the four of them could go out. Since Jack had no recollection of that sad dinner in Vancouver, he agreed. The next night he, once again, met Sadie Marks, the girl who would become the first and only Mrs. Jack Benny.

9

IN 1926 Jack had ended a four-year romance with Mary Kelly, the girl who had been Gracie Allen's roommate until Gracie married George Burns. Although deep down he had no real desire to be a married man and give up the easygoing life of a bachelor-actor, he was so in love with Mary Kelly that he did ask her to marry him many times. He knew his father, Meyer Kubelsky, would be mortified if he married a Catholic girl, and perhaps Jack knew his many proposals were safe because her Catholicism would never let her say yes.

Time after time Mary refused, and each time the tears flowed copiously, and although Jack shed as many of those heart-felt tears as she, he was to admit later that he had actually been relieved by her constant turndown. Finally, after they had agreed to disagree because their romance was going nowhere, Mary Kelly suddenly did an about-face and relented after a separation of several months. She sent Jack a wire and said she would marry him. But by this time he felt that marriage was out of the question for him and wrote her a long letter ending the romance once and for all.

When Jack met Sadie Marks again on that blind date with the Bernovicis, the world did not stand still, and if Cupid shot his little arrow, it not only didn't penetrate Jack's heart immediately, but missed him completely. He was not interested then in being serious, but he thought she was attractive and, more important, had a terrific sense of humor, which was high on his list of qualifications for a prospective date. Young Sadie was a hosiery salesgirl at the May Company, and the next day she told all her friends at the store about her meeting the vaudeville star Jack Benny, but they didn't believe her. Right after lunch in strolled Jack, wearing a natty straw hat, and walked right over to the hosiery counter. Sadie proudly introduced him to her friends, and then Jack asked for a date that night. He took her to the Cocoanut Grove at the Ambassador Hotel, the smartest dining and dancing spot in town. She was very impressed with him. Despite his sophisticated manner and his debonair exterior, Jack was really lonely for a simple Jewish girl with a similar background to his own, and since Sadie had a good sense of humor and was attractive, he found himself with her more and more until they were together every moment he was away from the theater and she was not behind the hosiery counter.

In the early 1950's Jack did a television show titled *How Jack Found Mary,* and their meeting was depicted in a humorous fashion. In the sketch he went to the May Company to buy a shirt for $1.99 and he gave the salesman $2. While he waited for the penny change, he saw Mary at the hosiery counter. On that show, Mary snapped, "Jack still has that same penny he got for change."

In future radio shows, Mary's sister, Babe, became a much-discussed character, although she never actually appeared on any of the shows. Many people thought that Babe was simply a fictitious role created to be the butt of jokes. "Babe," Jack would crack, "used to work in motion pictures under the name of William Bendix."

After Jack left Los Angeles on the tour, he called Sadie at least once a week, and one time when he had a three-day layover in San Francisco, he came to Los Angeles again to visit her. Although he liked her, his more serious thoughts were directed toward his career, as always.

In the latter part of 1926 Jack won one of the comedy leads in his first musical revue, a Shubert show called *The Great Temptations,* which opened for a successful run in Chicago. Jack did a strong eleven-minute spot in the musical, and the critics gave him excellent notices. He felt that he was off and running to bigger and better things. The last thing he was considering at that time was marriage. He was by then making $600 a week and having a wonderful time without too many responsibilities.

One day shortly after *The Great Temptations* opened, he ran into Babe, who was playing with her husband at a local vaudeville theater.

"Did you hear about Sadie?" asked Babe. "She's getting married to a very wealthy fellow from Vancouver."

"I just talked to her a week ago," said Jack, surprised, "and she didn't mention a thing about it to me."

"Well, she just decided because this man has been after her a long time, and now he's planning to come down to Los Angeles in a few weeks."

Jack called Sadie immediately, and when she confirmed the report, Jack insisted that she couldn't do that to him.

"Why don't you come to Chicago for a week or so and visit Babe and then we can talk about it?" he pleaded.

After a little convincing she agreed, and four days later she arrived. The first thing Jack did was to take her to Lake Forest, a beautiful Chicago suburb, where his father was living, and they spent a pleasant afternoon. Meyer quickly approved of Sadie, not only because she was attractive and personable, but because she was the first Jewish girl his son had ever mentioned to him, let alone brought for a visit. With a little urging from his father the reluctant Jack asked her to marry him.

His old friend Julius Synikan, still a clothing salesman in a Waukegan department store, insisted on giving the wedding, and with Julius as best man, his father and sister, Florence, at his side and Babe and Al Bernovici standing up for Sadie, a rabbi married Jack and Sadie in Julius' small bedroom in Waukegan's only hotel on January 14, 1927. As soon as the rabbi pronounced them man and wife, Sadie fainted dead away on Julius' bed, and it took them a half hour to revive her. The happy couple went right back to Chicago, where Jack just had time to get to the theater for the performance that night. And that's the way Sadie spent most of her honeymoon: sitting backstage at *The Great Temptations*.

Although the new Mrs. Benny had a great sense of humor, she didn't quite understand the easy camaraderie of showfolks and at first had a difficult time adjusting. Even in those days everyone tried to make Jack laugh because they loved to hear his great roars of approval and see him pound his thigh or the floor or table, whichever happened to be more available. The chorus girls in the show were no exception. About a week after they were married, Jack was getting made up in his dressing room one night and Sadie was watching when one of the chorus girls decided to play a big joke on him. Using a lipstick, she painted one of her breasts to look exactly like a pig, burst into the dressing room, pulled out the artistic breast and yelled, "Oink, oink." The girl didn't notice Sadie seated behind the door and screamed with laughter, waiting for Jack to give his customary roar. But poor Jack just sat there, looking embarrassed and uncomfortable until the girl turned, saw Sadie, and ran from the room. Sadie didn't talk to her husband for two days while he vainly tried to explain that it had been just a silly joke.

After a five-month run *The Great Temptations* opened in San Francisco. By this time Sadie had become bored and nervous from sitting backstage night after night. San Francisco was a welcome change from Chicago, and for the first few weeks she was busy shopping and visiting in the city where she had lived before moving to Los Angeles. However, one night, after several tiring evenings backstage, she and Jack had their first real argument, which resulted in their only separation during their forty-eight years of marriage. In the last few years of his stage appearances Jack often did a joke about divorce:

"Mary and I have been married forty-seven years, and not once have we ever had an argument serious enough to mention the word 'divorce' . . . 'murder,' yes, but 'divorce,' never."

The argument started as they were getting dressed to go out for dinner and Jack put on a very, very loud tie. Sadie objected to the tie, but Jack was stubborn and insisted on wearing it. The argument became so bitter over a silly tie that she finally said, "If you don't take that tie off, I'm leaving you and going home to my folks in Los Angeles."

Jack refused to remove the tie, never believing that she would go through with her threat, but she quickly packed, took a cab to the station, and did go home to Los Angeles.

Jack once told me that after a week of silence from both war fronts, the two of them stubbornly refusing to concede, he finally couldn't stand it any longer and mailed the tie to Sadie with a cute note which read: "I thought you'd like to give this tie to the Salvation Army. All my love, Jack."

She was back in San Francisco on the next train, and after a tearful reunion she presented him with a beautifully wrapped gift package. When he opened it, he got one of his biggest laughing fits, for Sadie had enclosed the same loud tie.

10

WHEN *The Great Temptations* closed, Jack booked a tour on the vaudeville circuit, but by now, realizing that it would be disastrous if his wife just tagged along, he wrote her into the act. Sadie had a very pleasant singing voice, and although she had never been on the stage before, she did not have stage fright. He wrote some put-down jokes and some "dumb" jokes, and with the excellent delivery she had right from the start, the audiences liked her. By the time they had toured for a season Sadie was getting big laughs on her lines and enthusiastic applause for the two songs she did every show, and she blossomed out as a full-fledged vaudeville performer.

One day Jack's agent, Tom Fitzpatrick, called with exciting news. Irving Thalberg had seen Jack and wanted him for Metro-Goldwyn-Mayer movies! This meant a new challenge in a new medium, motion pictures. Jack was thrilled, and he signed a six-month contract for $750 a week, heralding the start of another career for the handsome young actor. Sadie was equally happy because it meant that she was coming home and could spend time with her parents and her brother, Hilliard.

The Bennys rented a lovely home in Beverly Hills, and Jack was quickly initiated into the studio routine of publicity stills, biographical interviews, and general get-acquainted sessions with the big stars of MGM: Joan Crawford, John Gilbert, Greta Garbo, Lionel Barrymore, Wallace Beery, Conrad Nagel. It was a whole new world, this glamor arena of films and film stars, and at the beginning it was happy and exciting for the Bennys. But after the first two months Jack became discontented when he saw that the studio wasn't giving him leads in the big pictures they were making but instead used him as a master of ceremonies for industry dinners and Hollywood premieres. Finally he got a role, but only to play Jack Benny the comedian in *Hollywood Revue,* a musical revue utilizing all the stars MGM had under contract. Jack's part was to do a few jokes and then to introduce Conrad Nagel by saying, "And now I'd like to introduce one of the great stars of the day, a man with a name to conjure with, Mr. Conrad Nagel."

However, he pronounced "conjure" incorrectly as "conjoor," and when Mr. Nagel made his entrance, he called Jack on the mispronunciation, doing a whole routine on the correct way to pronounce the word. Then Jack left the stage, and Conrad Nagel proceeded to take over, introducing the other acts, including Cliff Edwards and his ukulele doing a chorus of "Singing in the Rain," which was repeated in *That's*

Entertainment. That was Jack's debut as a film player, and not a very auspicious one.

When *Hollywood Revue* was edited, the routine between Benny and Nagel was cut out, leaving Jack introducing him with "a name to conjoor with," which made no sense at all and moved one reviewer to comment, "If Mr. Benny plans to continue in motion pictures, we suggest he first learn how to speak English."

With no other pictures in store for him, Jack decided that the inactivity was hurting his career, so he went to Irving Thalberg to ask for a release from his contract. Thalberg did not plead too hard for the comedian to stay, so an agreement was reached, and as soon as the lease was up on their house, the Bennys were off to New York.

As I mentioned earlier, Jack Benny's career did not have the dramatic ups or downs which often mark the lives of famous personalities. But whether timing, fate, cleverness, or a combination of all three was responsible, Jack seemed often to be at the right place at the right time. As luck would have it, when the Bennys returned to New York, Earl Carroll was looking for another comedian for his new *Earl Carroll Vanities* and signed Jack for the gigantic sum of $1,500 a week, which for the year 1930 in the time of the Great Depression was a fortune.

Jack did just about everything in the show, a long monologue, as well as many different characters in all the sketches. In one sketch he entered a farmhouse carrying a girl in his arms and said to the farmer, "I've just resuscitated your daughter."

"By golly, then you've got to marry her."

For the early thirties this was very racy material, as you can imagine.

In another sketch, he played a detective, dressed in the stock derby hat and smoking a cigar. Although Jack was then thirty-six years old, tobacco had never crossed his lips and the first few days of rehearsal he became very nauseated from puffing on big black cigars. He pleaded with the director to eliminate the cigar and let the derby hat fully describe the character, but the cigar was a necessity for a detective, and the director insisted. After a few weeks Jack became more used to smoking, and little by little, he started to enjoy it. In no time at all he began to smoke cigars offstage and was an inveterate cigar smoker the rest of his life. Over the years, however, he never developed a taste for expensive cigars and appeared to enjoy a very cheap one just as much as an imported one. Although he would smoke, perhaps, several a day, he usually only smoked a few puffs and then would throw it away. People who knew him well knew this about him and would never give him the best cigars for gifts because he always reminded everyone what a waste that would be.

In 1948 Jack played the London Palladium. All imported items in England were very costly during that time right after the war. A good imported cigar was around $3, and Jack received many of them from his British friends. Those people, used to scarcities and deprivations of war, would smoke only a portion of such a cigar, then carefully clip off the end and store it in their pocket for a later smoke. When Jack would take his customary six or seven puffs and then throw away such a luxury item, his friends stared at him aghast that he could be so extravagant.

Although the job in the Vanities went smoothly and the money was the most he had ever earned, Jack started to feel uneasy as everyone began talking about the leading radio shows of the day. He listened to the little box as often as he could when he wasn't onstage. He heard names he had never before heard who were suddenly national stars, Gene and Glenn, Amos and Andy, as well as others who had had no background in show business. With his twenty years in the theater, Jack felt that he knew much more about comedy than these Johnny-come-latelies, and he waited anxiously for a chance to make his mark in the new medium. He wasn't the only one waiting; his friends Burns and Allen and Eddie Cantor and many others were also interested in breaking into this new area.

Jack's opportunity came in the latter part of 1931, when Ed Sullivan, then a columnist on the New York *Daily News,* invited Jack to be a guest on an interview program he was doing on a New York radio station. Jack's opening line on radio, a line which has been repeated thousands of times since, was: "This is Jack Benny. . . . There will now be a slight pause while everyone says, 'Who cares?' "

The reaction to the Sullivan interview was electric, and the advertising agencies started to discuss the possibilities of this new comedy prospect. The *Vanities* was due to go on the road, and Jack was torn between the security of the stage job and the vague possibility of a chance in radio. After discussing it with his wife, Jack decided to take a chance at radio, and since he had saved up some money, he felt he could afford to gamble. He went to Earl Carroll and asked for his release. Timing again or luck—Earl Carroll was anxious to save some money on the road tour and could easily replace Jack with a cheaper comedian, so a mutual agreement was readily arranged.

Jack made an audition record for an advertising agency and then took his wife to Miami Beach for a six-week vacation.

He had been in Florida a short time when he received word that he had been set to star in a new radio program with one of the top bandleaders of the day, George Olsen, and George Olsen's wife, the well-known singer Ethel Shutta.

11

CANADA Dry Ginger Ale was the sponsor of the radio show starring comedian Jack Benny, George Olsen and his band, and Ethel Shutta, and the program was scheduled to start in May, 1932, for seventeen weeks on CBS. As soon as he signed, Jack Benny, always the worrier, began to feel nervous about the forthcoming radio show. For a performer who had spent years developing a seventeen-minute act, he was terrified at the thought of having to deliver funny routines every week for seventeen weeks and come up with new material every time.

"There I was," Jack always said about that new career he started, "a man who would book three days in Scranton to break in one new joke before I'd try it in the big-city theaters, and now I would have to break in new jokes every single week to the whole country without any tryout at all!"

Jack went to his best friend, George Burns, for advice about a writer to help him since George had already launched the successful Burns and Allen show. George suggested that they share a writer George was using, a former vaudeville gagster, Harry Conn, who was being paid $35 a week by George. Jack hired Conn for an additional $50 a week, and they started to plan the show.

As was to be his custom for the rest of his radio and television career, Jack prodded Conn to come up with something new and different, to try to stay away from the ordinary formats of existing comedy programs. And even though they were to part four years later on unfriendly terms, Jack always credited Conn with being a brilliant writer and creator of many of the ideas that formed the Benny character and program conception that lasted through his lifetime.

Jack had been listening to the routine radio commercials on the other programs and felt that a comedian could inject some humor into the commercial to make it more palatable to the listener and do a better job of selling the product at the same time. Canada Dry reluctantly agreed to let him try it, and Harry Conn started to write.

On the first few shows, Jack would be introduced as "our effervescent comedian" by George Olsen, and then Jack would open with such lines as: "Effervescent for me, we would have a nice program tonight."

One of the first commercials they did with a comedy flavor had Jack reading a telegram supposedly written by the Canada Dry Ginger Ale sales manager in North Africa.

"I was driving across the Sahara Desert when I came across a party of people who had been stranded in the desert for thirty days without a drop of water, and they were ready to perish from lack of liquid. I gave each of them a glass of Canada Dry Ginger Ale, and not one of them said it was a bad drink."

The audacity of this commercial did not overly impress the sponsor, and when the next two "comic" commercials were broadcast, word came down from headquarters to eliminate the comedy and go back to a straight sell. But it had taken the public a few weeks to realize what was happening, and soon the letters started pouring in to Canada Dry, applauding them for their catchy and amusing sales pitch. The thousands of letters did the trick, and once again word came

61

down from the advertising agency, only this time it was to continue with the humorous commercial plan, which became a trademark for all the Benny radio and television shows thereafter.

Jack and Harry Conn also innovated the gag satirizations of current hit motion pictures, the first being a sketch of their version of *Grand Hotel,* called "Grind Hotel." They did such jokes as:

> SOUND: *Heavy knock on door.*
> ETHEL SHUTTA: Who is it?
> BENNY: It's the Baron.
> ETHEL: Which Baron?
> BENNY: From Wilkes Baron, Pennsylvania.

Satirizing motion pictures became an important addition to the many ingredients of Jack Benny comedy, and he used it throughout his radio and television career. In the meantime, many other programs picked up the idea, and it became standard comedy even on many of today's programs.

Another original idea that was started in the first year of the Benny radio program was the use of sound effects, which earlier were seldom if ever used on the air. Usually actors simply made entrances and exits, and the dialogue was supposed fully to describe the scene to the listening audience. Harry Conn started his characters knocking on doors and inserted the sounds of doors opening or slamming closed to indicate entrances and exits. This led to more sophisticated sound effects which became an integral part of radio and served to enhance the picture that the sound medium couldn't fully transmit by only the spoken word. The sounds of Jack Benny's Maxwell starting, sputtering along, and wheezing to a stop would get tremendous laughs in later shows without a word of dialogue.

At the end of his first short season George Olsen and Ethel Shutta left the show, as did the sponsor, Canada Dry. But General Motors signed Jack immediately to star in his own show, and he replaced his bandleader first with Ted Weems, then with Frank Black, and finally with Don Bestor.

Tenors were the singers in vogue at that time, and it was Harry Conn's idea to hire a boy singer. A young fellow named Frank Parker was chosen to complete the cast of the new Jack Benny program.

By then Harry Conn was Broadway's leading writer with his success on the new Benny program and the Burns and Allen show, which continued to be high on the popularity polls, but he wanted to be the sole writer for Burns instead of sharing the honors with a young man named Carroll Carroll who later was to achieve recognition as the writer of the Bing Crosby show.

"Conn came to me and delivered an ultimatum," says Burns. "He threatened to quit the show unless I got rid of Carroll as he wanted to write Jack's show and our show all by himself. Now, my advertising agency, J. Walter Thompson, was supplying Carroll to me for free, and I'm no fool, so I told Harry Conn he was free to write the Benny show by himself but Carroll was going to continue with me."

Conn went back to Jack and told him he would work for him exclusively, and Jack gave him a big raise and offered him extra money for writing material for his theater appearances which he was making while getting ready to start the new General Motors program on NBC.

One of the first bits Conn wrote for Jack for the theater was a Japanese wrestler sketch which ended up as a stage classic. For this act, Jack brought onstage a small Japanese man in traditional wrestler uniform and seven burly stagehands. He then explained to the audience that he had seen this man on a recent tour of Japan and discovered that he was the champion wrestler of the Orient and could easily handle any ten men. He then announced that the wrestler would dispose of the seven tough stagehands in exactly twenty seconds. He would give the signal to start, and the seven stagehands would advance on the wrestler and flatten him in five seconds, walking off, leaving the little fellow lying prone on the floor, while Jack looked at the audience with his helpless, frustrated expression as the curtain slowly descended.

He did the Japanese wrestler gag for many years on the stage, and in one of his early TV programs he repeated it with great success.

The new Jack Benny program started to climb in the ratings. His "Play, Don" to signal an orchestra number became a popular expression, and young Frank Parker was started on the road to stardom. But although the public liked the show, General Motors president William F. Knudsen did not like it and dropped it after the season.

Jack's disappointment at being dropped was tempered that year only by the fact that he had found a spot for his wife on the show. It came about when they were auditioning girls to play the role of a young fan from Plainfield, New Jersey, who was to read a crazy poem in tribute to Labor Day. Jack, knowing how well Sadie read lines, suggested that they try her out, and she read the script so well that she won the part of Mary Livingstone, the fan from Plainfield, a totally created character. The bit went over so well that another poem was written for the fan from Plainfield to read the following week. Again, the idea met with great success. Since it was awkward to have the "fan" keep returning each week, Jack hired her as his secretary, which gave a reason to write her in the show each time, and thus she became a regular member of the cast. Although Mrs. Benny has never been to Plainfield, New Jersey, she still receives fan letters from people who insist that they went to school with her in Plainfield.

12

THE year 1934 was a big one in the life of the Bennys.

First, they adopted a six-week-old girl, whom they named Joan.

And secondly, Frank Parker left the show to start his own program, such had been his popularity. Many people predicted doom for the Benny show with Frank Parker leaving. The tenor had become not only a singing sensation, but an important comedy element of the program, and some of the Broadway doomsayers thought that Jack would lose a big part of his audience without Frank Parker.

But Jack and Harry Conn found a young unknown tenor, Kenny Baker, and decided to try him. Sooner than even they expected, Kenny Baker took the fancy of the listening public, and eventually he became even more popular than Parker had been. That same year they hired a sports announcer, Don Wilson, who because of his girth started a series of "fat" jokes that were to continue for the life of the Benny programs.

The Bennys were leading a very active social life during this period, seeing all the Broadway shows and going out nearly every night to famous restaurants and nightclubs.

"There was one time," reports Jesse Block, "when the Bennys, Ida and Eddie Cantor, and Eva and I went out every single night for weeks. One week we went to Lindy's every night until finally Jack insisted we go to Ruby Foo's for Chinese food, which we all loved. But Eddie Cantor always ordered cornflakes and milk for dinner, and he was firm about going to Lindy's. After an argument, we decided to toss a coin. Eddie won, and off we went to Lindy's again. Jack told Leo Lindy what had happened, and when they brought Eddie his cornflakes, a troupe of Chinese waiters from a nearby restaurant paraded in, carrying steaming dishes of all sorts of delicious Cantonese food."

Although he had Jack by his side with his help, advice, and basic instincts as to what was right comedically, Harry Conn continued to write the half hour program every week by himself, which was a monumental job. The shows remained consistently funny and the ratings kept rising until the program was one of the leading comedy shows on the air. As the kudos kept coming in, Conn kept getting more egotistical and began to spread the word that he was the Jack Benny program and without him it would quickly drop out of sight. He was then making $1,500 per week, plus extra money for working on the Benny personal appearance shows.

General Motors had been replaced first by General Tires as a sponsor and then, in 1935, by General Foods, which signed the program to a long-term contract and assigned as the product to be sold on the show a gelatine named Jello, which at that time was far from one of the leaders in its food field.

With the signing of this contract, Conn became more arrogant with Jack because he felt that the comedian could not possibly do without him. One incident which helped bring much friction to the surface occurred when Mary Benny came in one day with her first mink coat, and Harry Conn's wife said, "If not for my husband, you wouldn't be wearing that mink coat."

On a vacation in Miami Beach, Conn ran into Meyer Kubelsky, who had retired and was living there. Conn told the old gentleman that if it weren't for him, Conn, Jack would be nothing. Naturally, Meyer was indignant and told his son about the remark, which helped create more animosity between the star and his writer. Toward the end of the 1935–36 season, Conn brought his resentment to the surface when they started to discuss a new contract, since Jack was going to the Coast to make a picture for MGM called *Broadway Melody* and planned to broadcast from Hollywood for the next year. Conn told Jack that he was totally responsible for his success and insisted on being an equal partner in the revenue from the show. Jack told him that it was ridiculous and refused to discuss such a contract. Jack was ready to give him a handsome raise, but Conn refused and went to Atlantic City with his wife.

Jack waited patiently for the script for the next Sunday's program, but Conn thought that this would be a good time to make the comedian realize his worth, and he not only didn't write the script, but refused to come to the phone to talk to Jack. When Thursday came and no script arrived, Jack called his good friend Phil Baker, who was starring in his own radio show. Baker let him borrow two of his writers, Sam Perrin and a young man named Arthur Phillips. Perrin was a former vaudeville drummer who had written some jokes for Jack years before for the stage and knew his brand of comedy. The two young writers huddled with Jack for three days and came up with a very funny script that was equal to one of Conn's.

Jack immediately sent a two-page vitriolic telegram firing Conn, and since there were only two weeks left in that season, he had Perrin and Phillips double from Phil Baker's program, and also hired another young team, Hugh Wedlock and Howard Snyder, press agents who wrote funny gags for the columnists.

As vaudeville entertainment was replaced by radio, the written word became more and more important, and the hiring of competent writers became an absolute necessity to a successful show. Fred Allen, one of the great comedians and

66

a good friend of Jack's, suggested that Jack hire another young writer named Ed Beloin for the following season. Jack paired Beloin with a Chicago writer, Bill Morrow. So with Beloin and Morrow, he had Wedlock and Snyder come to the Coast to help with the writing, and for insurance, he hired Al Boasberg, who was already on the Coast working for the Marx Brothers. He also arranged for MGM to hire Perrin and Phillips to write his comedy routines for *Broadway Melody*. Always the cautious man, Jack Benny had a very complete writing staff for the year. After the movie was completed, Phil Baker took up the option on Perrin and Phillips, and they returned to New York; Wedlock and Snyder went to work as motion-picture writers; and Morrow and Beloin continued to work as award-winning writers on the Benny show for the next seven years.

Ironically, Harry Conn went to work for Joe Penner, the "Wanna buy a duck?" comic for six shows, but they failed to get along. Then he wrote on the Eddie Cantor show for some time, after which he created his own show, *The Harry Conn Show,* which was similar in format to the Benny program but with unknown performers. Unfortunately, the critics destroyed his creation, and the public turned their dials away. From then on, Conn just drifted off, getting occasional work, and he ended up sadly, from time to time writing Jack for money loans. In the late 1950's Jack saw a Broadway play one evening and went backstage to congratulate one of the actors who was a friend of his. There he saw, much to their embarrassment, Harry Conn who was filling in for someone as a temporary doorman. This was their first meeting in many years and their last meeting before Conn died.

One of the last things Harry Conn wrote for Jack was an act Jack did on his personal appearance tours when he played motion-picture theaters with a stage show. This act was a satire of the three Boswell sisters, a leading singing trio of the thirties. Jack would announce that he was auditioning acts for his radio show and that the manager of the theater had assembled a different act to appear on each show so that Jack could see how they performed before an audience. Jack would emphasize that he hadn't seen the act he was about to introduce, and then he would read off a card the name "Coswell Sisters."

Three girls would enter dressed in funny frills and ruffles, one very fat, one very tough, and one young and pretty. The first few years he did the act, he used his old girlfriend, Mary Kelly, as the fat girl because she had reached 200 pounds, and by that time and size Mary Livingstone did not object to having her on the show. In later years he updated the act by calling it "The Landrew Sisters," then "The Guire Sisters," and finally "The Smothers Sisters."

As recently as the year before he died, Jack presented the Smothers Sisters in Las Vegas and other theaters with Iris Adrian as the gum-chewing tough girl, Peggy Mondo as the fat girl, and Chanin Hale as the pretty one. Highlights of the act included Jack looking over the three in amazement when they came on stage.

JACK *(to the fat one)*: Are you girls *really* sisters?

PEGGY: I am *(glancing at the others)*. I don't know about the other two.

JACK: Now, I don't want to get personal or anything, but have you always been that heavy.

PEGGY: I was even heavier, but last month I lost fifty pounds.

JACK: Oh, fifty pounds . . . did your doctor put you on a diet?

PEGGY: No, he took out my tonsils.

JACK *(to the tough one)*: I was wondering, have you girls had much experience?

IRIS: We ought to slap your face!

JACK *(to the pretty one)*: Say, you're the prettiest one of the three.

CHANIN *(glancing dubiously at the other two)*: Is that good?

JACK: How many boyfriends do you have?

CHANIN *(coyly)*: I'd rather not say.

JACK: Why, are you bashful?

CHANIN: No, married!

Then the three did a very bad song and dance to "Did You Ever See a Dream Walking?" with a marvelous brief operatic solo plus a fall onstage by the fat girl, concluded with the other two and Jack attempting to raise her from the floor. When they returned for their encore:

JACK: That's a pretty old song, isn't it?

IRIS: Well, we ain't exactly jailbait.

JACK (looking at her distastefully): You wouldn't be bait for a bear trap. But you girls are really pretty good.

IRIS: Never mind the commercial . . . do we get the job or don't we?

JACK: Well. . . .

CHANIN: We're not fussy about our salary.

PEGGY: Yeah, we'll work for our three meals a day.

JACK: Well, I wasn't planning to go *that* high (glancing at Peggy).

And that's the way the act went for almost forty years, with only a few new additions to the dialogue from the first time it was presented.

13

WHEN Jack decided to move his program to the West Coast for the 1935–36 season, he found Don Bestor, his orchestra leader, couldn't go with him. The account executive at Young and Rubicam, his advertising agency, found a brilliant young pianist, Johnny Green, who was conducting the orchestra at the St. Regis Roof. Johnny, just a few years out of Harvard, had already written many hit songs, including "Body and Soul," "Coquette," "I Cover the Waterfront," and "Out of Nowhere," and in addition to being a fine musician, he was excellent at all sorts of dialects.

"The agency man brought Jack to hear me play," recalls Johnny, "and between sets I sat with him and started to tell him some of my best stories. In no time at all I had him rolling on the floor, and by the time he left I was signed as the orchestra leader."

Johnny joined the Jewish dialectician on the program, Sam Hearn, who was famous for his greeting "Hello, stranger," which never failed to convulse audiences.

"I was portrayed as the classy Harvard man who looked down at Benny," remembers Johnny, "and we found a great deal of humor in this snob character. Sam did all the Jewish dialect work and a few other nationalities, and I doubled in all the other dialects. I remember we once did four broadcasts on which Jack supposedly was touring Europe. When he came to France, I was the French customs inspector who annoyed Jack, and in succeeding broadcasts, whatever country Jack was visiting, there I was, the French customs inspector, to harass him."

Jack used the same technique in later years with an actor named Frank Nelson, who annoyed Jack wherever he went, always greeting him with "Yeeeessss," a standard opening laugh. Nelson was the clerk, the waiter, the salesman, the floorwalker, forever looking down his nose at Jack and stopping him with irritating answers. One of the biggest laughs on a later broadcast was when Jack was late for a train and asked the ticket seller to validate his ticket. The ticket seller was Frank Nelson, who stalled Jack and acted nasty to him until another customer edged in and asked the ticket seller if the train on Track 8 was going to Glocca Morra. Nelson, suddenly courteous, answered that it was, and the other man asked, "How are things in Glocca Morra?"

When he was told that they are fine, he asked, "And is the little brook still leaping there?"

"Yes," replied Nelson.

"And does it still run down to Donny Cove?"

The man went through the entire lyric to "How Are Things in Glocca Morra?" while Jack looked on in complete frustration, making a brilliant piece of comedy.

During this first season in Hollywood, with the new writing team of Morrow and Beloin carrying most of the work load, the Jack Benny program was consistently in the top five ratings each week. The Bennys rented a lovely home in Beverly Hills, and life seemed now to be the frosting on the cake. Toward the end of that season Johnny Green was approached by Fred Astaire, who was starting a radio program with Charles Butterworth for Packard. They wanted Johnny as their musical director. It was arranged to broadcast this program on Tuesday nights so Johnny could double for Jack Benny's show. He called Jack for lunch to discuss the following season and they met at the Vendome on Sunset Boulevard, then the outstanding restaurant in Hollywood.

"Jack was very quiet when I told him about the *Packard*

70

Hour," said Johnny, "and he hemmed and hawed because he didn't know how to tell me that he couldn't use me the next season anyway. But then he finally explained that the agency had taken surveys, and they felt that I was too classy a performer to work against Jack every week, that, instead, he needed a brash, rough-talking man who could better act as a foil to Jack's character and thus bring more excitement to the show. And the man they had in mind was Phil Harris, who was then appearing with his band at the Aragon Ballroom in Los Angeles."

It was a correct evaluation, and Phil Harris, who did get the job, did bring an added dimension to the program. Johnny Green, who, as we all know, went on to a great musical career, was not in the least offended at being replaced and remained a very close friend of Jack's through the years.

14

THE famous Fred Allen-Jack Benny "feud" started in the mid-thirties and continued until Fred died twenty-five years later. Jack always said: "We never planned a feud, and if we had, it probably wouldn't have lasted more than a few broadcasts. We were actually into our feud for eight months before Fred and I ever discussed it."

The Benny show was on NBC from 7 to 7:30 P.M. every Sunday night, and Allen's program started at 8 P.M., one half hour after Benny finished. The feud started one night when Fred Allen presented a brilliant ten-year-old violinist, Stuart Canin, who played Franz Schubert's "The Bee." When he finished, Allen cracked: "Jack Benny should be ashamed of himself."

The following week, Jack did some jokes about Allen and insisted that he could play "The Bee" beautifully when he was only ten years old. On his next week's broadcast, Allen brought on a character actor who was supposedly an old neighbor of Jack's in Waukegan and swore that Jack hadn't

71

played well enough at ten to play "The Bee." The following week Jack brought on an actor who was supposed to have been his violin teacher when he was ten, and the "teacher" insisted that Jack could play the number then. And so the feud was off and running.

In addition to being a fine comedian, Fred Allen was a brilliant writer and a great natural wit. With his staff of writers to help, he came up with a series of devastating gags about Jack every week:

"Before shoes were invented, Jack was a heel. . . . His false teeth are so loose they are always clicking. . . . Jack has no more hair than an elbow. . . . He is so anemic that if he stays out at night, he has to get a transfusion so his eyes will be bloodshot in the morning. . . . I don't want to say that Jack Benny is cheap, but he's got short arms and carries his money low in his pockets. . . . When Jack Benny plays the violin, it sounds as if the strings are still back in the cat."

In the meantime, Jack was getting in his share of Allen squelches and ironically, many of them were about Allen's cheapness:

"Fred Allen is so tight, when he finally spent a five-dollar bill, Lincoln's eyes were bloodshot. . . . Fred is so modest, you could be in a bar with him all night and never know he had a quarter. . . . He has such high blood pressure that, in Technicolor, he photographs plaid. . . . Listening to Fred Allen is like listening to two Abbotts and no Costello. . . . He looks like a short butcher peeking over two pounds of liver."

Finally, Jack guest-starred on Allen's program for the first time, and their performance was a comedy classic. At one point Jack talked about his ad-libs, and Allen snapped: "You couldn't ad-lib a belch after a Hungarian dinner."

Jack immediately answered, "You wouldn't dare say that if my writers were here."

In 1939 Paramount had the world premiere of Jack Benny's picture *Man About Town,* in Waukegan, and the city planted a tree in the courthouse square in his honor. Very shortly after, the poor tree died, and no one could figure out why until Fred Allen, on his program, came up with the reason: "How could a tree live in Waukegan with the sap out in Hollywood?"

Fred peppered stingy jokes at Jack, and Jack kept coming

back at him with the same type of humor: "Fred Allen was so young when he started to save money . . . he wasn't even born yet. His father said to his mother, 'We'd better have him . . . he has $800 in the bank already.' "

"Fred was brilliant and had a much more difficult time with the feud than I did," Jack conceded. "I had a whole week after his show to plan my retorts, but Fred had only a half hour from the time I finished my program before he went on the air with a completely written and rehearsed show. And yet he managed to come up with hilarious gags in answer to me right after I'd finish . . . and he did it consistently, week after week after week."

In personal appearances years later, Jack did a big Fred Allen joke: "I was doing a benefit show where there were many important stars—Bob Hope, Bing Crosby—and I thought I saw Jane Russell. Then I put on my glasses, and it turned out to be Fred Allen! You see, the bags under his eyes are so low. . . ."

When Jack was nominated to open a March of Dimes drive, Fred said, "The dime hasn't been minted that could march past Jack."

Fred always said that "there are two kinds of jokes—funny jokes and Jack Benny jokes," but he admired Jack more than any other comedian and always conceded that most of the later successful comedy shows on the air owed their basic structure to the Benny format.

Fred and Jack exchanged appearances on each other's show and the listening audiences always looked forward to those programs. They also made one film together, *Love Thy Neighbor,* and before he died, Fred made one appearance on the Benny television program.

When Fred Allen died, the world of comedy lost a great performer, and Jack Benny lost a great friend.

In the early 1960's, when I was the executive producer of the Jack Benny program, I read a small notice in the paper that a violinist, Stuart Canin, was giving a recital at Town Hall in New York. After making certain that this was the same ten-year-old boy who had played "The Bee" on the Fred Allen show, I invited Mr. Canin, then almost forty years old and a professor of music at Oberlin College, to appear on the Benny program.

After telling the audience the story and producing the picture of the ten-year-old Stuart Canin, Jack brought on the violinist for a funny round of talk, and then proved to Stuart and the audience once and for all that he really could play "The Bee." During the eighteen years prior to his death, Jack did many benefit concerts, some of which are described later on, and "The Bee" was always included in any Benny concert program and was the solo number he played best.

15

BY the summer of 1936 Jack was riding high. His radio program had finally reached the number one position in the national ratings, and the Lyons Agency, which then represented him, had made a deal for three pictures at Paramount for $100,000 each. Mary's sister, Babe, who had divorced her first husband, married Myrt Blum, who had taken over as Jack's business manager. Jack went off on a series of personal appearances while Mary and her actress friend Frances Robinson went to New York to see the shows.

In New York, Mary and Frances met a young, personable bachelor named Fred De Cordova, a theatrical stage manager, and he became their escort around town until Jack arrived. Fred, who later became a very close personal friend and eventually Jack's producer-director for many years, looked forward to the arrival of Jack Benny, who by that time had achieved gigantic stature in show business.

"I was at El Morocco with Mary, Frances, Johnny Green and his then-wife, Betty Furness, and we were waiting for Jack who was due to arrive in New York that night," recalls Fred. "About ten o'clock in he walked with Myrt Blum, and he was greeted like a long-lost hero. When I was introduced to him, he barely gave me a short hello. When the waiter came for the drink order, Jack asked what we were having and Frances said that she was drinking Alexanders, so he ordered one. Then he started tablehopping, and each group bought him a drink, and Jack, being an amateur drinker, ordered an Alexander at each table. Now Alexanders are made of rich liqueurs and cream, and Jack must have had about ten of them. About midnight I went to the men's room, and there was this great star passed out on the floor, making my first meeting with him a memorable one. I called Myrt Blum, and with the help of the attendant, we managed to get him to a cab and to the Hampshire House, where they were staying."

During that same summer Jack, Johnny Green, and Jesse Block drove up to Saratoga Springs to see Sophie Tucker, who was appearing at the Piping Rock Club. They arrived at night, spent the next day at the races, and went to see Sophie that evening, planning to drive back after the show. In those days Saratoga Springs was a good six-hour drive from New York City. At 1 A.M. after the show was over and the three men were about to climb into Jack's roadster for the long drive back, Jack got into the driver's seat and Johnny asked Jesse to get in the middle. Jesse, who lived at the Park Central, a block before the hotel where Johnny was staying, said, "No, you get in first and let me sit on the outside. I get out first."

Jack laughed so hard at this ridiculous discussion that he couldn't drive the car for a half hour.

This one gag of Jesse Block's helped to make the two of them closer than ever as Jack told and retold the story hundreds of times.

When Jesse became a stockbroker in 1954, Jack called him on his first day in the office and said he was sending him $100,000 to invest.

"Please don't," pleaded Jesse. "I'm new, and I don't know enough yet."

"Then lose it for me," yelled Jack, and hung up.

Rarely did a week go by that Jack didn't phone his friend Jesse and although Jesse was in New York and Jack was in California, Jesse remained his stockbroker until his retirement in 1974.

During the 1937 season Jack was busy making pictures at Paramount and delivering fine, innovative radio programs weekly. Don Wilson's "six delicious flavors" sales pitch made Jello a household word, and the product was zooming toward the number one spot in the gelatine field just as the Benny program was in the audience ratings.

From time to time the weekly show was broadcast from New York. Once when the cast returned from a New York trip, they decided to do a show in which a Pullman porter in a train scene was needed. Many of Hollywood's top black actors were auditioned for this role, and Eddie Anderson, an obscure song-and-dance man, won the part. His name in the script was Rochester, and his gravel-voiced delivery brought howls from the studio audience. It was such a successful character that a few weeks later Jack and his writers, Morrow and Beloin, decided to bring Anderson back for a few more lines. In order to make a believable transition, they had him visit Jack at his home in Beverly Hills the next time Anderson's train came to Los Angeles. The audience reaction was so enthusiastic they decided to keep him on as a regular and, in another script, had Jack hire him away from the railroad to be his butler.

Rochester became one of the highlights of the program and his lines were quoted often:

"Hair? Mr. Benny has hair at home he hasn't even used yet. . . . One night I was walking in my sleep and Mr. Benny put a vacuum cleaner in my hand. . . . Is Mr. Benny tight? . Well, a little snug, perhaps. . . . If he can't take it with him, he ain't gonna go."

While shopping for a Christmas gift:

> SALESMAN: Is your boss a young man?
> ROCHESTER: No.
> SALESMAN: Is he middle-aged?
> ROCHESTER: No.
> SALESMAN: Is he elderly?
> ROCHESTER: Wrap it up.

In later years, when the militant black organizations objected to the "Uncle Tom" characters on many of the radio and television shows, there were very few complaints about the master-servant relationship of Benny and Rochester. This was because "Roch," as he was called in private, always stopped Jack with a put-down. He insulted Benny, and although it was done with great affection, Rochester always came up with the topper to the gag, often making Jack the silly one. His "Oh, come now, boss" was a sure laugh getter every time he did it. Although he was the servant, he was really running the house and making all the key decisions. Even though he complained that "my room is so small that . . ." and "the Maxwell is so old that . . . ," he actually loved his boss and wouldn't quit for five times the salary.

Their true relationship was best described in a show they did on radio one New Year's Eve, which was repeated several times on television. In that script Jack didn't want to go out with the gang to a party because he had a big date, and when the girl stood him up at the last minute, he came home in his white tie and tails just as Rochester was leaving for a black tie party on Central Avenue. When Rochester realized that his boss was going to be home alone on New Year's Eve, he refused to leave him and, instead, opened a bottle of champagne, and they toasted each other as the clock struck twelve and the orchestra played "Auld Lang Syne," a touching end to a beautiful show.

Rochester helped keep the show in the top position, and Morrow and Beloin continued to come up with new ideas and running gags which caused the listeners to tune in every Sunday. "Buck Benny" and Andy Devine and the Maxwell were only some of the fresh ideas that helped the Benny program maintain its quality of excellence every week and not fall into the rut that brought failure to some of its competitors. Jack and his writers were smart enough to be able to create characters and segments and then keep revolving them so that none became overplayed. In addition to his regular cast of star performers, all of whom had their individual styles, he had popular bit actors like Frank "that nasty man" Nelson, Sam "Shlepperman" Hearn, Mel Blanc, the man of many voices, two "Brooklyn" telephone operators at NBC—"Mr. Benny's line is flashing. . . . I wonder what Blue Eyes wants now?" He had the vault in his basement, and when the guard would say, "Halt, who goes there, friend or foe?" the audience pictured someone who had been down there since the Revolution. There was Carmichael, the bear, the French violin teacher, the parrot, and many others.

With so many situations, Benny was able to use the Maxwell, for example, only four or five times a season, yet the audiences pictured the Maxwell as being on practically every show. He did the same with the vault and operators so that there were always surprises, never boredom.

Jack told about a golf game he had with Jack Pearl when that comedian had achieved great success with his Baron Munchausen character, who used to ask program sidekick Cliff Hall, "Vass you dere, Sharlie?" This golf game took place in the mid-thirties when Pearl's show was top-rated.

"Let me make a suggestion," said Benny. "Your 'Vass you dere, Sharlie?' is sensational, but I think it would be even better if you skipped it for a week or two and then when you hit the audience with the line, it will be even funnier."

"Are you out of your mind?" Pearl answered. "'Vass you dere' is the biggest thing on my show . . . the listeners can't wait for it . . . they expect it. If I don't do it each time, they'll be disappointed."

Well, in a year or two, Jack Pearl's radio program was out of business, along with Joe Penner and his "Wanna buy a duck?" and subsequent shows that hit on a great idea but wore it to death.

But the Benny show, with its intelligent spacings of running jokes and situations, continued to ride high in the popularity polls, and General Foods couldn't supply the dealers with enough Jello to keep their shelves stocked. So, in 1940, they switched Benny to one of their other products, Grape Nuts.

During this same period the Eddie Cantor program was off the air, and Cantor complained to Jack that he couldn't find a sponsor because they objected to the many charity pitches he had made all through the years.

Jack called the account executives at Young and Rubicam, his advertising agency, and indignantly demanded that they find a sponsor for this great performer who had been a star in so many musicals on the stage and in motion pictures and who had contributed so much to radio entertainment. They did find a sponsor for Cantor, and he was ever grateful to Jack, continuing his humor and his handclapping songs and dances on his radio show for many more years.

In the late 1950's Jack went to visit Cantor in the Cedars of Lebanon Hospital after his heart attack.

"It was one of the saddest days of my life," reported Jack.

"When I came in to see him, he had already been in the hospital for nearly a month. He was sitting on the side of the bed, his feet dangling over the edge. 'Look at me, Jack,' he said. 'After a month here the doctors are finally letting me sit on the edge of the bed. Me, who used to dance across a thousand stages . . . and now this.' I had to fight to hold back the tears."

By 1938 Kenny Baker had become the brightest star of the Benny cast, eclipsing even the bubbling laugh of Mary Livingstone and the brash humor of Phil Harris, who by then had been developed as a drunken, woman-chasing bandleader. Kenny Baker was adored by the teenagers and mothered by the older women, and everyone was thrilled by his beautiful tenor voice. At the end of the season, when Jack's agent went to renegotiate Baker's contract, which had run out, they discovered that he had signed with Fred Allen for the following season, having created the impression with Allen that Kenny and Jack had agreed to end their business relationship.

When the news was announced, a deluge of letters poured in, decrying disaster for the program, and again the smart showmen predicted that without Kenny Baker the Benny show would drop from the number one spot.

Tenors from all over the country were submitted to Benny, but Jack remembered:

"I was listening to some audition records, and suddenly Mary perked up and asked to hear one particular voice again. He was a young singer named Eugene Patrick McNulty, who had been singing on a local New York radio station for twelve dollars and fifty cents a week. Mary liked his voice, so we had him come right out for a live audition, and when we heard him in person, we signed him immediately. He was renamed Dennis Day, and for the first few programs he was too scared to say a line. Then we had him say a few words on each show, and gradually, almost before we realized it, we had developed a 'dumb kid' character. For years he remained the 'dumb kid,' even after he was married and had eleven kids himself!"

Dennis became the most popular of all the tenors and eventually was signed for his own show. And with Mary, Phil Harris, Rochester, Don Wilson, the Maxwell, the talented

79

cast of supporting players, the Benny program continued making 30,000,000 people happy every week.

16

ALBERT CHAPEREAU, who claimed to be the Nicaraguan consul to the United States, was introduced to Jack and Mary by their best friends, George Burns and Gracie Allen. He was handsome and charming, and they took a great liking to him, having dinner with him and his wife very often when they visited New York City. That friendship was to be the cause of great unhappiness in Jack's life.

There are several versions that have been reported of a smuggling incident involving Jack and Chapereau, but as far as I can ascertain, the real story is as follows:

Jack Pearl introduced the Burnses to the Chapereaus, and George in turn introduced them to the Bennys. Mrs. Chapereau, an attractive, well-dressed young woman, always wore beautiful jewelry. Chapereau must have indicated that he had bought various pieces of jewelry for her very reasonably in Europe and didn't have to pay the duty since he was entitled to bring such items through U.S. customs in his diplomatic pouch.

Gracie admired a particular bracelet Mrs. Chapereau was wearing, and Chapereau offered to sell it to George for just what he had paid for it, $1,750. When Gracie told Mary about the wonderful buy she had made, Mary asked Chapereau if she could buy a pin Mrs. Chapereau had, and Jack bought that for approximately $750, which was what Chapereau said he had paid for it in France. Ironically, if Jack himself had purchased the pin in Europe and declared it to the U.S. customs' agents, the duty would have only been about $175. The mistake Burns and Benny made was that they failed to get receipts from Chapereau for the transactions.

Jack was back in Hollywood, making the movie *Man About Town*, in 1939 when U.S. customs agents arrived with a tip about the pin. Not believing he had done anything out of order, Jack readily turned the pin over to them. He was shocked when subsequently he was charged with having smuggled the pin through U.S. customs without declaring it. Because he was then the number one radio star, the story resulted in front-page headlines. Jack's Los Angeles attorney, Lloyd Wright, felt it was serious enough to hire the best legal help available for the New York trial, and so the famous "Wild Bill" Donovan, a war hero and brilliant attorney, was engaged to handle the case. Although Jack told his story exactly as it happened, the case was lost, and in addition to Donovan's fee of $50,000, Jack was fined $10,000 and given a severe tongue-lashing from the judge.

This was the only incident in his life of which I believe he was really ashamed, even though his intent was harmless. As a result, on hundreds of subsequent trips throughout the world, when he went through customs, he scrupulously listed each and every item even in cases where he was way under the allowable duty charge. On one trip to Canada in 1972 on which my wife and I were along, Jack, after a concert in Edmonton, bought two gifts for Mary, each around $100. Gift buying for Mary was a must on every trip he made. Since my wife had purchased nothing on that trip, she offered to bring one of the gifts into the United States on her own $100 exemption, but Jack refused even though we insisted that it was perfectly proper with the customs service.

When Jack Benny was a fan, he was an ardent one. Although the Chapereau happening colored the year 1939 dark for Jack, not all that happened that year was bad. He met Danny Kaye.

"It was at a benefit at Madison Square Garden," recalled Kaye, "and I came off the stage after being particularly good that night in one of my first appearances in the big time. Jack Benny was waiting in the wings to go on and came over and introduced himself and told me how good a performer he thought I was, which was like praise from Allah. The next year, 1940, I was performing at the Martinique, a smart supper club in New York, and just beginning to be well known in town, when Jack showed up on my second night. He started to laugh as soon as I came on and spurred the audience on as he had the most infectious and loudest laugh I ever heard. I

81

did everything I knew, and from then on Jack was my biggest booster and press agent. He came in every single night that week, bringing in new people to hear and see me, and he gave me great confidence."

A few months later when Danny was booked into Ciro's in Hollywood, Jack called and asked if he could introduce him on the opening night.

"The club was full of leading stars, and when Jack got through with his wonderful introduction, I was practically a hit before I opened my mouth."

Later, when Danny Kaye signed a contract with Samuel Goldwyn for pictures and moved to the Coast, he and Jack became fast friends. Jack always called him Dammy, which Danny came to love, and then Danny adopted a character for himself which used to fracture Jack. He became a Mr. Kaplan from Youngstown, Ohio, who worked for the Acme Rubber Company, but he only used this character for his friend Jack Benny. He would telephone Jack from time to time, and with a heavy Jewish accent, he would say it was Mr. Kaplan calling from Youngstown, and they would proceed to have a silly conversation. What made it sillier was that Jack would answer him as though he really were Mr. Kaplan in the Acme Rubber business. Wherever Jack made appearances, no matter in what country and how far away, a congratulatory telegram would come from Mr. Kaplan of the Acme Rubber Company in Youngstown.

"Jack had only one operation in his whole life," says Danny, "and that was a very minor one for removal of some nasal polyps at St. John's Hospital in Santa Monica. I was in New York when I heard about it and called him. The floor nurse took the call and explained that Jack couldn't talk because his nose was all packed with cotton. I made her promise to get a message to him that Mr. Kaplan of the Acme Rubber Company in Youngstown, Ohio, called to inquire after his health. When she conveyed those regards to Jack, he exploded with laughter, and all the packing came out of his nose, and a rush call had to be made to his doctor to repack it."

Another Danny Kaye party classic which he started just to make Jack laugh was the "busy eater" routine. One night at a particularly boring dinner party Danny found himself sitting across from Jack, who was having difficulty making conversation with his dinner partners. Danny started to do a hundred eating things at once, busily buttering the bread, sipping the soup, chewing a piece of celery, taking a bite of salad, all with short, quick moves until he had Jack on the floor. And from then on, at every dinner party the two attended, Danny repeated his busy eating, and Jack always roared, until many parties and hostesses were completely disrupted.

The Bennys had bought a house in 1937 at 1002 North Roxbury Drive in Beverly Hills. They paid the large sum of $68,000, which was a fortune for that time. They hired Julia Vallance, an English nurse, for Joan, who soon was enrolled in nearby El Rodeo grammar school. The Benny family was considered ideal, although Jack was so busy with his program and motion pictures that he didn't find as much time as he would have liked to spend with his daughter. He recalled once when she was six, he told her he loved her very much.

"I love you more," Joan answered.

"How can you say that? I love you just as much."

"I love you more, Daddy . . . because I loved you all my life and you didn't get me until you were already old."

Jack and Mary became leaders in the social life of Beverly Hills, and their beautiful home was often filled with celebrities: Robert Taylor and Barbara Stanwyck; the producer William Goetz and his wife, Jane Wyman; the Mervyn Le Roys; the Charles Vidors; and always, of course, the Burnses.

The Roxbury Drive home became the scene of many elaborate parties, and Jack always claimed that Mary gave the best parties in town. New Year's Eve at the Bennys' became a tradition, and the guests rarely left before 4 A.M. Fred De Cordova, who had come to Hollywood in late 1942 to work as a dialogue director at Warner Brothers, was invited to the Bennys' New Year's Eve party that year. It was his very first Hollywood party, and he came stag since he hardly knew anyone in town.

"I was thrilled," he said, "at the beauty of the home, the decorations, seeing all the big stars I had been reading about all my life. There was Clark Gable, Bob Hope, Bing and Stanwyck and Taylor and on and on. I thought it was the greatest night of my life, dancing with some of the girls who had been just a picture on a screen to me. I was standing at a bar in the garden having a drink when the lights went out at midnight, and I could see the shadows of all the famous couples kissing the New Year in. When the lights went up, I got a big kick out of finding myself standing next to Errol Flynn and Van Johnson, who had also come stag. Along came Jack, and when he spotted me, he said, 'This will teach you to come without a girl.'"

17

THROUGHOUT his career a Jack Benny trademark was the self-deprecating joke. Using such jokes as the ones about toupees, about being miserly, about not being able to ad-lib without a writer, Jack emerged so convincingly as a bald man, a cheapskate, a dumb actor that many of his fans really believed those to be his real-life characteristics. When he began to make movies, he continued that line of humor concerning his acting career until unintentionally he gave the kiss of death to offers for more acting jobs in films. Although his motion-picture career wasn't particularly distinguished, it was not as bad as his radio gags made it.

It started with a series of jokes about how terrible his movie *The Horn Blows at Midnight* was. It was far from an Academy Award picture—in fact, not very good at all—but when Jack said on his program, "When I did *The Horn Blows at Midnight,* it blew taps for me," it was the beginning of a series of jokes he did about the film. And to compound the problem, the Benny cast and guest stars were given deprecatory lines to read on the show about *The Horn* and his other films so that soon there was an aura of failure about his motion-picture career, when in actuality Jack's movies never lost money. Even *The Horn Blows at Midnight* managed to end up in the black, and a few of his films were very successful.

While he was at MGM making *Hollywood Revue of 1929,* he also appeared in the long-forgotten *Road Show* and *Chasing Rainbows.* Immediately thereafter he did *The Medicine Man* for Tiffany Studios, a small independent company. In 1933, for United Artists, he starred in *Transatlantic Merry Go Round,* and as Jack said later, "the less said about that, the better."

After he moved to California, where he made *Broadway Melody of 1936,* he was signed to a long-term contract at Paramount, and in his first film he was one of many radio stars who played themselves in *The Big Broacast of 1937.* He joined George Burns and Gracie Allen in *College Holiday.* It wasn't much of a picture, but Jack had lots of laughs during the filming with his old friends George and Gracie. Then came *Artists and Models* and *Artists and Models Abroad,* and his comment about them was: "One was good, and one was lousy." Which one was which I never got around to asking. *Man About Town,* in which he costarred with Dorothy Lamour, turned out very well, and this was the first picture he made that had a world premiere. The studio held the premiere in Jack's hometown, Waukegan, and it was complete with parades in his honor, thousands of fans lining the streets and big news stories about the "hometown boy who made good."

On the Benny radio program one of the best running gags was with a character named Buck Benny (Jack) and his sidekick, motion-picture actor Andy Devine. They did a series of satirical Western sketches which might have made a cowboy ashamed of his calling, but the public loved them. Paramount Pictures produced a very successful movie on Jack's theme, *Buck Benny Rides Again,* and then planned a sequel, but somehow the sequel never came about.

Then one of the bright young men at the studio had the idea of bringing Fred Allen to the Coast for a picture and casting Jack in it with him. The resulting movie, *Love Thy Neighbor,* like many a good idea, didn't quite work and was a critical failure, although it managed to make a profit.

By the end of 1939 Jack had completed his contract at Paramount, and his agent, Arthur Lyons, negotiated a two-picture deal at Twentieth Century-Fox at $100,000 for each. His first film under that contract was to be *Charley's Aunt.*

"I loved making *Charley's Aunt,*" Jack remembered, "because it was a classic and I wasn't going to be Jack Benny again. The only complaint I had about that picture was that with all the petticoats and underwear and girdle, I had the damnedest time going to the bathroom. And when they completed the picture, I remember seeing it for the first time in an empty projection room, and I didn't think anything in it was funny, including me. I was sick for a week. But then I went to the first sneak preview, and the audience started to laugh from the first funny thing that happened on the screen, and then they screamed throughout the whole show. I realized then that I couldn't judge a comedy without the laughs."

The picture was a big success for the studio, but it never offered another property for the second commitment. When Jack would go up to see the studio head, Darryl Zanuck, he was told that they were frantically searching for a good script for him, but nothing seemed to turn up. Finally, when his contract expired and he had not made the second picture, Lyons wanted to make the studio pay the other $100,000, but Jack refused to let him ask for it since he felt that they had tried but failed to find him the right story. However, it wasn't much later that he went to see a new Twentieth Century-Fox comedy, *Sitting Pretty,* which starred Clifton Webb as an aging baby-sitter. Jack was furious.

"It would have been a perfect vehicle for me, and as I watched the picture, I could just hear myself doing every line. I called my agent immediately and told him I had changed my mind and to get the money they owed."

They say that every comedian has a secret desire to play Hamlet. Well, Jack Benny was the one comedian who never wanted to play Hamlet but did. It was for the Ernst Lubitsch picture *To Be or Not to Be,* in which Jack costarred with Carole Lombard.

"When Ernst Lubitsch asked me to play the Polish Shakespearean actor," Jack once told Louella Parsons, "I was afraid. I told him that he needed a young, handsome leading man . . . a hero who would give the girls a thrill. Ernst said he had written it with me in mind and naturally I was flattered to do the picture with Lubitsch and Carole. If Lubitsch ever asks me to do another movie, I won't even read the script. I'll say 'Yes' before he can say his own name."

In the film, Jack is a member of a touring Polish Shakespearean company, and at the outset they are doing Hamlet with Jack in the title role. The time of the film is 1941, and the setting is Warsaw. The city is overrun with Nazi military officers, and the Shakespearean troupe becomes involved with the Polish underground. Through a series of situations, mostly funny, sometimes exciting, the actors of the troupe end up impersonating Nazi officers, Jack becoming a colonel.

When Jack's father, Meyer Kubelsky, saw the picture, he walked out of the theater refusing to speak to his son because he saw him in a Nazi uniform in the first scene. When Jack tried to explain, Meyer coldly said, "I never thought I'd live to see the day my own son would wear a Nazi uniform."

After an hour Jack finally convinced the old man that it was only playacting and he actually was on the side against the Nazis in the story. Eventually, he took his father back in the theater and explained the whole thing to him as they watched it.

Jack was very nervous to be working with Lubitsch, who was a brilliant director, and from the first day on the set he started to bite his nails.

"About the third day of shooting," Robert Stack recalled, "Jack was pacing up and down and, without really thinking, came over to me and asked for some suggestions on how to play a certain scene. I was dumbfounded and said to him, 'But this is only my second film, Mr. Benny,' and then he realized what he had done and walked away in embarrassment."

The night after *To Be or Not to Be* was completed, Ernst Lubitsch gave a party at his Bel Air home for the cast of the film. Naturally, Carole Lombard came with her husband, Clark Gable, along with many other well-known stars, directors and producers. The director, Billy Wilder, a friend of Lubitsch's, was standing with a group that included Jack, the host, and another Hollywood director.

"This director kept talking about himself and all his pictures," reported Wilder, "and poor Lubitsch couldn't get a word in. After a few minutes of this, I noticed that Jack Benny had quietly walked out of the room for a few minutes and then had returned to our group and was listening while this director continued the monologue of his accomplishments. About a half hour later a telegram arrived for the talkative director, and it was handed to him in the middle of a verbose sentence. It read: 'Why don't you shut up and let Lubitsch get a word in?' Jack never said a word, but there was a twinkle in his eye as the director excused himself and left the party."

Carole Lombard's tragic death in an airplane crash a few weeks after completion of the picture cast a pall over the film, and United Artists could not promote it properly. Although the film was received enthusiastically by the critics, it was not a smash hit at the box office at that time. It wasn't until much later that *To Be or Not to Be* became appreciated as one of the motion-picture classics. It is still shown every year in France at many of their leading theaters, and it is revived at cinema festivals in England. It is shown in the United States regularly and is an important feature in most university cinema courses.

Jack continued his round of the studios and, in 1942, signed a long-term contract with Warner Brothers, selecting as his first film for them an adaptation of the Broadway play *George Washington Slept Here.* The leading comedy role in the play was the role of the wife, while the husband played the straight man. For the film, all they did was reverse the roles and Jack Benny took the comedy part, with Ann Sheridan as the wife who fed the lead lines.

On Broadway the character actor Percy Kilbride had played the nasal down-east farmer and had been a comedic sensation. Jack went to Jack L. Warner and asked him to bring Kilbride out from New York for the picture, but Warner refused.

"I want *you* to be the comedy star of this picture," Warner explained, "and Kilbride was so funny in the play I'm afraid he'll get bigger laughs than you."

"Listen, J.L., when Phil Harris, Dennis Day, Rochester, and Mary stop getting the big laughs on my show, then I'm in trouble."

Percy Kilbride did play the movie role and was an hilarious performer and did get tremendous laughs. But as Jack predicted, it only helped the picture, which turned out to be one of his better films.

After *The Meanest Man in the World,* a fair film, Jack was one of a score of stars cast in *Hollywood Canteen,* in which he did a short comedy spot with concert violinist Joseph Szigeti. He performed a number which he had originally done with Jascha Heifetz on a *Command Performance* radio broadcast to servicemen and many years later at Carnegie Hall with Isaac

Stern. The two men played a violin duet, each taking a short solo part. When Jack completed his particularly flat, scratchy solo, he turned to the audience and said, "Now honestly, can you tell the difference?"

After *The Horn Blows at Midnight,* which was filmed in 1946, Jack had no more roles in motion pictures for twenty-eight years, except for an occasional cameo which never amounted to more than a day's work. Whether the producers decided that films were not his cup of tea or whether his own self-disparaging remarks about his films were the cause of his lack of offers, we'll never know.

The Sunshine Boys, of which more later, might have been a glorious finish to his motion-picture career, but sadly, it was never to be. A month before rehearsal was to start, Jack Benny died, and the record books will state that *The Horn Blows at Midnight* really did blow taps to his motion-picture career.

18

"WAR is hell," someone once said, but the World War II years were perhaps Jack Benny's most enjoyable as a performer because the enthusiasm, laughter, and applause of the countless sailors, soldiers, and marines he played to were like music to his ears. Jack always said that he and Bob Hope used to argue about who was the biggest ham, and some wag once said about Jack, "Every time he opens the refrigerator and the light goes on he does a five-minute monologue."

In 1941, before the United States had entered the war, Jack took his program on a tour of army camps and naval bases and the audiences of thousands of troops sent roars of laughter out after each gag. Jack loved every minute of it. After the U.S. entry into the war he devoted most of his efforts to entertaining the servicemen at the camps and made countless appearances for war bond drives in the major cities of the United States and Canada, and wherever he went, he also visited hospitals to cheer up the wounded troops.

Early in the war one of the top men in Washington, D.C.,

called Jack with a bright publicity idea to get people to contribute to a scrap-iron drive. His suggestion was to have Jack donate his mythical Maxwell to the scrap-iron drive. The Maxwell, a creation consisting of Mel Blanc's voice, plus tricky sound effects, conjured up a picture of an old car with a wheezing motor, rattling bolts, and flapping fenders and was without a doubt one of Jack's best gags. Asking him to give it up was like asking Groucho Marx to give up his mustache. But he agreed. On the program on which the donation was made, the climax of the show came with Jack in bed, haunted by dreams of his car but happy that it had been converted into one of our own U.S. war planes. Then came sound effects as plane after plane came roaring across the Pacific supposedly on the way to Japan, until the very last plane came . . . wheezing instead of roaring and with rattling bolts and flapping fenders . . . and no words were necessary to explain precisely from what scrap iron that B-29 had been made.

There is no question that Bob Hope was the leading entertainer of World War II, traveling everywhere for the servicemen. But although he never received as much publicity, Jack Benny was not too far behind. In the summer of 1943 he spent nine weeks overseas, trouping in Central Africa, North Africa, Egypt, the Persian Gulf, Tunisia, Sicily, and Italy. In his company were harmonica genius Larry Adler, songstress Wini Shaw, and actress Anna Lee. At their first stop in Africa, in Acra, they met the Yacht Club Boys, who were on the last night of an eight-month tour. Jack persuaded their pianist, Jack Snyder, to stay on with his show. Since he had his own plane and two pilots, Jack joked that now that there were five of them in the troupe, they should name the plane "Five Jerks to Cairo," and the next morning when they came down to the field for takeoff, that name in large letters had already been painted on the side of the plane.

They traveled to many camps, giving shows to as few as 250 men and as many as 10,000 at a time. Although most of the other entertainment companies came dressed in khaki, Jack always felt that the soldiers saw enough uniforms every day and would appreciate civilian clothes and insisted that the girls wear evening dresses and the men wear nice suits, shirts, and ties.

Jack was not usually a great tourist, but he found the Arabs most interesting and was so absorbed by the customs of the country that he was having the time of his life by the time the "Five Jerks" arrived in Cairo. At the same time he found Larry Adler to be a very amusing fellow, and by the time they arrived in Cairo, Larry had replaced George Burns, at least temporarily, as the funniest man in the world. As Adler tells it:

"We had gone to a nightclub in Cairo to watch an extremely boring belly dancer who took two encores, each encore being an exact duplicate of her original. I whispered to Jack that the girl was in danger of getting into a rut. Now that line's not all that good, but it just happened to hit Jack the right way. He could see that belly going up, doing a slight twist at the top, and then coming down again, not only then but into infinity, like a satellite lost in space. Within five minutes he was laughing so hysterically that Arabs in the audience were giving us very nasty looks. We left and went back to the Shepheard's Hotel, and Jack was still laughing. He couldn't stop, and I was beginning to be alarmed. I finally located a flight surgeon who gave Jack a mild sedative injection. You've got to be careful telling a joke to a man like that."

Larry Adler also remembers that Jack went around to hospital wards taking names, addresses and phone numbers, and when he returned to the States, he would call each family and give them personal news of their sons.

After five weeks of hard work in Africa, he took a four-day trip to Jerusalem and Tel Aviv, then a part of Palestine, to rest as well as to perform in a show at a rest camp for American servicemen and another at a British camp. While there he spent some time with Henrietta Szold, then an eighty-two-year-old woman about whom Wendell Willkie had written in his *One World*. Born in Baltimore, Maryland, she had been a national president of the Hadassah but had been living in Jerusalem for twenty-four years before the war. She impressed Jack very much, so much, in fact, that he spoke about her at every Bonds for Israel and United Jewish Appeal rally he attended thereafter.

After his rest stop he took his troupe to Iran and Iraq for a series of the "hottest shows I ever did." Jack reported that the temperature was never less than 100 degrees, and in one city, Abadan, he did a show at ten o'clock in the morning when the temperature was 140 degrees.

Jack was one of the first performers to arrive in Sicily. He did shows at Catania, and Lentini and then made a surprise flight to Crotone, Italy, where he gave a performance for the 59th Fighter Squadron of the Seventh Army just before they left for the Battle of Salerno. When he returned to Palermo, Sicily, to entertain the troops there, he spent an interesting two hours with General George Patton right after the famous slapping incident and found the general to be "a very emotional character."

By the time he left for home the only shot he had heard fired was one night in Africa when he was returning to his camp after a performance and a nervous young sentry thought the driver hadn't given the proper signal and fired a shot to stop the jeep. After they explained who was in the car, they proceeded, and a black cat crossed the road. Jack yelled, "Now he tells us."

At the finish of the trip, Jack wrote: "I came home fifteen pounds heavier, and it was the most thrilling and memorable trip I have ever had in my life."

In the summer of 1944 he went to the South Pacific, entertaining GI's in New Guinea, the Marianas, the Marshalls, the Gilberts, the Solomons, Kwajelein Atoll, and Hawaii. Larry Adler joined him again, along with Carole Landis, Martha Tilton, and the Army Air Force Band.

Except for some topical and local references, Jack did essentially the same jokes and show he did the year before. In his monologue, he would always tell about the First World War in which he was a sailor: "In those days, they used to place you according to what you did in civilian life. If you were a mailman, you were put in the infantry; if you were a cowboy, you went into the cavalry; and if a mechanic, you became an engineer. How I ever ended up on a *fairy* boat, I'll never know."

About his cast, he would comment: "I don't know how much liquor Phil Harris drinks, but you can name any patent medicine and he'll tell you how much alcohol it contains. . . . Rochester once described his girl to me. He said, 'Picture a Hershey bar with the almonds in just the right places.' . . . One day Dennis said to me, 'Have a nice trip, Mr. Benny,' and I was halfway through packing when I realized I wasn't going anyplace."

With Carole Landis, he would do a hilarious love scene: "Now, when I kiss you, think of me as Clark Gable or Taylor. I mean Robert Taylor—a tailor I could be."

After Martha Tilton would sing several songs, Jack would discuss her encore:

BENNY: What are you going to sing as an encore?

TILTON: I'm going to do . . .

BENNY: Now for this number, how would it be if I accompanied you on my violin?

TILTON: Well, I don't know how to say it, but the arrangement is all set and the violin would interfere.

BENNY: Well, for someone who didn't know how to say it, you phrased it beautifully. Sing your lousy encore.

When Jack arrived at the first camp in the South Pacific, there was a giant sign at the entrance reading WELCOME FRED ALLEN, and the soldiers watched expectantly to see how Jack would react. Naturally, Jack let out a roar and told them it was the funniest thing he had seen in years.

"Then it seemed that practically every camp had the WEL-COME FRED ALLEN sign," said Jack, "and the boys always waited for me to break up . . . and I always did as I couldn't let them down."

While in New Guinea, he met Dr. Charles Mayo, head of the famed Mayo Clinic in Rochester, Minnesota, and he spent two days in his company there. In 1953 when Danny Kaye wanted to go to the clinic for a checkup, Jack called Charles Mayo, after not having spoken to him since New Guinea, to arrange for his friend to be taken care of by the doctor personally. Jack didn't speak to him again until 1962, when he decided to go for a checkup himself. He called Charles Mayo: "Hello, Charlie, this is Jack Benny."

"What," yelled Dr. Mayo, "again!"

Twenty years after his South Pacific Army tour we filmed a Jack Benny television program, with Martha Tilton as a guest, and they reminisced about their New Guinea tour. On the television program, Jack is supposed to be doing a show for the GI's, and in the middle of his performance, he picks up his fiddle and "General MacArthur" (an actor) gets up and walks out of the theater. As Jack starts to play, two Japanese soldiers come out of the jungle and offer to make a deal: They'll surrender if he'll stop playing.

After six weeks of grueling shows in the steaming jungles, General MacArthur arranged for the comedian to fly to Sydney, Australia, for a five-day rest and recreation period. Although Jack was a happily married man and very much in love with Mary, like many men, he never lost interest in looking at pretty girls and even enjoyed a mild flirtation from time to time. He loved the city of Sydney and its people, especially the attractive female drivers assigned to drive VIP's around. He often spoke enthusiastically of his Australian visit and expressed a great desire to return one day.

Back in the jungles, he continued his two shows a day, and one night before he left, he heard about a young enlisted man named Jack Paar, who was making quite a reputation for himself as an entertainer. Jack Benny went to see him, and after watching him carefully, he decided to tuck this clever, young man in the back of his mind for future reference. Three years later he hired him as his summer replacement on the radio, giving him his major start in show business.

The last show Jack did was at famed Bougainville, where Rand Smith, a baritone working in a small USO unit, recalls: "We were doing four shows a day, playing in ninety-five-degree muggy heat to about five hundred men at every performance. We all shared the same Red Cross billet, and the first thing Jack did was put us back to back with him, playing to five thousand men at each performance instead. He gave each of us a great spot in his show and told the GI's, 'These are the bums you ought to thank for staying out in this washing machine with you, not me. I'm going home tomorrow.'"

A few months after Germany surrendered in 1945, Jack went to occupied Germany for the summer with Larry Adler and Ingrid Bergman, and they played all over the shattered country wherever the GI's needed entertainment. One day in Frankfurt, Jack visited General Eisenhower, and Larry Adler accompanied him to the meeting. He was flattered that Ike took time out from a very busy schedule to spend an hour with him and even more surprised when Ike asked Jack for an autograph for a relative.

Ten years later Jack had a private visit in the White House

with President Eisenhower, and out of the blue Ike asked, "What was the name of that harmonica player who came with you when you visited me in Frankfurt?"

The director Billy Wilder ran into Jack in Berlin that summer, and Jack invited him to come with him to Nuremberg, where he was doing a big show on July 4.

"I went," recalls Billy, "because I had seen the Leni Riefenstahl film, *Triumph of the Will,* where Hitler made his initial speech about Nazism from a platform at the top of the stadium to thousands of cheering Germans, and I was curious to see how it would look with Jack there. Well, there were at least forty thousand soldiers in the audience, and it was thrilling to see them laughing and cheering and applauding. After the show Jack had to urinate, and I suggested we go up to Hitler's platform at the top of the stadium and relieve ourselves there. When we stepped onto the platform, we found that many of the soldiers had already had the same idea and we stepped into ankle-deep urine and had to throw our expensive shoes away and salvage new ones from the Army."

Jack went back to Germany in 1948, after playing the Palladium Theatre in London, to perform in the American zone of occupied Germany. On this trip, which was my first Army tour with Jack, he brought his wife, Mary Livingstone, Phil Harris and Alice Faye, Marilyn Maxwell, and the left-handed guitar player Frank Remley, who achieved fame on the radio show as Phil Harris' hard-drinking buddy.

We played in Frankfurt, Wurzburg, Nuremberg, and Munich with each of us assigned a special car and army driver so that we could motor from city to city. The weather was perfect for the week, and the opportunity to see some of the German countryside made it an interesting experience for us, as well as enjoyable for the military we entertained. Jack was thrilled to have his wife with him for the first time on an overseas tour.

When the Korean War broke out, Jack immediately volunteered to go, and in the summer of 1951, he assembled a troupe that included Errol Flynn, Marjorie Reynolds, Harry Kahn, an upside-down writer, tap dancer Dolores Gay, and Frank Remley, who was a lovable man and great company for Jack.

He opened the show in Tokyo for the GI's who were stationed there, and Jack worked hard with his writers on a rou-

95

tine for Flynn, who was the swinging star of the year. He introduced him:

"I'm very happy that Errol Flynn could make this tour with us . . . and I don't know whether you fellows know this or not, but he comes under somewhat of a handicap. You may have read that a few months ago he hurt his back. Flynn said it was from a fall . . . imagine, from a fall . . . that's like Phil Harris saying his eyes are bloodshot from reading . . . I'm sure that you're all familiar with those rumors and stories of Flynn's romantic escapades. Ordinarily, publicity like this would hurt a movie star, but it hasn't affected the loyalty of his fans. As a matter of fact, Errol was recently voted the number one male star by the Los Angeles Girls' Home for Juvenile Delinquents . . . Anyway, fellows, it gives me great pleasure to introduce someone who has the unique distinction of being the only man who is mentioned in both *Who's Who* and *The Kinsey Report*—Errol Flynn."

FLYNN: Say, Jack I was just listening to that introduction you gave me and I think it's very unfair.

BENNY: Unfair?

FLYNN: Sure. . . . You stand up here and give these fellows the impression that I'm a wolf. You practically tell them that I like to chase women, that I'm not particular who I make love to, and I'll go out with anything as long as it's in skirts . . . and I'm angry.

BENNY: You are?

FLYNN: Yeah, I wanted to tell them myself.

BENNY: Well, I'm sorry, Errol.

FLYNN: Anyway, Jack, do you think we should be so crude in front of these gentlemen?

BENNY: Errol, if they've seen those Army health movies, nothing we say can shock them . . . believe me. But say, Errol, weren't you wearing a mustache yesterday?

FLYNN: Yes, but I took a swig of that GI coffee, and it was gone.

BENNY: But where else can you beat those PX prices?

FLYNN: Jack, don't tell me you've been buying at the PX?

BENNY: No, Errol, selling . . . selling.

FLYNN: So you're beginning to act like you did on our last USO tour.

BENNY: You mean in the last war?

FLYNN: Sure, remember the day we hit the beach with the men at Anzio?

BENNY: How can I forget it? What a landing. Everything was so perfectly timed. At twelve one the artillery barrage started . . . at twelve two the boats came in . . . at twelve three the troops came ashore.

FLYNN: And at twelve four the beach was cleared and Benny had the first coffee and doughnut concession in southern Italy.

That was the way the routine started, and the GI's loved it, but then Flynn's back really did go out on him, and he had to leave the show before it went on to Korea.

For four weeks Jack worked harder and slept less than he had ever before done. He did shows all day and every night, and in between he visited the hospitals, sleeping an average of four hours a night in small tents up near the battle lines. The boys were disappointed that Errol Flynn wasn't along, but Jack explained it, and one great joke emerged from the situation. He said, "When I was in Tokyo with Errol Flynn, I used to get hundreds of calls about him from mothers looking for their daughters. Flynn got one call about me . . . from a daughter looking for her mother."

When Jack returned home from Korea, he was so exhausted that the doctor ordered him to bed for a week. As a result, when the stars started to go to Vietnam to entertain during that war, although Jack, then in his mid-seventies, was extremely anxious to go again, his depleting experience during the Korean War kept him at home.

19

DURING Jack Benny's tenth year on NBC the network gave an anniversary dinner for the comedian at the Biltmore Bowl in Los Angeles. Many of the important radio stars of that time were invited to be on the dais, and it was at that dinner that Niles Trammell, president of NBC, presented Jack with the 7 P.M. time period for his weekly show. This meant that Benny owned the time, so to speak, and would continue in that hour no matter who the sponsor might be. This was publicized as a historic agreement in radio, one that had never before been made with any star and never would again be made. In actuality, it was accomplished by a simple letter from Niles Trammell promising Jack that time period.

It all came about because several offers had been presented to Jack, and he decided that perhaps a new sponsor might bring added excitement to the program. NBC was anxious for him to continue with General Foods because that package had been a successful one, so in order to induce Jack to keep selling their product, the network made the offer of the time period, and he accepted.

The year 1943 was not the best of years for the comedian. It started with the first and next to last serious illness of his life when he was stricken with a severe case of pneumonia in Chicago while on a tour of army camps. He was too ill to be moved from his hotel suite and was placed in an oxygen tent for a long time, unable to perform on his radio program for six weeks. But he was fortunate to secure Robert Taylor, Orson Welles, and Jane Wyman to host the show several times each during his illness.

Right after that Dennis Day went into the service, a loss that again threatened to hurt the show. He was replaced by a young tenor named Larry Stevens, and although Stevens had all the talent necessary for the job, Jack never really tried to give him too strong a buildup because he knew that Dennis would be back to the show in time.

Although the penurious violinist continued to star in one of the leading shows on the air, his program had dropped from its exalted number one position, while other, newer shows like the Bob Hope show and the Edgar Bergen-Charlie McCarthy show had come along to supplant Benny in the top spot.

Then came the final blow. His brilliant writers Morrow and Beloin left the program. Morrow entered the service, and with his leaving, Beloin decided that this was his opportunity to accept one of the many motion-picture writing jobs he had been offered.

For a short time Jack felt that same sinking feeling he had had when Harry Conn left him, but by this time he had much more confidence in his ability to assemble a good program with help from writers.

He hired four writers, which gave him enough manpower to replace the two men who were leaving. He first brought in Sam Perrin, the writer who had helped him when Conn left, and Perrin's partner, George Balzer, a young fellow who had been working on various radio shows with him. Also hired was Milt Josefsberg, for many years a Bob Hope writer. Then Jack took a gamble on a young Texan, John Tackaberry, who had had little experience but had submitted some funny material which impressed Jack.

At this time Jack decided that it was desirable to change sponsors, especially since he had offers from five different advertisers. He narrowed his options down to two, the Campbell Soup Company and the American Tobacco Company for Lucky Strike cigarettes. Even though many people warned him that George Washington Hill, the president of the American Tobacco Company, was a very difficult man and would drive him crazy with interference and changes in his show, Jack had enough confidence in himself to feel that he could handle the man. And the fact that Hill agreed to hire the Steve Hannagan publicity office to publicize the program helped him choose Lucky Strike, since Hannagan had popularized Miami Beach and the Indianapolis 500 Races so successfully that Jack felt he would be instrumental in bringing his show back to the number one spot again in the Hooper ratings.

"I don't care what problems anyone else had with George Washington Hill," Jack always said, "I found him to be a simply wonderful man as far as my show was concerned. I didn't meet him until four months after I started working for him. We had lunch one day, and he told me how much he enjoyed my programs, and I told him we were very fortunate in having had a run of very good shows, but that sometimes we weren't always so lucky. He said to me, 'Well, Mr. Benny, I only know one thing. Had your shows been bad, they never would have blamed you. They would say that so-and-so George Washington Hill was to blame for that.'"

The four new writers fell into the rhythm of the show, and with the wealth of characterization that had been established over the years, as well as the wonderful cast and supporting players, their job was made much easier. Although he took no credit, Jack acted as editor of the writing, and his innate sense of comedy helped keep the show's quality at a high level. The four men were very funny at the writing sessions, and sometimes one would drop a line that would have Jack laughing helplessly on the floor. When he'd recover, he'd often turn the line down because, although hilarious, it didn't belong in that particular sequence.

Even though the writers and Jack were producing very funny scripts each week and Steve Hannagan and his men were publicizing the show regularly, the program hit a real slump by 1945, and for the first time in ten years it dropped out of the first five in the ratings. It was a nervous time for Jack, and always the pessimist, he began to worry about where this drop might end.

The writers were concerned, too, and one day at a writing session one of them suggested that perhaps if they had some kind of contest on the show, it would not only give them a few good programs, but might also spur some added stimulation to a sluggish season. Another writer said, "They're always asking people to write in 'I like such and such toothpaste because' in twenty-five words or less. How about us asking them to write in in twenty-five words or less why they hate Jack Benny?"

"Everyone laughed at this joke, except me," Jack mused. "I held a perfectly straight face. When the others noticed I wasn't laughing at this insult, they quickly stopped. There was an apprehensive moment of silence after which I said, 'That's it, fellows, that's what we're going to do.'"

The writers looked at Jack as if he were crazy, but he insisted that they go ahead with it, and then they tempered it by taking out the word "hate," and the contest ended up as "I can't stand Jack Benny because" in twenty-five words or less with $10,000 offered in prizes. The contest received tremendous publicity and lasted for six very funny programs. Fred Allen was announced as the official judge, and a staff of twelve secretaries was recruited to handle the mail. Jack wondered if his being Jewish might encourage some anti-Semitic responses, and he asked the girls to pull all such letters, but out of the 270,000 letters that were received, there were only 3 which mentioned that subject.

The winner was Carroll P. Craig, Sr., of Pacific Palisades, California, who won $2,500 with this poem:

> I can't stand Jack Benny because,
> He fills the air with boasts and brags,
> And obsolete, obnoxious gags,
> His cowardice alone, indeed,
> Is matched by his obnoxious greed,
> And all the things that he portrays
> Show up my own obnoxious ways.

The winning poem was brilliant because in a few words it gave the prime reason for the popularity of the Benny program which captured the idiosyncrasies and foibles of most of us or, if not of ourselves, of an uncle or friend.

One answer that judge Fred Allen did a doubletake on was: "I can't stand Jack Benny because he helped build up Fred Allen, and *him* I can't stand."

That contest received widespread news coverage and gave the Benny program the shot in the arm it needed to zoom upward once again to be in contention for the top rating.

About this time Mr. Kitzel was introduced to the program, portrayed by a former photographer on the New York *Daily News*, Artie Auerback. Mr. Shlepperman (Sam Hearn) had been off the show for some time, and the Jewish-accented Mr. Kitzel soon became a program favorite with his "Hallo, Mr. Benny" entrance and the song that John Tackaberry wrote for him: "Pickle in the Middle." Soon the whole country was laughing and singing his little song:

> Pickle in the middle with the mustard on top,
> Just the way you like it and they're all red hot.

In 1946 Jack's agent, Arthur Lyons, signed him to a new three-year contract with the American Tobacco Company for $22,500 a week, and by the end of that season, with options for increased salaries for his cast coming up, Jack realized that he would end up making only $2,000 per show for himself, which was much less than most of the other radio stars were making for themselves. The top agency in the country at that time was the Music Corporation of America, known in the industry as MCA, and Jack went to see Taft

Schreiber, MCA's vice-president in charge of radio, with his problem.

"Jack walked into my office one day," recalls Schreiber, "without any solicitation from any of us. We had just made a big deal for the Amos and Andy program, selling it to CBS, and Jack seemed impressed with that. I told him we would love to handle him, but not if he had another agent. It was then that he paid off Arthur Lyons so we could sign him with MCA."

The first move Taft and MCA made was to form a company, Amusement Enterprises, Inc., which would produce the Benny program as well as other shows, motion pictures, and anything else they could create. Jack Benny owned 60 percent of the stock; Myrt Blum took 30 percent; Lloyd Wright, Benny's lawyer, received 5 percent, as did the accountant Sylvan Ostreicher. Taft then renegotiated the contract with American Tobacco, with Jack getting $10,000 per show for his services and Amusement Enterprises receiving $27,500 to pay the expenses of the rest of the show—a healthy raise.

The company was ready to operate in June, 1947, and that's when I was hired as publicity and advertising director.

20

WHEN Amusement Enterprises was formed, MCA suggested, and Jack immediately agreed, that they hire one man to publicize Benny and the program instead of the large Steve Hannagan organization, and that one man should be selected from the motion-picture industry rather than the radio field since the agency felt that film publicity and exploitation and promotion were much more advanced then. I had been employed as a publicist and exploitation director and a publicity director for many years at movie studios, including Warner Brothers, Samuel Goldwyn, and Columbia Pictures, and when I was offered the opportunity to work in a small organization as opposed to the larger studio departments I had been used to, I leaped at it.

Although at the time I knew it was a forward step for me, I could not realize that it was the beginning of a relationship that would span almost twenty-eight years and that soon I would come to love Jack Benny as I would a father or a son, a father because he was so much older than I and a son because he always seemed so helpless and dependent in everything but the creation and performance of his program. His helplessness was communicated to everyone else, too, and just as I found myself worrying about him during all my waking hours, I soon discovered that many others were fretting over him, too, even total strangers. I used to become anxious about him when we were at airports waiting at the gate for the plane's departure. Invariably, he'd wander off to buy a newspaper or magazine, and as the time for the takeoff approached, I knew he could never find his way back to the proper gate alone. When I first started to travel with him, I'd scurry all over the airport looking for him, but finally I learned to relax in the certainty that someone would befriend the unprotected star and get him to the plane on time. And to verify my faith, he always showed up with a guard or a pretty girl or some stranger steering him to the right place at the right time.

The first office of Amusement Enterprises was in a small two-story frame building in the 400 block of North Bedford Drive in Beverly Hills. My secretary and a bookkeeper were in the downstairs offices, and I occupied one of the two offices upstairs. The other one was shared by Jack and the writers and Bernard Luber, a man who was hired to bring in motion-picture deals and other properties.

Our company packaged the program that replaced the Benny show that summer of 1947, a quiz show called *Let's Talk Hollywood,* but I concentrated on getting the publicity and promotion on the Benny program ready for a September start. I spent hours with the comedian and found him warm and very friendly, and within a few weeks I felt that I had known him for years. And despite his supposed lack of humor offstage, I discovered that he did say funny things even though he wasn't trying to be funny every time we were in a group or at a luncheon. "I'm only funny when I get paid for it," was a standard comment of his, and funny he was when he was onstage or on radio. There were some comics who killed them at the dinner table but didn't get a laugh onstage, and fortunately, Jack didn't fall into that category.

One day, after a few weeks, when I thought that things were rolling smoothly and that I had got to know Jack well, I heard his footsteps coming up the stairs to my office. But instead of his usual springy step, he seemed to plod the stairs slowly, one by one. He walked into the office and sat down opposite me without a word of greeting. I offered an opening line of some sort, but he didn't answer and just sat for several minutes, looking glum and not speaking. I couldn't understand what was happening. Was he getting ready to fire me? What had I done that could have displeased him so much? Was there an item in one of the columns that I shouldn't have planted? While those disquieting thoughts were running through my mind, Jack rose, mumbled a brief good-bye, and left.

Immediately I went to Myrt Blum and asked him to clarify my position and to explain Jack's peculiar behavior. To my astonishment, he just laughed. "Jack isn't like you or me," he said. "Jack gets highs that are much higher than most when he's exuberant and exhilarated—they can last for days and sometimes weeks. But when he hits a low, and it might be for no reason we know of, he is impossible to talk to."

That was my introduction to Jack's low mood, a condition I was often to find him in through the years. We talked about it frequently, and Jack said that he had been that way all his life. I learned with the passing of time not to worry about it if he became sullen and silent.

One of the champion worriers of our time, Jack was enraged when Hedda Hopper referred to him as a great worrier in her syndicated column, and he came storming into my office complaining about that description. This happened during the first month I was with him, and not yet understanding his many foibles, I didn't know what to make of his deep concern about such an innocuous item. But he kept worrying about it, all the while denying he was a worrier.

"Take Bert Lahr," said Jack. "Now *he's* a worrier about everything. As soon as he reads a script, he worries if the show will be any good, and when he starts rehearsals, he worries about the critics, and if the show's a hit and looks as if it'll run a long time, he's already worrying what the critics will say about his next show."

Jack worried about the Hedda Hopper line for weeks until I finally told him I would phone her about it.

"Why, that's ridiculous that he's not a worrier." Hedda laughed. "He's the champion."

But she promised not to upset him with that line again, and when I told Jack I had straightened it out, he stopped worrying about being called a worrier—but not about the multitude of other details that seemed to plague him constantly.

Although he was a mild-mannered man on the surface and most people thought he didn't have an angry bone in his body, quite often Jack would explode. Even though it wasn't a frequent happening, when he would become incensed, it was the anger of a person accustomed to keeping the plug over the boiling water—when the plug was pulled, watch out! Knowing this about himself, he warned people close to him how really angry he would become on occasion. The first time I saw it happen was during a Saturday rehearsal when Mr. and Mrs. Ronald Colman were the guests on the program, probably their second or third guesting. It was the routine to read the radio script while sitting around a table on Saturdays at noon, and then Jack and the writers would polish it after hearing it read, giving them all day Sunday to rehearse and perform the show.

Rochester was very often late for rehearsal, but usually not more than five or ten minutes, but on this day we waited about twenty minutes for him. Jack became more and more embarrassed to hold up the reading with such luminaries as the Colmans until he decided that the reading should start without Rochester. They went through the entire program, and by the time it was finished it was one o'clock, and still no Rochester.

"Let's write him out of this show," fumed Jack, and the writers agreed and left to go to the script room for the rewrite. Just as they reached the other room, Rochester arrived, explaining that his plane from San Francisco was late. Jack glowered at him and then, in a voice chilled with anger, said, "You're finished on this show, Rochester," and quickly walked away, leaving Rochester openmouthed.

Rochester was written out of the program, but he came to rehearsal the next day and tried to speak to his boss. Jack remained tight-lipped, refusing to talk to him. Finally, Mary took Jack aside and persuaded him that he was breaking poor Rochester's heart, so Jack relented, and Roch was back on the show. By the following week Jack appeared to have forgotten all about it, and the two were again best of friends.

Rochester had great respect for Jack for many reasons. When they went on the road in the 1940's, there were a few unpleasant instances in which a hotel refused to accept Rochester. Jack, when such an unfortunate thing happened, would have the entire company move to another hotel. He left orders, when reservations were made in advance, to be sure that Rochester would be a welcome guest if the hotel wanted the Benny troupe.

The Colmans started on the Benny show as very reluctant guest stars. Jack originally offered them the job because he had a very good idea involving an austere British couple, but since Colman was one of Hollywood's finest dramatic actors, he was hesitant about appearing on a comedy program. However, his agent, Nat Wolf, convinced him that he was too elegant and restrained and that a Benny show exposure would do a great deal to enhance his versatile image with Mr. and Mrs. Average American.

Their first appearance was hilarious, and the contrast of Jack's boorishness and the Colmans' suavity produced a perfect laugh combination. From that time on the Colmans always looked forward to an invitation to the Benny show.

The longest laugh on that program, and one of the longest on any Benny program, occurred when Ronnie and Benita were talking about Jack and his orchestra leader while Benita was eating an apple.

"Benita," he asked, "have you ever seen Phil Harris' musicians?"

"Please, Ronnie," she answered, "not when I'm eating."

This first broadcast went on before I joined him, but Jack explained the background on that joke to me in detail. It was one of his great pleasures to study the anatomy of his jokes, or anyone else's for that matter, discussing and dissecting to savor every nuance that he could find in it.

"Now that joke about Phil's musicians is a pretty good one if it was just set up on that program," Jack explained. "But the audience had ten years of jokes about Phil Harris and the drunken bums that made up his band. They pictured Phil,

Remley, Sammy, the drummer, and all the rest going out and getting loaded and doing crazy things as soon as the show was over. So when she delivers that punch line, you can picture these drunken guys and how this tasteful English lady reacts at their mere mention."

The show the Colmans rehearsed that brought about poor Rochester's temporary dismissal was equally funny. It involved Jack receiving a cocktail invitation from the Colmans by mistake, and their displeasure on his arrival was heightened by this short sequence:

COLMAN: Well, the cocktails are ready. A toast! Benita, your health! *(Sound: Tinkle of glasses)*
COLMAN: Wellington, happy days! *(Sound: Tinkle of glasses)*
COLMAN: Benny, good luck. *(Sound: Glass breaking)*
BENNY: Whoops! Too hard . . . I'm sorry, I didn't mean to break your glass.
BENITA *(sadly)*: Oh, and that set was one hundred fifty years old.
BENNY: Well, I'm glad I didn't break any of your new stuff!

On that program, as well as succeeding ones, the Colmans were pictured as living next door to Benny, and this was so real to the radio audiences that hundreds of tourists who discovered where Jack lived also rang the doorbell of the harassed next-door neighbors until they had a sign painted at their bell: "Ronald Colman does NOT live here."

21

THE Jack Benny program hadn't been in first place in the Hooper ratings for many years when I started on the show, and in a youthful burst of bravado I told Jack that I would get the show back on top.

"You'll never do it, kid," he said. "They don't want to see me in first place again."

Who "they" were, I didn't know and I'm sure he didn't either, but I worked hard seven days a week, the writers were brilliant week after week, and by such constant effort, great shows, and good luck, we moved back into first place within four months, putting me into first place in Jack's eyes from then on. Now Jack's only worry became how to stay in the top spot, and he worked harder than ever, with the writers developing and perfecting every script.

Although the jokes were important, the situations were more important, and the staff would spend more time building an attitude or character than on the joke itself. What also elevated his program above most others was that he was able to seize on a situation or sometimes a mistake and build it so that the audience realized what he was doing and kept rooting for him. Jack explained some of these techniques best in a lecture he gave in 1964 to a group in his hometown, Waukegan:

"In one show, we were building a joke in which *I* had the big payoff—the funny line. It was such a good joke I could hardly wait to say it. Mary had the last line of the buildup. She was supposed to say, 'I'll have a *swiss cheese* sandwich.' Now it's time for her line, and I'm waiting with the big joke to follow. When the waiter said, 'And what will you have, miss?' Mary said, 'I'll have a *chiss swiss* sandwich.' Well, the audience just roared. Knowing that my joke was now ruined, I looked at her and said, 'A *chiss swiss* sandwich?' and the audience again roared. She said, 'I didn't say that.' I said, 'Yes, you did.' The audience was now laughing harder than ever. Mary again said, 'I did not. I said *chiss swiss* sandwich.' When the audience heard her make the same mistake, they screamed. Now of course, I realized I had something going for me, and intermittently during the last fifteen minutes of the show, I'd just look at her and say, '*chiss swiss* sandwich?' and each time I did it the audience would laugh harder than ever. I knew that by doing this, I was destroying the material that had been carefully prepared and rehearsed, but the audience, knowing that they were seeing an ad-lib situation develop right before their eyes, laughed much more than at anything in the prepared script.

108

"And this wasn't the only time. I remember once we were doing a broadcast and had a joke in which I went to great length to explain that comedy pictures don't win Academy Awards. I pointed out that only dramatic pictures won the Oscar. And to make my case stronger, I said, 'The only way to win an Academy Award is to make a picture with absolutely no laughs at all in it.' And Mary was supposed to say, 'Your last one darned near made it,' but instead, she said, 'Your *darn* one last near made it.' Now, there's a line that makes no sense at all, but the audience, appreciating the humor of the mistake, roared so that we could hardly go on with the show.

"Once Mary was supposed to say, 'My car was up on a grease rack.' I'm sure you agree with me that it is not a difficult line. But leave it to Mary. We go on the air, and when it's time for her line, she says, 'My car was up on a grass reek.' Again the audience howled. Now this is a type of humor that you cannot write and rehearse because it gets its strength from its spontaneity. As I said, you can't write these incidents, but you can capitalize on them. To show you what I mean, since Mary had made several of these errors, my writers and I decided to prepare a show in which I woud bawl her out for making these mistakes. We were in Palm Springs, and during the first twenty minutes of the show, I kept saying to Mary from time to time, 'The word is grease rack. It couldn't possibly be anything else!' And I continued to harp on the fact that there was no such word as 'grass reek.' I repeated it over and over, all the while getting laughs. After this was well planted, and believe me, it was, the Palm Springs chief of police came on. We had a routine, and at the end of it, I said, 'By the way, Chief, have you had any emergency calls that were unusual?' He said, 'Well, yes, Jack, I have. Only last week we went out on a call. Two skunks fighting on someone's front lawn.' I said, 'Two skunks fighting on someone's front lawn?' And he said, 'Yes, and boy, did that *grass reek!*' Now, Mary jumped up, and as previously prepared in the script, I had to apologize to the audience for embarrassing her.

"I recall one time we were just going off the air and didn't have any idea of what we were going to do next week. During the closing commercial my writers and I were in the control room discussing possibilities for the next program. Nobody had an idea, so we decided to meet in the morning. Just then, Don Wilson's voice came blaring out of the speaker, and instead of saying 'Be Happy, Go Lucky', he said 'Be Lucky, Go Happy.' We just looked at each other, and I said, 'That's it . . . that's the show we'll do next week.'"

Early in 1948 Ralph Edwards started a contest on his *Truth or Consequences* program to identify "The Walking Man," who was Jack Benny. The first person to write in the correct name of the Walking Man would win $10,000, but each letter writer was asked to insert $1 or more in his envelope for heart research. Secrecy was essential, and the only people who knew who the Walking Man was were Mickey Rockford, an MCA agent; me; Ralph Edwards; his producer; and a sound engineer on the Edwards staff. Since programs were done live in those days, Jack had to go to a house in Laurel Canyon every Saturday where he walked on cue while Ralph Edwards recited a short poem clue. As the weeks went by, interest in the Walking Man grew until the whole country was talking about it. It wasn't until the eighth broadcast that someone guessed correctly that it was Jack Benny. By that time, ironically, *Truth or Consequences* had supplanted Jack Benny as the number one program in the ratings, but the tremendous publicity Jack received personally as the Walking Man soon pushed his show back on top, where it remained for many, many years. In the meanwhile, $1,800,000 was raised for heart research, an amount which exceeded everyone's expectations. And with that money the Heart Fund was started.

Twenty years later I accompanied Jack to the twentieth anniversary dinner of the Heart Fund, which was held in Miami Beach. Ironically, the secondary Heart Fund award went to Dr. Michael De Bakey, the first man in the United States to transplant a heart successfully; the award of the *first* Golden Heart went to Jack Benny because of his being instrumental in raising the sum of money necessary to launch the organization.

A member of the supporting cast who kept getting more important on the Benny program was Mel Blanc, the man of many voices. Originally, Mel was hired because he could make the funny sound that was supposed to be the voice of Carmichael, the bear, and this was his only contribution to the program for a long time.

"Finally I went to him," recounted Blanc, "and I said, 'Mr. Benny, I can talk, too.' This was good for a five-minute explosion from Jack, and the next thing I knew, I was the voice of his long-suffering French violin teacher. I followed that by being the train announcer with the famous 'Train leaving on track five for Anaheim, Azusa and Cucamonga.' And then I did what was perhaps the funniest character of all, the Mexican in the 'Sí-Sy' routine."

Johnny Carson, who was an astute judge of comedy even when he was a student at the University of Nebraska, recently listened to a tape he made when he addressed his radio class when he was a senior at the university.

"I was always interested in radio comedy, and I used the Jack Benny show as a prime example of fine comedy and comedy writing, especially in the way Jack and his writers played a running gag all through a program and then made it pay off at the end. I had taped the 'Sí-Sy' routine from Jack's satirical version of the motion picture, *The Treasure of Sierra Madre,* which was the first time the Mexican routine had ever been done, and I pointed it out as an example of a perfect comedy spot."

The routine was performed many times on radio and then again on television when Jack would run into the Mexican character in all sorts of places, a department store, railroad station, or airport. It went like this:

> BENNY: Does this train go to Chicago?
> MEL: *Sí.*
> BENNY: Is it on time?
> MEL: *Sí.*
> BENNY: What's your name?
> MEL: Sy.
> BENNY: Sy?
> MEL: *Sí.*
> BENNY: Are you married?
> MEL: *Sí.*
> BENNY: What's your wife's name?
> MEL: Sue.
> BENNY: Sue?
> MEL: *Sí.*
> BENNY: Does your wife work?
> MEL: *Sí.*

BENNY: What does she do?
MEL: Sew.
BENNY: Sew?
MEL: *Sí.*

Naturally, the pauses, the stares at the audience, Mel Blanc's monotone delivery—all added greatly to the hilarious reaction to that dialogue.

Mel Blanc continued with his many characters and voice effects for the life of the Benny program except for the long months he was laid up after nearly dying in a terrible automobile accident.

"The doctors practically gave up on me," Mel remembers, "and when they finally pulled me through, they found that just about every bone in my body was broken. When they let me go home, I was in a hospital bed in traction, completely immobile, with both arms and legs suspended in air. Jack saw me that way the day I came home and then got the biggest laugh I ever heard from my wife when he came to visit a few days later. When she opened the door, Jack inquired, 'Is Mel home?'"

During the 1940's Jack added the Sportsmen Quartet to his cast to do many of the commercials, capitalizing on the singing commercials that had become so popular on radio. Don Wilson would introduce the quartet's commercial, and Benny would get annoyed with their jingles and try to keep them off the show, but Don would trick him by various means to sneak the product plugs in. Usually, he would convince Jack that they were going to sing a straight song, which Jack would approve, and then they'd gradually turn it into a commercial. Finally, on one program, Jack got so mad at them, that he fired them, and then the script called for him to be summoned to the phone by Vincent Riggio, then the president of the American Tobacco Company.

BENNY: Oh, oh, my sponsor. . . . Hello, Vince . . . Vincent? . . . Oh, Mr. Riggio. What can I do for you, Mr. Riggio? . . . You've been listening to the show? . . . Wasn't it great? . . . Oh, . . . I shouldn't have what? . . . But I had to fire them. That quartet was the worst. . . . You didn't think

112

so? . . . Well, everybody's entitled to his own opinion. That's why they put rubber mats around cuspidors. *(silly laugh)* What? . . . I guess you're right; it didn't get a laugh either. . . . But about that quartet, Mr. Riggio, I felt that. . . . I know but. . . . But, Mr. Riggio. . . . I know, but . . . Yes, but. . . . You might be right, but . . . but . . . but . . . but . . . I know, but . . . but . . . but . . . but . . . but . . . but. . . .

And that's the way the program ended—on dead air.

Cleveland Amory reported in his *Saturday Evening Post* article:

The psychology of this laugh, Benny feels, was that his audience was amused not only by what they imagined Mr. Riggio was saying, but also at Benny's own gall in allowing so much "dead air" or at least air dead of anything but studio laughter. As Benny read the script, the space between the two most separated "buts" was timed at fourteen and a half seconds. "I don't know how I did it," Benny concludes earnestly. "We've repeated sequences like it since but never one with that much space. If you don't believe fourteen and a half seconds is a long time, take out your watch, read the script and time it for yourself.

Jokes about the sponsor were common on the program, and the integrated commercials continued to be a special highlight and gave the sponsor a good ride for his money as the middle commercial was usually as funny and entertaining as anything in the program. One of the most entertaining was the commercial which featured the Ink Spots and their hit recording of "If I Didn't Care." In this number the second chorus consists of the soprano singing the lyric while the bass recites the lyric and the others hum. The number had been so popular via their hit recording and past radio appearances that the audience really responded when the bass went into the commercial for his recitation.

This led to one of Jack's most embarrassing moments a few months later when he was performing at a big benefit at the Shrine Auditorium in Los Angeles. While waiting to go on, he noticed four black performers seated nearby, also waiting for their turn on the show. When Jack caught their eyes, he coyly started to sing, "If I didn't care. . . . If I didn't care," and all the while he was rolling his eyes and smiling in conspiracy.

Finally, one of the quartet spoke up: "I think you've made a mistake, Mr. Benny. We're the Mills Brothers."

22

THE audience in the radio studio numbered about 150, and although their laughs were usually very good, they didn't give Jack the satisfaction he received from the big theater audiences he had grown up with. And after the years of entertaining the troops, Jack needed the continuous stimulation of big live audiences. Whenever he could therefore, he appeared at benefits, and he generally took Phil Harris with him because together their humor blended beautifully, especially on the stage. One of the routines they did on a tour of theaters for the March of Dimes went in part like this:

JACK: Phil, what makes you think that people would rather see you than hear me play the violin?

PHIL: Look, Jackson, these people want youth . . . vitality . . . beauty . . . they want me. *(Phil dances)*

JACK: There is the biggest ham I've every known in my life. Phil, what makes you so conceited?

PHIL: I'm not conceited. I'm just irresistible. *(Dances)*

JACK: I'd give a thousand dollars if he fell off this stage. . . . You know, I'll never understand you if I live to be a hundred years old.

PHIL: You ain't got far to go.

JACK: All right, all right. . . . But I'll never understand how Phil got such a beautiful wife like Alice Faye.

PHIL: Well, wait a minute, what's wrong wth that? I've got a right to be married, ain't I?

JACK: That's not what I mean, Phil. . . . What I can't understand is the proposal. How did the proposal take place?

PHIL: Oh, the romance. . . . You want a little romance, huh?

JACK: Yes, yes, Phil, tell me how the proposal took place.

PHIL: Well, it was a beautiful night . . . full moon . . . one of those nights . . . and you know how it is . . . when you're surrounded by those beautiful blue eyes.

JACK: Yes.

PHIL: That gorgeous blond wavy hair. . . .

JACK: Yes.

PHIL: I'm not going too fast for you, am I?

JACK: No, no, go ahead.

PHIL:Those luscious lips . . . and . . . er . . . and . . . er . . . and . . . er . . . Well, that's what I mean. . . . What would you do in a case like that?

JACK: I don't know, Phil, I guess I'd get down on one knee and propose.

PHIL: That's exactly what Alice did. *(Dances)*

"Jack and I did our own routines in lots of theaters," Phil Harris remembered, "and we were a good team and always kept the audience laughing. But one night we did a big show at Carnegie Hall for the March of Dimes, and I must have been marching to the bar too often, because when Jack brought me on, I started to ad-lib a whole routine about Alice and Tyrone Power, who had been in a picture with her. In my condition, I thought I was pretty funny, but the audience didn't, and I really laid a bomb that night. Well, Jack called me in the next morning, and for the first time since I was with him, he really laced into me and told me to stick to the script word for word the next night when we were to do the show in Boston. I stuck to the script in Boston, and I was the biggest hit I had ever been, and the audience just wouldn't let me off. And as they kept applauding me, Jack whispered, 'If this keeps up, I'm going to make you go back to the Carnegie Hall routine.'"

In June, 1947, Jack presented a stage show in two motion-picture theaters, surrounding himself with powerful attractions, including Phil Harris, Rochester, the Sportsmen Quartet, and Marjorie Reynolds. Playing with a film, he broke the all-time record at the Chicago Theater, and then appeared at the Roxy Theater in New York for a week and broke that record, too.

On our way to perform at the Palladium Theatre in London in 1948, he booked a week at the Fox Theater in Detroit and a week at the Palace Theater in Cleveland. This was the first time I was publicizing a theater engagement, and knowing he had broken all records the year before, I felt that if he didn't do that kind of business this time, it would be a reflection on me.

I arrived in Detroit four days before the opening and impressed on the theater people that we had to work harder on this engagement because we were opening on a Wednesday instead of their customary Thursday opening. Everyone cooperated beautifully, and every section of the newspapers was covered: drama, radio, news and even the women's section, with a beauty-tip interview with Phil Harris. The NBC station kept plugging the opening, too, and when the cast arrived, this time with Marilyn Maxwell as the girl singer, the pictures and stories were on the front pages.

The show opened on Wednesday and was as good as any Jack had put together. It moved briskly with songs and comedy, and everyone in the cast thwarted Jack, who was never allowed to play his violin. Finally, when the others had been cleared from the stage, Jack announced that he would play his theme, "Love in Bloom," and as he started, the lights went down, the screen came down, and the newsreel started, leaving Jack a pitiful figure trying to play against the terse, loud clarity of a news commentator's voice and the roar of the background sounds, until in complete frustration, he sadly turned and walked off the stage. In order to ensure the finish, Jack always had them cut the newsreel so that it started with a particularly noisy event, usually something like the Indianapolis 500 with the sound turned up.

Business was just fair that first day, nothing like what it had been on opening days the year before, and after the final performance that night we all gathered in the Benny suite to discuss the problem. Everyone had suggestions. There should have been more and bigger ads (the theater had overspent on advertising), more publicity (everything had been covered), business was off because of a strike (there are always strikes in Detroit), and an agent who had cabbed in from the airport that afternoon said he didn't see any twenty-four-sheet billboards (too costly for a one-week engagement). The meeting ended with no solutions and Jack glumly forecasting the end of his popularity and me feeling guilty that I must have contributed a poor effort.

The theater opened with a film at 9 A.M. with the first stage show starting about 10:45. They had six shows daily and seven on Saturdays. The next morning, which was Thursday, very concerned after a sleepless night, I arrived at the theater at 8:45 for a meeting. To my amazement there was a line of ticket buyers stretching around the block, and happily, this line remained permanently at the box office for the remaining six days of the engagement. The only problem we had was that too many people stayed for two or three shows while anxious customers waited in line. I quickly had a few thousand copies made of an autographed picture of Jack, and as soon as the stage show was over, we had someone announce on the public address system that the first 200 people to come to the stage door would get an autographed photo. That would usually clear out the diehard fans and make some room for the ones in line.

The record of the theater had been set a few years before at $72,000, and despite the slow start, our show grossed $95,000. *Billboard,* the theatrical publication, commented on the figure, stating that we really only grossed $88,000. However, our figure was correct, of course. *Billboard* simply couldn't believe that our show could have broken the previous record by such a margin.

The incident impressed on me that fact that habit plays a most important role in the entertainment pattern of the American public. Even though all our publicity was aimed at a Wednesday opening—the Tuesday ads said "Opening Tomorrow," and the Wednesday ads said "Opening Today," and the date was repeatedly printed and announced—the public automatically was programmed to Thursday, the regular opening day, and that is when they came.

After another record-breaking engagement at the Palace in Cleveland, Jack was so happy with the show that he decided to keep it intact for a date at the London Palladium. From Cleveland, the group, consisting of Jack and Mary Benny, Phil Harris and Alice Faye, Marilyn Maxwell, the left-handed guitar player Frankie Remley, and I, stopped in New York and then boarded the *Queen Elizabeth* bound for England.

We arrived in Southampton, and as soon as we docked, our London agents, Lew and Leslie Grade, came on board with more than a score of British press and photographers to interview Jack. The interviews were not too much different from hundreds we had before and after, but one question shattered us for a moment when a newsman asked if Jack had always been mean. Jack looked at me with that helpless expression, and I quickly answered, "Why, no, he's never been mean. As a matter of fact, he is a very nice, kindly man and always has been."

"But we remember him from his radio programs as being very mean," insisted the reporter, and Lew Grade quickly interrupted to explain to the visiting Americans that "mean" meant "stingy" in England.

The first night in London I had dinner with Jack and Mary in their suite at the Savoy Hotel, and all through dinner Jack worried his way through his routines, wondering anxiously whether or not the British people would know him well enough to understand all his humor, which depended so much on an intimate knowledge of his foibles and pretensions.

After dinner Jack and I took a walk on the Strand, which was fairly deserted at that time of night. The first person we saw walking toward us was a typical English gentleman in a bowler hat and a large black umbrella hooked over his arm. As he passed, he did a double take and said, "Mr. Benny?"

Jack nodded his head, and the man asked, "Did you bring Rochester?"

We told him we did and as we walked away, I said to Jack, "Are you still worried that they don't know you?"

The show Jack assembled for the Palladium was a rewrite of his regular stage shows with new jokes added, and the British audiences loved it. During his opening monologue, Jack said:

"I'm living in a very modest place. I have a room overlooking beautiful Claridge's Hotel. I thought it was better than paying Claridge's prices and overlooking the dump I'm living in. Claridge's is much too high-class for me; it's so ritzy I understand that all the old managers are buried in Westminster Abbey. And it's so terribly expensive. I went into Claridge's for lunch the other day—all I ordered was a fruit salad and coffee, and I had to book another week at the Palladium.

"But anyway, it's so nice to be back here. I have been reading in our trade papers that you have had so many American artists here at the Palladium. You see, we have a reciprocal agreement with England in which we send you American acts and you send us British entertainers. And it works out very well. Why, only last month at the Roxy Theater in New York, you sent us Danny Kaye. He calls himself Danny Kye now.* You know, I have never met anyone who is as crazy about the Palladium as Danny is. When you talk to him, no matter what subject you get into, it always ends up with the Palladium. All he thinks and talks about is the Palladium Theater. Now I'm going to tell you something you won't believe. I met him on the street one day—I had an appointment so I said, 'Danny, what time is it?' and he said, 'Six and eight thirty.'†

"The other day I was waiting on the street for someone who was picking me up, and I noticed a man standing in back of me, so I moved to the corner, turned around, and there was the same fellow right in back of me again. So I turned to him and said, 'Look, mister, why are you always standing in back of me?' And he said, 'I don't know what you're queuing up for, but being second isn't bad.'"

The Phil Harris routine was essentially the same as the ones they did in the States and included exchanges like this:

JACK: You know, folks, since Phil made that picture *Wabash Avenue,* I haven't been able to do a thing with him.
PHIL: Thank you, Jackson. You know, I was really great in that picture, wasn't I? What a lover!
JACK: Lover! Phil, if you're such a great leading man, how come at the end of the picture, Victor Mature wins out?

*Danny Kaye had created a sensation when he played the Palladium the year before—1947.
†The two shows nightly at the theater started at 6 P.M. and 8:30 P.M.

PHIL: He didn't win, Jackson. He lost.
JACK: What are you talking about. He got Betty Grable.
PHIL: I know . . . but he wanted me!

After the Benny-Harris routine, Phil would sing three songs and invariably would finish to tremendous applause as Jack would come out clapping his hands halfheartedly. This jealous reaction would lead to more applause until Phil would raise his hands for silence and then say, "Don't worry, folks, I'll be back . . . because this old man needs me."

And as he made a slow exit with some grinds and kicks, with sound effects from the drums, the laughs would be tremendous as Jack would look with feigned irritation at the spot where Phil had exited. Then Jack would turn and stare at the audience, and then back to the exit, and back to the audience, and as long as he wanted to continue this maneuver, he could keep the audience laughing. I think the longest laugh I ever heard in a theater happened one night when Jack was in a particularly good mood and kept that laugh going for a very long time, and just as it was dying down, a Cockney voice from the second balcony called out, "For God's sykes, Mr. Benny, sye something."

The show opened to wonderful reviews in all the London papers, with headlines like THE IRRESISTIBLE JACK BENNY IS A NATURAL and OH, GOOD, MR. BENNY, OH, VERY GOOD! Beverly Baxter, the reviewer for the *Evening Standard,* caught one facet of Jack's impression on the audience with these few paragraphs from his review:

It was in one of these pauses that a young man in the row behind touched me on the shoulder and said, "Excuse me, could you tell me who this is?"

I said that it was Jack Benny.

Ten minutes later, while Mr. Benny was looking at his fingernails as if he had never seen them before, the same young man leaned forward and asked me when the man on stage was going to do something.

As quietly as possible, I explained that Jack Benny never did anything, which was his peculiar genius. "Thank you," whispered the young man, who was perfectly sober and had very good manners.

120

The engagement was a sellout at every performance, and Benny returned to the Palladium in 1950, again with Phil Harris, and in 1952 repeated his success, that time with Dennis Day.

23

DURING the summer of 1948 Jack's company, Amusement Enterprises, presented Jack Paar as the summer replacement for the Benny program, and it proved successful enough to find a sponsor for the winter season. At the same time the company produced a motion picture from the Craig Rice mystery novel *The Lucky Stiff,* starring Dorothy Lamour, Brian Donlevy, and Claire Trevor. We also bought a series of filmed Italian operas, which were planned for television.

With this activity, MCA, the agency, offered the company for sale to NBC, and when they hesitated for a time, feeling no immediate compulsion to purchase a company whose major asset, the Jack Benny program, was already on their network, MCA quickly went to William S. Paley, chairman of the board of CBS. In November, 1948, CBS bought Amusement Enterprises for $2,400,000. The story was a big one, and the reporters filed items daily as rumors of the negotiations persisted, but because of the delicate nature of the network switchover as well as the capital tax gains of the sale, we wished to keep a low profile. When the sale was finally consummated, the agents and the lawyers insisted on a "no comment" to the press. However, because of the magnitude of the deal and all the resultant queries, I felt compelled to issue some quote from Jack Benny on his reaction. His comment was announced as "I wonder if they have free parking at CBS?"

Although it has never been officially announced, the rumor was that the only hitch in the deal was the sponsor, the American Tobacco Company, which had the number one program on NBC and had nothing to gain by a network switch, but perhaps a great deal to lose. It was my understanding that in order to get the sponsor to agree, Bill Paley guaranteed them a refund of $3,000 for every point the Benny show might drop from its closing rating on NBC, this payment to cover the first eight weeks of the CBS series scheduled to start on January 4, 1949. In any event, the orders came from high up to go all out on the campaign to promote the switchover.

In conjunction with Victor Ratner, vice-president of advertising and promotion for CBS, and his staff, we lined up a gigantic campaign. As well as regular press releases and Jack Benny interviews, we made a special series of radio commercials plugging the show, and CBS blanketed the air with them all through December and until our opening broadcast. During the final week Benny popped in on almost every CBS program with a gag or two, plugging his forthcoming appearance.

One of the highlights of the promotion was a tie-up we made with the March of Dimes. We had a Jack Benny Covered Wagon travel across the country, collecting money for the March of Dimes, carrying a Jack Benny safe with 1,000,000 pennies in it which the comedian was donating to the drive. A sign on it said: "This is my safe. Keep hands off. Jack Benny." A recording by Don Wilson urged contributions while interjecting mentions of the new CBS program. I arranged for Stan Margolies, a film studio press agent, now a producer, to go out ahead of the wagon with Arthur Wilde, then and now a motion-picture publicist, to travel with the wagon that covered thirty-six cities in thirty days. Slick Airways shipped the wagon from city to city, and then it was trucked to the outskirts of the city, where teams of horses or mules were attached to the wagon for the trip through the main streets up to the city hall. The covered wagon ended up in Washington, D.C., a few days before our opening broadcast, and Vice President Alben Barkley was handed a check for $100,000 that had been raised, as well as the 1,000,000 pennies from Jack.

While our campaign was going on, NBC didn't sit idly by, but instead decided to put the Horace Heidt program in the 7 P.M. Sunday spot, opposite Jack on CBS. Heidt was host of an amateur program that had been on NBC at a later hour on Sunday and had done very well in the ratings despite the poor time spot. So NBC ran publicity heralding "Horace Heidt moves to the No. 1 spot in radio," insinuating that the time period was what brought the majority of the listeners to a particular program.

The theme of our opening show was "Do I get free parking at CBS?" and although everyone from Bill Paley on down was confident about the quality of the program, all were very nervous about the rating. We had closed at NBC with a Hooper rating of 24.1, which was considered phenomenal, but our opening rating on CBS amazed even the most optimistic when Hooper announced a fabulous 27.8. The rating continued very high for the rest of the season, making everyone, especially the CBS treasurer, very happy.

When this windfall of money came from CBS, Jack's agent, Taft Schreiber, advised Myrt Blum to buy 50,000 shares of CBS stock, which was then selling at about $17 per share. He felt that Jack could only help CBS and would contribute greatly to the development of the number two network. But Blum was cautious and wanted more security for the star, so instead went for more conservative investments.

"If they had listened to me," said Schreiber recently, "that stock today, after the various splits, would have been worth over twenty million dollars."

Jack took a capital gain on the Amusement Enterprises sale, and the Internal Revenue Service immediately sued on the grounds that it was a personal holding corporation and the gain should be treated as straight income. Jack's lawyers took the position that actors shouldn't be discriminated against just because of their profession but should be entitled to set up a company in the same manner as any other businessman. After a lengthy trial the Benny position was upheld, and this victory was very important for actors who, in the future, would form their own companies more and more frequently.

The Benny changeover to CBS made a great impact on the radio industry, and very soon other NBC programs, including Burns and Allen, Bing Crosby, and Red Skelton, followed Jack. Within one year CBS, which had been a poor second, became the number one network in the ratings, and *Fortune* magazine credited the Benny move to that network as the prime reason for the turnaround.

Jack and his boss, William Paley, resumed their friendship and spent a great deal of time together. At a CBS dinner, when called on to speak, Jack said, "Bill Paley is not only the greatest boss I ever had, but he's the most brilliant, honest and warm human being I've ever met. And I'll say that to his face—even if it costs me my job."

Although CBS was delighted with the final results of the Amusement Enterprises purchase because of the success of the Benny show, it didn't fare too well with the other assets of the company. *The Lucky Stiff* turned out to be a disaster at the box office; the Jack Paar program was dropped, and he went to New York to make his reputation as a host on the *Tonight* show; the Italian opera films never saw the light of day again; and *Let's Talk Hollywood,* the 1947 summer replacement program, never sold again as a radio program.

24

THE program continued at CBS at its usual high level, and Jack remained the same cheap, toupee-wearing braggart, although the humor had to be more sophisticated every year in order to hold the audience. As Jack once explained it, "I must be cheaper now than I was ten years ago in order to get a laugh. It's not funny now if I leave the table and give the waiter a nickel tip, which was a laugh years ago. Today I must maneuver it so that somehow I get the waiter to give *me* a nickel tip."

A great example of a cheap routine, according to Jack, was one he did about the Acme Plaza, a run-down hotel that he supposedly lived in when he visited New York. For years the cast did jokes about him staying at this fleabag, and Jack always defended it for various reasons. On one broadcast, he was asked directly why he stayed there.

JACK: Okay. Once and for all I'll explain my loyalty to the Acme Plaza. Years ago, when I started in vaudeville, I couldn't get work, couldn't pay my rent, and didn't have what to eat. The manager of the Acme Plaza not only let me stay there rent-free, but every morning he'd place a tray outside my door, and it had orange juice, coffee, and a doughnut so I wouldn't be hungry—and not once did the manager ever embarrass me by asking for money. Now the least I can do to show my loyalty is to stay there.
MARY: Jack, I never knew that. And to show how I feel, I'm going to stay at the Acme Plaza, too.
JACK: Thanks, Mary, that's very nice. But if you should run into the manager, don't tell him I'm working now.

Long before Frank Sinatra came back with his blue eyes, Jack was doing his "blue eyes" jokes and each year came up with a new topper to describe how blue his eyes were: "Bluer than the thumb of a cross-eyed carpenter. . . . Bluer than the feet of a French grape crusher. . . . Bluer than the thumb of a hitchhiker in Alaska. . . . Bluer than the seat of the fourth man on a three-man bobsled."

One day the comedian was playing golf with his friend Norman Krasna, the playwright. Jack told Norman that he had a wonderful comedy line for his next program when he would say to someone, "I need you like a moose needs a hat rack."

"I told Jack that the line wouldn't get a laugh," Krasna related, "because it was what I call a 'picture' joke, and even though it was a clever line, by the time the audience would create the picture it would be too late for the laugh. Well, Jack thought I was crazy, accused me of not knowing what I was talking about, and insisted that it would get a big laugh. Jack did the joke the next Sunday and got no reaction. The following day we played golf, and he didn't say a word for the first two holes and then started to explain why the joke didn't work—a slight distraction in the audience—and then said he would do it again the following week and show me that I was wrong. The following Sunday he used 'the line again and again got nothing, and after a pause, said, 'That's funny. Norman Krasna thought it would get a big laugh.' This was such an inside line that, of the thirty million listeners, only his writers and I knew what he was talking about. The following week he was doing a golf sketch, and right in the middle of it he yelled, 'There's Norman Krasna over there,' and then proceeded to throw the 'He needs me like a moose needs a hat rack' line at me and then had Mel Blanc do his 'Woody the Woodpecker' laugh, which was supposed to be me. The topper to this running gag was that *Variety* finally ran a box on their front page which said that I insisted the line was funny which was why Jack kept repeating it."

During this period in radio many advertisers frequently offered writers gifts, their products, liquor, and even money, to insert jokes in the scripts that mentioned the name of their product, which is why the Santa Fe *Chief*, 4-Way Cold Tablets, Bendix washers, to mention only a few, were heard day after day on comedy shows. This practice continued when television became popular until it was made illegal by an act of the Federal Communications Commission. But for many years the comedy writers, the Benny writers included, had a field day. Sometimes they spent hours trying to think of funny jokes to build around a plug product, which is why you might have heard Dennis Day say, "Gee, Mr. Benny, they must be showing a sea picture on this television set. All I can see is water."

And Jack would answer, "Silly kid! You're looking at the Bendix."

One time, they inserted the following joke in a script but it was not a "plug":

JACK: You were supposed to call me last night at my hotel, the Sherry Netherland. Why didn't you do it?
PHIL: I was so full of Sherry I couldn't say Netherland.

After this routine one of the writers rushed over to see the manager of the Sherry Netherland and asked him what they did for actors, and the manager answered, "We applaud them."

After many years of the plugs, the writers finally did the best one of them all, and again, it wasn't a plug.

JACK: I'm tired, Rochester. Run upstairs and plug in my General Electric blanket.
ROCHESTER: But, boss, we ain't got a General Electric blanket.
JACK: We've got one now.

The president of GE heard this gratuitous mention and had one of his executives call me the next morning and insist on presenting blankets to the cast and writers.

Jack had tremendous regard for his writers, always giving them credit for much of the success of his shows and treating them with courtesy and respect at all times. Even though he came up with funny ideas for complete shows and was a fine editor, he couldn't write the humorous lines for the program, nor could he say funny things in front of the writers, just as he couldn't be funny in front of Mary. There were some people to whom he could write very hilarious letters and some to whom he could say funny things, people like a nurse, a barber, the bank teller, a guitar player. Once he was getting a series of shots in his posterior twice weekly, on Tuesdays and Thursdays. The nurses would alternate the cheeks so that he wouldn't be sore on one side. Neither Jack nor the girls could remember which cheek had had it the time before, so one day he broke up the entire staff in the doctor's office when he dropped his pants and they saw printed on one cheek "Tues" and the other "Thu."

His dentist, Dr. Charles Pincus, told about the time his nurse spelled "honor" as "horror" and Jack said to her, "Can you imagine if you had to spell Funk and Wagnall?"

After a big laugh in the office, Jack said, "You'd never be able to spell 'Wagnall.'"

But in front of his writers Jack could only laugh at their funny lines, and very rarely did he even try to come up with one of his own. One day during a rehearsal of a radio program, Jack called the *four* writers onto the stage and said, "I want to give Mel Blanc credit. I want a line for the tag of the show that says the part of the violin teacher was played by Mel Blanc."

127

One of the four writers took the script and quickly wrote on it: "The part of the violin teacher was played by Mel Blanc."

Jack said thanks to the boys and the four walked off the stage. As they exited, one remarked, "Jack, I think two of us could have done that."

Of course, when he realized how ridiculous the whole thing was, he collapsed with laughter, and the rehearsal had to be halted temporarily.

Another time Jack stopped the rehearsal to complain that he didn't think a line was funny, but the writers argued that they thought it was. The discussion went on for a time until one of the men said, "Well, the four of us could be wrong."

And that line ended the discussion and sent Jack off into a floor-pounding laugh.

Jo Ehre, the wife of psychiatrist Sam Ehre, longtime friend of the Bennys, related an incident that was similar to the one about the Mel Blanc tag line. It occurred when the Ehres were visiting the Bennys.

"We were in the den of their old home on Roxbury Drive with Mary and Jack. Sam and I were going to Palm Springs, and Jack wanted us to play golf as his guests at his club there, Tamarisk. Mary said, 'Jo has to have *my* caddie. He knows the course inside and out, and it makes a big difference to my game.' Came one of Jack's long, famous pauses, hands to face, then: 'How do I do that?' Mary said, 'Jack, you see that phone over there? Go to that phone, call Tamarisk, say, 'This is Jack Benny. My friends Dr. and Mrs. Ehre are coming out to play golf as my guests. Mrs. Benny wants to be sure Mrs. Ehre has *her* caddie.' Another long pause, blank look, hands to face; then Jack walked to the phone, picked it up and verbatim, every inflection the same as Mary's, made the call. I don't know if it will read so, but it was incredibly funny."

In the same way that he could get laughs on the stage simply from a look or a grimace, Jack made the most of long pauses on radio, and this, combined with the use of sound effects and the ability to get humor out of his character and the characters he had built over the years for his cast, contributed to a steady series of successful shows. Once, when John Crosby, then the leading radio critic in the country, heard a particularly funny show, he called me for a copy of the script in order to quote some of the jokes. In his column the next day, he wrote about hearing the funny show and then reading the script and not finding one funny thing to quote.

Jack always believed that the play was the thing, even in comedy, and he didn't care who got the laughs as long as the show was funny. The cast of the Eddie Cantor program always complained that whenever one of them got a big laugh at rehearsal, Cantor would immediately change the dialogue so that he could take the funny line. But Jack always maintained that he didn't care if he didn't have one joke on the show himself because if the program was funny, he would get the credit anyway.

One of the most daring programs he ever did on radio concerned a sight-seeing bus driving by the homes of Hollywood stars. The driver of the bus pointed out various stars' homes and then pointed out the home of Dennis Day, whereupon the music dissolved into a scene between Dennis and his mother. On then to a scene at the home of Don Wilson, next to a rehearsal at Phil Harris' house, and finally, when the bus arrived at Jack Benny's house, the listeners heard his voice say, "Driver, here's where I get off," and that ended the program. That one line was all Jack said on the entire half hour.

Bill Paley telephoned him right after the broadcast.

"Boy, you've got a lot of guts," Paley commented.

"I wasn't afraid to do that show with only one line," Jack said later, "because don't forget that Dennis, Don, and Phil talked about me the whole time that I wasn't on, and that satisfied the listeners."

25

JACK BENNY'S frequent appearances at the Palladium in London inspired one of the best jokes he did for years afterward:

"Now, when I played the Palladium, I was a big hit just as Bob Hope and Danny Kaye were. But somehow they did much better socially than I did. Danny often was invited to the palace by the then Princess Elizabeth and Princess Margaret and went to many parties and important affairs with them. And Bob Hope was very friendly with Lord Mountbatten and many a time played golf with him. Now those things never happened to me. Almost, but not quite. . . . Once, I was invited to dinner at Number Nine Downing Street."

But Jack did walk with kings, and throughout his lifetime he was welcomed by lords and ladies as well. In 1952 Prince Bernhardt of the Netherlands met him at the Palladium and was so charmed by Jack that he invited him to the royal palace in Holland to visit with him and Queen Juliana. Jack's four days as their only guest at the beautiful summer palace was a happy occasion of which he often spoke.

Jack's knowledge of politics was minimal, to say the least. His life was so filled with show business that he had neither the energies nor the desire to pursue other interests in any depth. In spite of this, he did become acquainted with several United States presidents, and even though he was not a member of any political party, he would comment, "I am neither a Democrat nor a Republican. I'm a registered Whig. . . . If it was good enough for President Fillmore, it's good enough for me. . . . Now don't laugh about President Fillmore. . . . after all, he kept us out of Vietnam!"

The first President he was introduced to was Franklin Roosevelt. Even though he never knew him very well, he did entertain for him a few times. After the much-publicized eviction by Roosevelt's order of the chairman of the board of Montgomery Ward from his office for defying the government during World War II, Jack gave Roosevelt a hearty laugh at a Washington dinner when he said, "How do you like this suit I bought yesterday at Montgomery, Roosevelt and Ward's?"

Harry S. Truman was the President Jack was closest to from the time he was the Vice President until his death. In 1943 at a Washington press club affair at which Jack entertained, he posed for a photograph playing the fiddle accompanied by Truman at the piano. The picture was printed in newspapers and magazines for many years thereafter. In

1949 I went to Washington with Jack when he was to be master of ceremonies at the White House photographers' dinner for Mr. Truman. The day of the dinner Truman invited Jack for a private visit to his office at the White House, and Jack insisted that I go, too. The three of us were alone in that historic office. I don't know about Jack, but I was very awestruck and nervous. However, in just a few minutes, Truman had put us completely at ease with stories about the vaudeville acts he had seen as a young man in Kansas City. Jack loved the conversation and recounted some of his classic show business stories. Then Truman shocked us by saying that he had always had a secret desire to get a job playing piano in a whorehouse. Not wishing to impose on Truman's hospitality, Jack and I kept trying to take our leave, but the President laughed and told us to stay as long as we liked. That night at the party I was particularly interested in Mr. Truman's reactions as Jack told his stories and played his fiddle, and it was obvious to everyone present that the President enjoyed every moment of it.

It was a Jack Benny habit to shun large, fancy parties after doing a performance. He usually liked to find some small diner or café to eat a snack. And his tastes in food were very plebeian. Every time he would have a cup of coffee, a piece of pie, or a bowl of soup at such an eatery he always claimed it was the best coffee, best soup, or best pie he had ever had.

After that press club dinner there were various parties being held at our hotel to which we had been invited. But Jack refused them all, suggesting that we go out to grab a bite elsewhere. A few streets from the hotel we found a little diner, just the kind that Jack seemed to like, and we ordered ham and eggs. They were moderately good, but Jack, as usual, extolled the virtues of those ham and eggs, saying that they were the greatest and talking about that "sensational" neighborhood diner often.

Six years later we came back to Washington for Jack to perform at the White House Correspondents' Dinner for President Eisenhower. After that dinner, he said, "Let's skip all the parties and go back to that wonderful diner for those great ham and eggs."

By that time I had completely forgotten all about that diner, let alone where it was located, but out we went in our dinner jackets, and wandered up and down darkened Washington streets until we finally found the right place and Jack could have his great ham and eggs.

In 1959, after he had been appearing gratis for various charities as violin soloist with symphony orchestras, Jack had lunch in Beverly Hills with Mr. Truman and offered to perform with a symphony to raise money for the Truman Library in Independence. Mr. Truman was delighted and arranged for the Kansas City symphony to play with him, but after a few weeks Mr. Truman called the comedian and suggested, "Listen, Jack, the library has plenty of money but the Kansas City Symphony needs it badly, so would you please do the concert for their fund instead of mine, and if you do, I'll be the general chairman of the event?"

"Okay, Mr. President," answered Jack, "I'll do it for them if you'll play a number with me on the program."

But Truman said he would never play the piano in public. However, he offered to conduct the orchestra for a number, and so it was a deal.

I had arranged with the symphony manager to meet us with a car at the airport when we arrived, and to my amazement, when we exited from the plane, there was the former President waiting for us. After Jack scolded him for coming all the way to the airport, we drove back to the Muehlebach Hotel with him, and for the two days we spent in Kansas City, he stayed with us nearly all the time.

Jack delighted the audience with his violin comedy, but the real star of that evening was Mr. Truman when he closed the concert by conducting the orchestra in "Stars and Stripes Forever," waving the baton slightly off the beat but managing to stay with it to the finish, bringing the audience to its feet for a long, standing ovation.

After the concert Truman and his wife, Bess, came up to our suite in the hotel for sandwiches and coffee and the four of us talked about politics, Truman candidly discussing the 1960 election possibilities. I told him that I had heard that Joe Kennedy would spend $10,000,000 to get his son John elected President, and Truman laughed.

"He hasn't a chance," Truman insisted, "because no Catholic can possibly get enough votes to be elected."

Jack and I became political pundits for the next year as we explained to our friends, on expert authority, why John

Kennedy could never get the Democratic nomination. Mr. Truman was very grateful to Jack for helping the symphony raise $54,000, and so, later, when I was desperately looking for exciting guest stars to ensure top ratings for our television program, I suggested that Jack call Mr. Truman and invite him to be on the show. Jack stared at me as though I had two heads.

"We could go to Independence," I insisted, "and tape a scene right in the library. I think he would like the whole country to get a look at that library. It'll only be a day's work, and he just might get a kick out of it."

"But you can't ask a President to be a comedian," answered Jack. "He'd never stand for it."

"Well, I think he would," I said, "and anyway, what have you got to lose by asking? The worst he can do is turn you down."

After a few days of argument I finally picked up the phone and called Rose Conway, Truman's secretary, and told her Jack wanted to speak with the President. I handed the phone to Jack. He explained as best he could what we wanted, at the same time acted a bit apologetic for being so presumptuous.

Without hesitation, the President said, "Of course, I'd be delighted, Jack."

And Jack quickly asked, "Why not?"

They both laughed as they realized how wrong Jack's anticipation had been, and I began to make the arrangements immediately to go to Independence the following month to tape the scene.

After a morning rehearsal at the library on our first day in Independence, we broke for lunch and about ten of us went with Mr. Truman to a nearby Howard Johnson's coffee shop. Mr. Truman drove Jack, me, and Seymour Burns, our director. Another car carried the two writers we brought, Sam Perrin and George Balzer. When we entered the coffee shop, the hostess was all aflutter when she saw Mr. Truman and his entourage, since the room was fairly crowded and there would be difficulty seating twelve people together.

"Why didn't you make a reservation, Mr. President," she asked, "and I would have had a table for twelve waiting for you?"

"Well, I'm in show business now," Truman answered with a twinkle in his eye. "You know the crazy hours we keep."

At lunch Truman regaled us with his warm and witty anec-

133

dotes. When the check came, Jack made a grab for it, but the waitress gave it to the President.

"Let us take it, Mr. President," I said. "We are on an expense account."

"No," said Truman, "you can't pay a check when you're in Independence."

We brought the press from all over the country, and Truman was obviously enjoying his excursion into show business during the taping despite the reporters and photographers who crowded him at every turn. It was a big news story, a former President turning comedian on a commercial TV show.

The scene we shot there, which constituted about half the entire show, consisted of Truman showing Jack through the library and pointing out the various exhibits of highlights of his Presidential years. When they came to a bust of Abraham Lincoln and Jack said that Lincoln was his favorite President, Truman asked him why.

"Any man who would walk five miles through the snow, barefoot, just to return a library book so he could save three cents—that's my kind of guy," answered Jack.

A few days after we returned to the Coast, Seymour Burns phoned to tell me that because they had used the wrong microphones, which kicked the sound off the marble floors and walls of the Truman Library, not only was the sound muddied, but the picture was affected. This was very upsetting because I knew that Jack wanted it to be perfect for the President and had been telling everyone what a great show we had. The CBS technicians went to work on the problem, but since it had been shot on tape, there wasn't too much they could do other than improve it only slightly. Meanwhile, Jack kept pressing me to see a preview of the completed show, and I stalled him with all sorts of excuses until finally, nearing the air date, I ran out of excuses and scheduled a showing in a CBS projection room for Jack and the four writers.

The program was excellent, but the sound in the Truman Library scene was distorted and the picture was still poor in places. When the lights in the projection room came up, there was silence, and Jack just looked straight ahead at the screen, not saying a word for minutes. No one else spoke either. Jack then turned to Seymour Burns and me.

"That's the worst thing I've ever seen. I won't allow it to go on the air."

There was little any of us could say, but nonetheless we tried to tell him it wasn't as bad as he thought and since we were stuck, we had to make the best of it. Jack was as depressed as I had ever seen him and simply refused to listen to any excuses. He was adamant that the program would *not* go on. Finally, I suggested that we let CBS work on it again and try to improve it further, and that's the way we ended that session.

Although Jack was ready to scrap that program, I tried to find some solution, even if it meant returning to Independence. But Truman was on his way to New York, and it was impossible to get back there in time to reshoot the scene by our scheduled air date. And we couldn't change the scheduled air date because we had covers and stories on the program that had gone to press in just about every newspaper TV magazine in the country.

We failed to improve the sequence, and under protest, Jack allowed it to be aired, all the while predicting disaster. Wonder of wonders, it was very well received, and several reviewers wrote that it was refreshing to see flaws in the film and sound instead of perfect studio quality, showing the viewers that the show was obviously done on location at the library. Our rating was the highest for any program that week, so all was well that ended well.

On Jack's behalf, I sent a contribution to the Truman Library for $10,000 in gratitude for Mr. Truman's appearance on our show. In addition, I sent a check to Mr. Truman for $155, which was the union scale minimum payment for an actor in a TV production. Shortly thereafter, I received this letter from our former President:

September 25, 1959

Dear Mr. Fein,

Thank you very much for the check I earned as a scale actor in your production. It will be put to good use.

I was very pleased to learn of the proposed $10,000 contribution to the Library. I had never thought Mr. Benny was *so* liberal, but we need it and it will be very welcome, indeed.

Sincerely yours,
Harry S Truman
(signed)

And, in his own handwriting, Mr. Truman wrote the following postscript:

"Jack now has a walking testimonial to his real liberality if he needs such testimony."

Jack was now in the Truman camp, and the following year he was the only Hollywood star invited by Truman's cronies to attend their annual birthday luncheon for him at the Muehlebach Hotel in Kansas City. Truman loved those luncheons more than anything they gave for him in Washington or New York, and Jack was always happy to be included, turning them down only when his schedule interfered.

Whenever we were in the area, we always dropped in on the former President at his home in Independence, and he seemed to appreciate that Jack would take the time to visit him and Mrs. Truman. In 1966, when we were at the All-American Fair in Wichita, Kansas, Mr. Truman had just returned to his home after a long hospitalization, but when Jack called and asked if he could visit, he was told to come right along. When we finished that engagement, we drove to Independence, where we were received by Mrs. Truman and the President. This time, though, Mrs. Truman did all the talking. The President just smiled and twirled his thumbs continually throughout the visit, hardly speaking, and we were very concerned about the state of his health.

A few years later, we again came to Independence, and although he looked older, he seemed to be the old Harry Truman again, bright, warm, and cheerful. That was the last time we saw him, and happily, that was the way we remembered him.

26

PRESIDENT Eisenhower and Jack Benny were never very close except for a few meetings throughout the years, but Jack loved to tell about a golf game they had once in Palm

Springs years after Ike left the Presidency. The President hooked a long drive, and in exasperation, he said, "The *one* thing I've really wanted to do my whole life is to straighten out my hook."

Jack just looked at him and then said, "Now look here. You've graduated from West Point, you've been a four-star general, you've been commander in chief of the Army, you've been president of Columbia University, you've been President of the United States. . . . I'm sure there was something else you've wanted to do in your whole life besides straighten out that hook."

Lyndon Johnson was another casual friend of Jack's, and even though Jack knew him slightly when he was in the Senate and a Vice President, he saw a little more of him when he was the President and entertained for him a number of times. At one $1,000-a-plate dinner for the President in Washington, a chair was left empty at each table so that Mr. Johnson could spend a little time at every table during the dinner. Jack was seated that evening at a table with Adlai Stevenson, Averell Harriman and the Sargent Shrivers. When the President came to sit with them, he repeatedly referred to Jack as "Mr. Benny." When he moved over to the next table, Jack remarked to his tablemates, "I wish he'd call me Jack instead of Mr. Benny. Every President I've known has called me Jack."

Mrs. Shriver, the former Eunice Kennedy, queried, "And what did President Lincoln call you?"

Before Jack could think of an answer, Adlai Stevenson snapped, "Lincoln called him Kubelsky because Jack hadn't changed his name yet!"

Jack loved to tell that story to his theater audiences because it was one of many good examples of his theory that the best laughs come from true stories. Frequently, he told another story involving President Johnson, but this one did not really happen but was created simply for the joke.

"I was invited to a party at the White House by President Johnson," Jack would say, "and I arrived very late because I had done a concert at Constitution Hall that evening. As I walked up the steps to the White House carrying my fiddle case, a Secret Service man yelled at me, 'Hey, fella, what have you got in that case?' Thinking that since he didn't recognize me, I'd have a little fun, I answered, 'A machine gun!' and the Secret Service man responded, 'Thank God, I thought it was your violin!'"

Jack did not know John Kennedy very well until he became President, but John Kennedy knew Jack very well—and, at one point in his life, was very unhappy about him. During the 1960 campaign we were waiting in an airport when we met Bobby Kennedy, who was also between planes. He told Jack that his father, Joseph Kennedy, was most likely the biggest Jack Benny fan of all and that when the boys were in their middle and late teens, Sunday night at seven was a "must listen" at their home. The senior Kennedy would gather the whole clan in the den, and whether they liked it or not, they had to listen to the Benny program and no one could say a word. Bobby said that sometimes they would have dates and be anxious to be off, but his father wouldn't allow it until the show was over.

In Jim Bishop's book *A Day in the Life of President Kennedy,* he reported that although he rarely looked at television, the one show the President tried to catch from time to time was the Jack Benny program. Perhaps, that was a holdover from his father's influence, but nonetheless, Jack was flattered.

When Jack was invited to be one of the masters of ceremonies at the big birthday party for President Kennedy at Madison Square Garden in May, 1963, he jumped at the chance and decided to bring Kennedy a birthday gift. For years Jack had been gifting special friends with a gold money clip on which was engraved the famous Benny caricature done by the well-known artist Bouché. But for this gift Jack was able to find a caricature of Kennedy in a newspaper, and on the other side of the money clip he had that engraved. Off we went to New York to join the scores of celebrities who came for the event. It proved to be the party of the century with Marilyn Monroe singing "Happy Birthday" to the President and entertainment featuring motion-picture, stage, and opera stars.

Maria Callas flew from Paris for the event and was staying at the Pierre Hotel, where we were also living. When Jack met her at the hotel, he acknowledged the introduction, but she said, "We've met before, Mr. Benny. Don't you remember?"

Jack rarely forgot an attractive woman, so it was unusual that he failed to remember meeting her. Then she reminded him.

"I made my first radio appearance as a contestant on a *Major Bowes Amateur Hour*," she told him, "and you were one of the judges. I came in second because you were the only judge who voted for me!"

Jack realized that it would be too hectic to give the President the gift at the show, so he decided to present it to him afterward at the intimate party given for him by Arthur Krim, president of United Artists and chairman of the event. That party was attended by about sixty people, including Vice President Lyndon Johnson, Adlai Stevenson, Cabinet officers, Bobby Kennedy, the Kennedy sisters and their husbands, and about fifteen stars. Why I was included, I'll never know. As soon as Jack arrived, he went over to President Kennedy, who was standing at the bar, offered his congratulations, and reached into his pocket for the gift—only to discover that he had left it at the hotel. The followup to the story, which Jack once tape-recorded, went as follows:

"But the next day Peter Lawford came up to my suite at the Pierre to have a drink, and I said to him, 'You know, Peter, I did this stupid thing. I brought a gift for the President last night, but I forgot to bring it with me to the party,' and Peter said, 'Wait a minute. His father is in the New York Hospital and Jack is there with him now. Give it to me. I'm going over there and I'll see him.' So I did. I gave Peter the clip. But I wrote a little note and put a dollar in the clip. The note said, 'Dear Mr. President, Happy Birthday. If you don't need this, send it back. The dollar, I mean, not the clip.'

"And then I got this letter, written by hand, on dirty hospital stationery. 'Dear Jack,' it read, 'I appreciate your sending me the money guard. Would you believe what Peter Lawford did? I know you must have put at least $500 or more in that money guard, but when it arrived, it was only $1. I am sending you an extremely rare tiepin which cost $750 to pay for your ticket. I have also asked Milt Ebbins [Peter Lawford's agent] to take care of it as I know you can trust agents. My father told me this when he was young. Yours sincerely, Jack Kennedy.'"

A month before John Kennedy's assassination, he attended a $1,000-a-plate dinner at the Beverly Hilton Hotel in Beverly Hills. In order to get the ballroom, a high school prom that had had the room booked for months was ejected by the Democratic organizers. After a protest broke in the newspapers, the hotel found another room for the prom, but not until after much embarrassment for the President.

At that dinner also, there was one empty chair at each table for the President, and when he came to Jack's table, after he was introduced to each guest, he turned to Jack and said, "I wish you'd do me a favor."

"Mr. President, I'll do anything you ask," answered the comedian, "but I wish you'd at least say hello to me first."

Kennedy laughed, said hello, and then asked Jack to go with him to the room where the high school prom was being held and help him make up with the kids he displaced. You can imagine how thrilled those young students were with Kennedy's appearance and then his introduction of Jack Benny as "my younger brother, Ted."

Two days after the assassination, some of the prom kids came to our office in Beverly Hills to give Jack a flash picture one of them had taken of the two Jacks. We had the picture framed beside the handwritten note from Kennedy, and those were among Jack Benny's proudest mementos.

Richard Nixon was a Congressman and Senator from California, yet he and Jack never spent any time together until Jack was honored in 1959 with the Laurel Award, which was presented at a small dinner in Washington. Jack was thrilled to receive this award, which previously had been given only to serious musical artists. On this occasion, the Vice President of the United States, Richard M. Nixon, would make the presentation.

I was then president of J & M Productions, the company that produced the Benny program, and had been traveling with Jack on a hectic two-week schedule terminating in Washington for the dinner before going back to our homes in California. At that time there were no nonstop jet flights between Los Angeles and Washington, D.C., and one had to arrive and depart from the Baltimore Airport if he wished to fly nonstop. At that, there were only two nonstop flights daily to the Coast, one at 10 A.M. and the other at 3 P.M. I had booked the afternoon flight as we would be up late that night and the Baltimore Airport was a long drive from our hotel.

At the dinner Jack was seated on one side of the ballroom with Nixon and some other dignitaries, while I was seated on the other side with a group that included two Senators and a Congressman. After a short time, Jack came over to my table and told me, "Irving, Richard Nixon says we're on the wrong plane. He makes the trip all the time, and he always takes the ten o'clock flight."

"No, Jack," I said. "We're on the right flight because we would have to get up too early in the morning to make the ten o'clock plane, and it's silly because we have nothing to rush home for."

That seemed to satisfy him, but a few minutes later he showed up again at the table, this time with Richard Nixon in tow.

"Listen, Irving, Dick here says we should definitely take the ten o'clock flight . . . it's better," said Jack, and Mr. Nixon quickly interjected his reasons over my objections.

Finally, I stopped the discussion when I said, "Jack, are you going to listen to a vice president or a president?" While Jack gave one of his roars of appreciation for that line, I must say that Nixon really laughed loud and hard, too, and for the remainder of the evening, every time I danced by him or walked near his table he would salute me with a "Hello, Mr. President."

In the late sixties we were doing a television special titled *Jack Benny's Twentieth Anniversary Special* on which we brought back all the Benny radio cast. Jack and I tried to persuade Mary to make a short appearance on the show, although she had retired from show business in 1958. One day, President Nixon phoned to thank Jack for having appeared with Bob Hope at a Fourth of July rally in Washington, and when Jack told him that he was having trouble convincing Mary to appear on his anniversary special, Nixon said, "You tell Mary that the President is making a personal request that she appear. Tell her this is a command performance."

I don't know whether or not that's what did it, but Mary did appear in a sketch, and Jack always credited the President for making it happen.

141

27

JACK eased into the medium of television very slowly, getting his feet wet with four programs for the 1950–51 season, then progressing to six the next year, nine the next, and then for many years starring in thirteen shows a season, one every other week. For the first five years he continued to do his weekly radio show, and for the added work, he hired two young partner writers, Al Gordon and Hal Goldman, for $200 a week each, to help the other four writers. From the time they were hired, Jack referred to Goldman and Gordon as the new writers, and years later, when this team became seasoned, high-salaried, Emmy award-winning TV writers, Jack still called them the new writers. One day in the fall of 1974, when we were beginning work on a TV special that was destined not to be taped because of Jack's death, a staff meeting was scheduled, and Jack told his secretary, "Don't forget to phone the new writers about the meeting Saturday."

The early television programs, with a few variations, were photographic versions of the radio shows, and Jack retained all the characteristics he had built up in his years in radio: the cheapskate, the braggart, the blue eyes, the toupee, and the age gags.

The perennial "thirty-nine-year-old" jokes started, as did most of the Benny routines, by accident. Sometime in the late 1940's a nurse in a sketch asked him his age, and after a pause, he said, "Thirty-six." Now, this may not be the funniest thing you ever heard, but the studio audience at the radio show, looking at a man they knew was in his fifties, laughed at the mention of "thirty-six." For the rest of that season and on into the next, they repeated situations that called for giving his age, and it was always funny. The following year, on his birthday, he turned "thirty-seven" and managed to stay there a few years, and then he became "thirty-eight." When he reached "thirty-nine," that number seemed funniest of all, so he decided to remain that age as long as he could. But after he was "thirty-nine" a few years, he did a radio program on which his birthday came up and the script called for him to turn "forty," a time of great unhappiness for him. However, just before the end of the program, a telegram came from his sister in Waukegan telling him that there had been a mistake on his birth certificate which they just discovered and that actually he had been born a year later, so, he had just turned "thirty-nine." After that, he didn't bother to have any more birthdays and simply kept on being the oldest "thirty-nine-year-old" in the world.

Jack wrote an article for the now defunct *Collier's* magazine in which he listed many rules on "Turning Forty," including:

> When in the company of younger people, ask their advice on everything. Pretty soon they'll begin to believe they're older than you are.
>
> Stay slim. Thin people always look younger. Connie Mack is 91 but he's so slender, nobody figures him to be more than 88.
>
> Avoid reminiscing about the past. If the name Lincoln comes up in your conversation, be sure it's the car you're talking about, not the President.

The "thirty-nine-year-old" gag became so well known nationwide that a small Texas newspaper once ran a headline, reading simply: MERCURY REACHES BENNY, with no further details necessary.

When Groucho Marx was a guest on the Benny TV program while his own program, *You Bet Your Life,* was very popular, the sketch involved a thinly disguised Jack Benny going on *You Bet Your Life* as a contestant who learned that the jackpot question was worth $3,000. The jackpot question turned out to be "What is the real age of that famous comedian Jack Benny?"

That posed a classic problem for the comedian—should he expose what a fraud he had been all those years about his age, or should he tell the truth and grab the money? While the audience laughed, he puzzled out his dilemma, and the longer he puzzled, the funnier it got. That was one of the longest laughs ever on the program. Finally, he meekly answered, "thirty-nine," thereby losing the jackpot. When Groucho finally found out who he was, he asked him, "Jack, you had a chance to win the jackpot. Why didn't you give your right age?"

"Groucho," Jack answered, "where else can you buy twenty-two years of life for just three thousand dollars?"

Several years later Jack was persuaded to turn "forty" for a television special which would get a lot of interest and excitement. Chrysler sponsored the CBS Special, *Jack Benny's 40th Birthday.* For that program, we brought back all the old radio cast, including the bandleaders. The program was much-discussed and had ample publicity, but somehow it didn't quite come off, and then a Boston newspaper printed an editorial urging Jack to stay at age "thirty-nine" because that image helped keep all of us young and thinking young. The column ended with a plea: "Please, Mr. Benny, don't turn '40,' stay '39' forever." He promptly forgot about his fortieth birthday and remained at age "thirty-nine" from then on until the end.

When I mentioned the laugh that Jack received when he looked at the audience after Groucho asked, "What is the real age of Jack Benny?" it reminds me that Jack and I often discussed which laughs were the longest of the many he received during radio and television. Once Hank Grant, the columnist on the *Hollywood Reporter,* asked me if Jack would write a guest column for him when he went on vacation. I suggested to Jack that he do one about the biggest laughs from the programs, and this is what he wrote:

About 20 years ago on one of my programs I did a gag that got a terrific amount of nation-wide publicity and is still getting it whenever a columnist discusses the great jokes of the past. The gag, which supposedly got the longest laugh that I have ever received in radio or television was:

Holdup Man: Your money or your life.
Jack: (long pause—in fact one of my longest).
Holdup Man: Quit stalling—I said your money or your life.
Jack: I'M THINKING IT OVER!

Now here's another one we did that was good for a 20-second audience reaction (and that's a long time):

Mary: Jack, why don't you stop being so stingy?

Jack: Mary, I'm not stingy, and you know it!

Mary: You're not, eh? . . . Last year when you were going to have your appendix removed, you wanted Rochester to do it.

Jack: I DID NOT. I merely asked him if he knew how.

Here's one we did on television. The scene was my dressing room. Rochester had just taken a quarter out of my pants' pocket to tip a Western Union boy. About a minute later, I entered and picked up my trousers to put them on. As I held my trousers in front of me, I "weighed" them for a couple of seconds. Then I turned to Rochester and said: "ROCHESTER, WHO TOOK A QUARTER OUT OF MY PANTS' POCKET?" This was about a 15-second scream.

Here's another one: Mel Blanc played the part of my French violin teacher who was always disgusted with my tone and technique. During one of my lessons, the following episode took place:

Jack: Professor LeBlanc—do you think you can ever make a good violinist out of me?

Mel: I do not know. How old are you?

Jack: Why?

Mel: HOW MUCH TIME HAVE WE LEFT?

Mary Livingstone got a laugh with ONLY THREE WORDS. She got it through her delivery in a very funny situation. Dorothy Kirsten and Don Wilson were discussing different operas.

Don: Oh, Miss Kirsten, I wanted to tell you that I saw you in "Madame Butterfly" Wednesday afternoon and I thought your performance was simply magnificent.

Kirsten: Well that's awfully kind of you, Mr. Wilson, but who could help singing Puccini? It's so expressive—particularly the last act starting with the allegro vivacissimo.

Don: Well, that's being very modest, Miss Kirsten, but not every singer has the necessary bel canto and flexibility or the range to cope with the high tessatura of that first act.

Kirsten: Well, Mr. Wilson, didn't you think in the aria

145

"Un Bel Di Vedremo" that the strings played the con molto exceptionally fine, with great sostenendo?

Jack: Well—I thought . . .

Mary: OH SHUT UP.

Now, Hank, because of this very humorous situation, Mary's simple three words—"Oh Shut Up"—practically stopped the show. If I had to choose only one bit as being the funniest, that's the one I would have to pick.

28

THE first time Jack Benny disagreed with me (we were to have many disagreements later in our long association) was in 1950, and it concerned a promotion idea. I called my friend Vic Ratner, former advertising VP for CBS and then vice-president of advertising for Macy's, and suggested that he run full-page ads of a photo of Jack shopping at Macy's, with no copy other than a headline stating that this proved Macy's sold for less . . . Jack Benny shopped here. Naturally, I wanted a good credit in every ad to plug our Sunday program. Vic jumped at the idea and approved it immediately, but when I discussed it with Jack, he was very lukewarm, voicing reservations that it might be cheapening. I finally convinced him, and we went ahead with the project, although his approval was only halfhearted.

The following week we went to Macy's, where Jack posed for a photograph with a crowd of women shopping at a counter selling men's underwear. Jack was very lackadaisical about the photo session, and the next day when I brought the ad proof for him to approve, he wanted to cancel the deal. The headline read MORE PROOF THAT MACY'S IS VERY KIND TO THE POCKETBOOK . . . JACK BENNY SHOPS HERE! I told him that the space had already been bought by the store and it would be very unfair to back out at such a late date. He agreed, but with a complete lack of enthusiasm, insisting that the ad had no class and would embarrass him.

The next day the ad broke full page in the New York *Times* and all other New York papers, and even though I saw Jack several times that day, he never once mentioned it. That night I took him to a benefit at the Waldorf-Astoria Hotel, where he made a short appearance, and since he was meeting some friends later at the 21 Club, I dropped him there on my way back to my hotel.

At eight o'clock the next morning, the phone rang, and it was Jack.

"Irving," he said, "can you come right over? I've got something important I want to tell you."

I quickly showered, shaved, dressed, and rushed over, worried that there had been some repercussions over the Macy's ad and wondering whether I had been right in pressuring him into it. When I arrived at his suite, he took me into his bedroom and closed the door.

"Let me tell you something," he began. "As soon as I walked into Twenty-one, the first person who came over to me was Leland Hayward. He couldn't get over that Macy ad. He asked me whose idea it was, and when I said it was yours, he told me it was a stroke of genius. The next fellow I saw was Billy Rose. Now you know what kind of a showman Billy is and how brilliant he is. Well, Billy told me that the Macy ad was the greatest ad he had ever seen and he'd like to hire the fellow who thought of it. And then, for the rest of the evening, all I heard at Twenty-one was about your Macy ad. Isn't that terrific?"

From then on, any time anyone mentioned advertising Jack would bring up the greatest ad ever done—the Macy ad he was featured in.

The following year, in order to promote one of Jack's television programs, I went back to Macy's. Vic Ratner was no longer there, and the new man turned me down on another ad. Without any hesitation, I stepped across the street to Gimbels, told them I had given an ad to Macy's the year before and in order to be fair, I wanted to give them too the opportunity to use Jack Benny in an ad. Their full-page ads in all the New York papers headlined: JACK'S NO DUMB BUNNY . . . HE SHOPS AT GIMBELS.

Jack always talked about the wonderful coffee and pie served at the Automat in New York, but after he became a star, he was embarrassed to be seen in one, especially with his tightwad character. But every time we passed one he looked in longingly, commenting on the good pie and coffee. When Rogers and Cowan, the PR agency, was publicizing the Benny program for the American Tobacco Company, we were looking for a new idea at a time when every motion-picture studio and television show was giving elaborate parties at 21 or Four Seasons or some other elegant restaurant to kick off a new season. We thought it would be fitting, as well as original, to have Jack's party at the Automat. Knowing this would be a tough one to sell to Jack, I asked Henry Rogers to join me at a meeting with our star. After much discussion Henry and I finally overcame enough of his objections to proceed with the party plans, with the cooperation of CBS.

Elaborate engraved invitations went out from Jack inviting the press, photographers, and the brightest stars in New York to a black tie party at the Automat at Forty-eighth Street near Fifth Avenue. The idea caught fire, and suddenly everyone was trying to wangle invitations. The night of the party a red carpet was rolled out from the entrance to the curb, where uniformed parking attendants assisted the formally attired celebrities from their limousines. It was the sight of the year to see the Rolls-Royces driving up to the Automat and Jack Benny handing each arriving guest a $2 roll of nickels for the food slots in case they didn't want to partake of the elegant buffet. An orchestra played for dancing and everyone, especially the press and photographers, had a ball until 3 A.M. The press coverage all over the country was fantastic, and that party became one of the most talked-about affairs of that year and many years to follow.

There were many times, however, when Jack himself would come up with exciting ideas that created publicity for him. One in particular he thought of when the *$64,000 Question,* starring the late Hal March, was the talk of television, and the contestants on that show were winning a great deal of money. Jack called Hal March and told him his idea, and they placed big ads heralding the appearance of Jack Benny on the program as a contestant. His category was the violin.

The first question, for $64, was usually a very simple one allowing a contestant to get rolling. I don't recall the exact question Jack was asked, but it was as easy as, and might actually have been: "Who is the famous eighteenth-century violinmaker whose first name was Antonio?" Jack promptly answered, "Stradivarius."

"Right," said March. "You now have sixty-four dollars, would you like to try for a hundred and twenty-eight dollars?"

"No," answered Jack.

Hal March looked at him in amazement as the audience screamed.

"But no one stops at sixty-four dollars. Everyone goes on for a little while," protested March.

"No," answered Jack. "I'm quitting right now. Give me my sixty-four dollars, and let me go."

March tried to get him to try at least for $128, but Jack would take no chances and would not leave the stage until March pulled $64 out of his own pocket and gave it to him.

One "cheap" idea that we both loved but never got around to doing, was a tie-up with the Treasury Department. We learned that periodically the government burns up the old and torn bills in a furnace in Washington. I had it arranged once or twice for Jack to shovel that money into the fire, all the while looking extremely unhappy and pained. However, each time we were in Washington, it seemed that something would come up on our schedule preventing us from working in this extra stunt.

29

JACK BENNY was honored at hundreds of dinners throughout his long career. Dinners were given in his honor many times by the Heart Fund, the Cancer Fund, the March of Dimes, to name just a few of the scores of charitable institutions to which he gave time and money. The only times he refused to be a guest of honor were at stag dinners because of something that happened at one. He had spoken at quite a few stags until one night the Writers Guild gave a dinner for two of his writers, Hugh Wedlock and Howard Snyder. Jack did some funny, albeit dirty, jokes, unaware that someone was secretly recording the whole show. It was released as a private recording without the permission of the participants, and Jack heard from friends all over this country and as far off as England who were slightly shocked that the mild-spoken, clean-cut comedian could say such words. He was so upset that from then on he made it a rule to turn down all requests to speak at stag dinners, no matter how close he was to the guest of honor.

Of all the dinners given for him, the ones that gave him the most satisfaction were those given by members of the theatrical profession, because Jack loved everything that had anything to do with actors, just as he loved all actor and vaudeville stories. One of his favorites was the joke about the two headliners who meet and one says, "Charlie, did you hear about Harry Sloane, the juggler?"

"No," the other replied, "what happened to him?"

"He died in St. Louis."

"He always did."

The first big dinner given for Jack was in 1929, when he was honored by the Lambs Club, a theatrical organization that numbered George M. Cohan and other theatrical greats as members. Jack felt very important as speakers ribbed and extolled him all evening, and just as he was feeling like the King of Broadway, Willie Collier, the toastmaster, read a wire from Jack's wife, Mary: WHEN YOU COME HOME TONIGHT, BE SURE TO TAKE OUT THE GARBAGE.

A dinner that was probably the highlight of them all was the one the Friars Club of New York gave for him in January, 1952. At most of the previous Friars' dinners, the dais was predominantly filled with comedians, but I wanted Jack's dinner to be something special so I asked the Friars to invite some illustrious guests who were not in show business in order to give the dinner a different look. We had met Bernard Baruch on the *Queen Elizabeth* on a trip to England, and I suggested that they ask him. To the surprise of all of us, he accepted. We also invited Mayor Vincent Impellitteri of New York and Governor Thomas Dewey, as well as Jack's good friend Helen Hayes. Naturally, the dais also included Bob Hope, Fred Allen, and Milton Berle, with George Jessel as toastmaster.

Several weeks before the dinner Governor Dewey had to

cancel, and when Jesse Block, who was in charge of the entertainment, phoned me on the Coast to ask for suggestions for a replacement, I proposed they send a wire to Adlai Stevenson, who was then the governor of Jack's home state, Illinois. The summer before, Jack was scheduled to star at the Illinois State Fair in Springfield, and I received a letter from the governor, of whom I must confess I'd never heard, asking if he could have a small cocktail party for Jack when we arrived. When I asked Jack, he wondered if Adlai was a man or a woman and whether he should bring a box of cigars or an orchid corsage. In any event, Jack did attend his party and the two men took a liking to each other. So when Jesse sent the Friars' invitation, Governor Stevenson gladly accepted.

We were in New York preparing a TV program at the time of the Friars' dinner, and Jack invited his writers and staff to the dinner. The boys hadn't brought tuxedos with them, so they had to rent the dress clothes for the evening. They found a small, inexpensive rental shop which had a rather large selection of tuxedos, mostly old and worn. They complained to Jack, with humor, that they had rented very old tuxedos, and when he asked them how old they thought the suits were, one of the boys answered, "I'll tell you how old mine is, but you won't believe it. I put my hands in the pocket and there were some notes written on a piece of paper that said, 'Fourscore and seven years ago.'"

With all the comedians at the dinner, there were many funny speeches, but one of the most gratifying spots of the evening was Fred Allen's speech. Fred, an outstanding wit, had been on a decline for a number of years, ever since his radio program had been badly outrated by a game show called *Stop the Music* and was finally dropped. He had made two attempts at television, but both formats had failed, and he hadn't worked for some time before that dinner. Since he was to make a speech about his friend Jack Benny, the entire audience was rooting for him to be good. He wasn't good; he was brilliant. Fred made one of the funniest speeches of his life and when he finished, the whole audience rose and gave him a cheering, standing ovation.

Then Jessel introduced the next speaker, who was sitting next to Fred Allen.

"And now the next speaker, a man with a spot I wouldn't

give to a leopard, the governor of Illinois—Adlai Stevenson."

Stevenson rose and received a smattering of polite applause since just a handful of the 1,200 in attendance had ever heard of him. It was just six months later that he was nominated for President on the Democratic ticket. Stevenson looked at the audience and then said, "Ladies and gentlemen, I was sitting next to Fred Allen and during the dinner I looked at his speech and he looked at mine, and we thought it might be fun if we exchanged speeches. So now I would like to read Fred Allen's speech."

That opening was so clever and the laugh so big that from then on everything he said was funny. Adlai Stevenson in later years would of course prove to be not only an astute politician, but a bright humorist as well.

Another Friars Club dinner given for Jack which he thoroughly enjoyed was for his sixty-third birthday in 1957 at the Beverly Hilton Hotel. All proceeds of the $100-a-plate dinner went to the Heart Fund, and all Hollywood turned out to honor him that night. Again George Jessel was the toastmaster, and a dazzling dais included California Governor Goodwin Knight, Irene Dunne, and Deborah Kerr, all of whom turned comic for the evening. Admiral J. B. Pearson, Jr., was there to speak about Jack's Navy career; Dean Martin came to sing a funny lyric to "I Could Have Danced All Night"; Frank Sinatra recited an hilarious poem; Tony Martin rendered a beautiful version of "Love in Bloom."

Ronald Reagan was then the host of the *G.E. Television Theater,* and he too turned comedian for the night with a routine that included: "Jack wound up at Warner Brothers because there was a man in high office [Jack Warner] who liked to tell funny stories, and particularly he loved to tell stories to people who liked to laugh . . . and here was a man who would laugh when George Burns says 'Hello.' 'How are you?' makes him hysterical. This employee-employer relationship would have developed into something akin to Damon and Pythias except for one small matter. Just as the trumpet shattered the walls of Jericho, so did the horn that blew at midnight split a pair of Jacks."

Reagan ended his speech with: "His violin always plays off-key, but his humor is never off-color."

George Burns said a few words about his old friend that night and then added, "Jack and Mary and Gracie and I were

152

going to dinner one night and Gracie asked Mary, 'Is Jack really thirty-nine?' and Mary said, 'Ridiculous.' Then she asked, 'Is he really cheap?' and Mary said, 'Ridiculous!' And then she asked, 'And how is his sex life?' and Mary said, 'Ridiculous!' "

Bob Hope was the next to the last speaker, and he said, "I'm on so late my clothes and material are out of style . . . Last time Jack paid one hundred dollars a plate, it was to his dentist, Dr. Pincus. . . . I don't know how old his is, but a couple of years ago he went to Rome, saw the Colosseum, and said, 'It's nice if you like modern.' . . ."

Art Linkletter, then the host for *People Are Funny*, said, "We have been friends because we are not in competition. I do the kind of show he could never do—a giveaway. It has often been said that Jack Benny is the greatest entertainer in the world. And tonight I think we should honor the man who has said it—Irving Fein—he said it over and over and over and over again."

Jack closed the dinner very late in the evening, and he began with: "I was thirty-nine when the first speaker got up. . . . Wasn't Deborah Kerr wonderful in *Tea and Sympathy*? I almost appeared in the film, but I felt I was too old for the boy's role, and the studio felt I was too old for the husband. They weren't looking for that much sympathy. So we had some tea and went home. Irene Dunne always wanted me for her leading man, but the studio kept sticking her with leading men like Cary Grant and Clark Gable. . . ."

After a long speech in which he talked about everyone on the dais, Jack finished with: "I'm not really thirty-nine because I couldn't have made this many friends in thirty-nine years."

During the last ten years of his life, the dinners in his honor came more often than he liked, and in the final two years it seemed that every week some charity or organization wanted to do him honor. But Jack turned most of them down as he started to be embarrassed at all the plaques and tributes he was collecting. One he couldn't turn down was when Greg Garrison asked him to be honored by his friend Dean Martin on Martin's *Comedy Hour Special Roast* which was telecast in February, 1974.

Dean opened the program this way: "Being a great comedian wasn't Jack's whole life . . . he loved the violin. . . .

He always dreamt of being a soloist with a concert orchestra. Two years ago he was invited to Israel to perform with the Israeli Philharmonic. When Moshe Dayan heard him play, he took the patch off his eye and put it over his ear."

Jack's good friend symphony conductor Zubin Mehta was a big hit with these remarks: "Throughout Jack's violin solo at the Hollywood Bowl, the audience was glued to their seats. That was the only way he could get them to sit down. There was one especially memorable moment . . . when Jack began a very difficult passage from Mendelssohn's Concerto, everyone in the orchestra turned and looked at Jack in wonder and amazement . . . they were playing Beethoven's Fifth at the time! . . . And there's one particular moment during that concert that I shall recall as long as I live. It's when the entire audience jumped to its feet and shouted, 'More! More!' It was right after Jack had announced there would be a five-minute intermission!"

Demond Wilson, son of *Sanford and Son,* did a routine about racial jokes: "You know, Jack's show did a lot for the image of black people in America. You ready? Before Jack came along, everybody thought blacks were only fit to be shoeshine boys and railroad porters. The Jack Benny program proved to America that they could also be chauffeurs, dishwashers, houseboys!"

When Jack Benny closed that program, he thanked all the guests who made speeches, including Jimmy Stewart, Pearl Bailey, George Burns, Mark Spitz, Rich Little, Joey Bishop, Wayne Newton, and Jack Carter with comments like:

"I am in the most difficult position of any personality that has been roasted on the Dean Martin show because nearly everything they said about me is true. I am cheap, stingy, frugal. . . . I was going to say penurious, but nobody on this dais would know what I was talking about. Now what do I have in common with Mark Spitz? I had a swimming pool for forty years, and it was only used once. . . . My cat fell in it. . . . Now you all know the closest friend I have in this whole business is George Burns. And we're around the same age, give or take a few minutes. And we have a lot in common. The other night we went to see an X-rated movie, and we both fell asleep. Now Zubin Mehta flew all the way to Tel Aviv to conduct the Israeli Symphony for me. Asking Zubin, that great conductor, to conduct for me really takes guts. It's like asking Van Gogh to paint 'Merry Christmas' on the window of the May Company. . . . Dean, I've really appreciated this evening's tribute. Let's face it—all of us in show business enjoy recognition. And believe me, it wasn't easy for me to make it in Hollywood. I can't drink like you do. I can't act like George C. Scott. And when it comes to Frank Sinatra . . . well, good night, folks!"

30

THE fans of an actor or comedian can make a big star of the performer if enough of them go to his motion pictures, see his shows, or turn to the TV channel on which he can be seen. Conversely, if they don't pay or look, then no one may want to hire that performer. The fans can be a great source of joy to the star, feeding the ego, making him feel loved, important, clever, but they can also be a great annoyance. Signing autographs can be the biggest bother in the world, depending on the circumstances and some performers refuse to sign them. However, one star once summed it up realistically: "I'll start worrying when they stop asking."

In February, 1955, Jack and I went to Miami Beach to attend a United Jewish Appeal dinner. We arrived at the Saxony Hotel, headquarters for the event, at 11:30 P.M., and there at the entrance was a Maxwell, and nearby were hundreds of fans, mostly elderly and Jewish, waiting for the comedian. They pounced on him like locusts, and it took three burly room clerks, the hotel manager, and a guard to rescue him. This was his first visit to Miami Beach since 1932, and it was almost impossible for him to walk down the street without spending hours signing autographs and listening to bad jokes. Jack was very unhappy with this excessive attention.

After the UJA affair we had two free days before going to New York for another dinner, so we decided to go to Havana, where neither of us had ever been. Jack, usually not an enthusiastic tourist, couldn't stand the thought of spending the next two days in Miami, where his overzealous admirers wouldn't allow him to relax. In Havana the head of the Cuban Tourist Bureau escorted us everywhere, making certain that we had the best suite at the Nacional Hotel, dinner at a gourmet restaurant, shows at the two leading nightclubs, the Tropicana and the Sans Souci. I had a marvelous time. But something strange happened. Not one person asked Jack for an autograph; no one stopped him on the street; he was not recognized or catered to at the nightclubs or in the restaurant; actually, it seemed that we got special attention only because of our escort. The reason for this, of course, was that our TV shows did not reach Havana and no one remembered Jack from his movies. Finally, after looking bored and depressed for the two days, he said to me, "Let's get out of here. No one knows me, and I hate it."

A similar episode occurred on our way back from Australia in 1964, when we decided to stop off in Tahiti for a four-day rest. The city officials had been notified of our flight, and when we arrived at Papeete, there was a photographer and a reporter waiting. As Jack and I descended the stairway from the plane, both of us with dark hair and tortoise-rimmed glasses, the photographer grabbed *my* arm and said, "Stand right over here, Mr. Benny. We want to take your picture."

I had to explain which one of us Jack Benny was, and that started our vacation on the wrong note. To compound the trouble, the following day we went into a shop to buy some perfume for our wives, and when Jack gave his name for the bill of sale, the saleswoman repeated, "Bemmy . . . Bemmy? . . . How do you spell Bemmy, please?"

That vacation lasted only two days, and from then on the mere mention of Tahiti brought a string of disparaging remarks from Jack.

Jack Benny, from his early radio days, was a favorite of the fans, and even in later years when he wasn't the number one comedian, he always had a diehard corps of fans who never missed anything he did. But sometimes even Jack's patience was tested by the idiocy of some of the letter writers, as well as certain in-person boors who could drive a celebrity to distraction.

Many high-salaried stars get letters asking for money, and

Jack received such letters regularly. One time a fan wrote asking him for $5,000. Jack wrote back: "I have just fired my four writers because obviously my image is not coming through."

Another time when he received a letter asking for an extraordinary amount of money, Jack answered the man: "I have a sister in Chicago who lives on nothing but bread and milk; she has no money for a warm coat for the winter, and is being evicted from her apartment for nonpayment of rent. I'm not helping her, so what chance do you think you have?"

A farmer wrote to George Burns and Jack Benny asking them for $50,000 so he could buy some tractors which he needed for his farm. The farmer said that to prove he was honest, if they would send the money, he would send them pictures of the tractors he had bought. George suggested that they send the man a *picture* of five $10,000 bills!

Once a lawyer in Cleveland wrote that he thought it was disgraceful that Jack had Rochester sleep in a room without a window and that Jack only paid Dennis Day $12 a week and made him mow the lawn as well. Jack wrote a long letter in return, telling the lawyer that Rochester lived in a home with a swimming pool, had a 50-foot boat, owned racehorses, and had a butler of his own. And Dennis had two gardeners to mow his own lawn.

Some fans were so nervous at seeing him in person that unintentionally they would say or do something silly in their embarrassment. Once Ralph Levy, who was directing the TV show at the time, was coming down in the elevator with Jack at the Grand Hotel in Rome when an American woman practically fainted when she saw Jack and then asked him, "How's Gracie?"

Film director Mervyn Le Roy tells of the time he was walking down the street in Palm Springs with Jack one evening and a man stopped them and asked, "Aren't you Jack Benny?"

When Jack nodded yes, the man said, "Well, good luck to you anyway."

Another time I was walking on Fifth Avenue in New York with him and a woman rushed over and gushed, "Mr. Benny. . . . Oh, you're my biggest fan!"

Many years ago a fan once asked Gracie Allen, "Is Jack Benny really tight?" "Am I stupid?" Gracie asked the fan.

When we were in San Francisco for a benefit, a young couple stopped Jack at the entrance to the Fairmont Hotel and asked for an autograph. He responded with a little joke and they were obviously thrilled. The girl told him, "Mr. Benny, we were just married three days ago, and meeting you is the most exciting thing that's happened to us on our whole honeymoon."

Jack just stared at her for a minute until she realized what she had said, and when she blushed, Jack gave her a hug and kiss, shook the young man's hand, and told them he certainly hoped that their meeting him *wasn't* the *most* exciting thing on their honeymoon.

A story Jack loved to tell on himself was about the time a woman came up to him in a hotel lobby in Phoenix.

"Mr. Benny, you look exactly like my father," she enthused, "exactly. I can't wait to tell him I met you. I'm so thrilled because you're the spitting image of him, short neck and all!"

There were two types of fans who annoyed Jack the most. One was someone he might have met twenty or thirty years before for a split second whom he was expected to remember now. A man would approach Jack, pump his hand in greeting, and tell him how happy he was to see him again. Then he'd ask Jack if he remembered him. Jack would stall, saying the man looked familiar, but he couldn't quite recall. This kind of man would generally put Jack on the spot, trying to make him guess where they had once met. Jack would finally give up, and then the fan might tell him that he'd been the driver of a car that took him from the plane to his quarters in Frankfurt, Germany, in 1945. One man kept him guessing for a long time and seemed very insulted that Jack didn't remember he was a guard on Guadalcanal in 1944 who, on seeing him, asked, "Who goes there?" and Jack answered, "Fred Allen."

The other kind of autograph hunter who bothered him was the one in a restaurant who would shove a menu in front of his face just as he was taking a bite, to ask him to sign on the menu. Oftimes he was asked to sign three or four menus each course!

We were doing a radio show from the American Legion Hall in Palm Springs one time and we had to turn off the air conditioning during the broadcast as the noise of the fan came through the microphone. The hall was stifling by the time we finished the broadcast, and we all rushed outside for a breath of fresh air. Suddenly, Mary passed out cold and fell to the ground. Jack rushed over to her. As he bent down to her prone body, a fan slipped a book between Mary and Jack and asked for an autograph.

From 1958, when Mary retired, she stopped accompanying Jack on the road and seldom attended the benefit dinners at which he was honored. Occasionally she would travel with him to New York, London, or Las Vegas, but usually Mary restricted her social activity and public appearances with Jack to their select coterie of friends. As the years passed, Jack was seen more and more often without Mary, attending different affairs, ball games, movies, concerts with me or someone else with whom he worked. Because of this, the female next to Jack, whether it was my wife or another friend, was often mistaken for Mary.

Once in New York Jack and my wife were leaving the Plaza Hotel in evening dress on the way to a dinner to honor him. As they entered a waiting limousine, the autograph seekers gathered around, pushing books and pens into his face. One eager fan rapped on the car window and gestured toward my wife for her signature. Jack rolled down the window and yelled, "Go away! She's nobody."

Mary was out of the limelight so long that there were other times when someone would approach Jack and inquire about the old cast—Rochester, Dennis Day, Phil—and then in a somber tone with a face filled with sympathy, ask, "How long has it been since Mary passed away?"

There were many times, however, when his admirers were a source of great satisfaction to him. One such very moving time occurred in Colorado Springs when Jerry Lavin, a friend from Chicago, was walking through the grounds of the Broadmoor Hotel with Jack, when a lady asked him for a favor. She said her daughter, eighteen years old, had been blinded in an automobile accident a month earlier and would like to meet Jack. Of course, Jack said yes.

"I stood by as he walked up to the girl, a lovely young lady," was the way Jerry related the story. "She asked Jack if she could touch his face, and then she ran her hands very softly across it, getting a picture of him with her sensitive fingers. Afterward she said, 'Thank you, Mr. Benny. You've made me so happy.' He cried like a baby."

Jerry told the story to Mort Edelstein of the Chicago *Daily News* after Jack's death, and Edelstein printed it in his column. Ten days later Edelstein received a letter from a gentleman named L. E. Whittaker, president of a savings and loan company in Beatrice, Nebraska. The letter read:

DEAR MR. EDELSTEIN:

A copy of your editorial dated December 30, 1974 was sent to us by friends in Chicago. In that editorial you referred to an incident of the young lady who had been blinded and asked to meet Jack Benny. That young lady was our daughter Nancy.

Nancy has been unsighted for one year. During that period of time, she completed her high school, she has learned Braille 1 and 2, she has completed ten college credit hours with an "A" average, and is looking forward to the future with great anticipation. I'll always believe that part of her courage came from that brief moment of attention she received from Jack Benny.

What an interesting world we would be living in today if more great people with this overwhelming charisma were also blessed with the sincere empathy that Jack Benny had. That small gesture by this great man lifted Nancy at a time that she desperately needed lifting.

31

THE many faces of Jack Benny created for the stage, radio and television were all good for laughs: the toupee (he didn't really wear one), the "thirty-nine-year-old" gag, the braggadocio, the blue eyes. But the one characteristic that was steadfast and true throughout his career, the one he relied on when the chips were down, was the "cheap" character.

Jack age nine.

Jack at fourteen.

Jack, right, with his partner
Lyman Woods in 1916.

Jack and his first partner,
Cora Salisbury, in 1913.

Jack when he used the name
Ben K. Benny during his early
years in vaudeville.

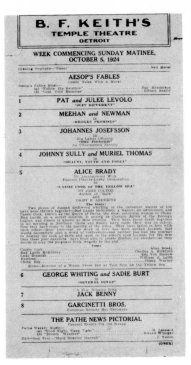

Bing Crosby, Jack, and George Burns in
an old vaudeville routine for a TV show.

"A few minutes with Jack
Benny," 1924.

Jack Benny, his trusty old Maxwell, and Rochester, in 1948.

Jack and Gregory Peck in a song-and-dance routine for a Benny special.

ack and Fred Allen on the tage of the Roxy Theater n 1947.

Jack fiddling in front of Albert Hall, London, while rehearsing with the London Philharmonic. Author passing the hat.
Photo: Thames Television Picture

At a Benny rehearsal. Jack, Fred Allen, writer Seamon
Jacobs, and author. *CBS photo by Gabor Rona.*

Jack Benny and his friend Ed
Sullivan.

Jack and George Burns imitate
the Smothers Brothers on the
Smothers Brothers Show.

Queen Elizabeth, King George VI, and right to left: Jack, Dinah Shore, Allan Jones, and Gracie Fields. At command performance in November, 1951.

Jack and Mary.

Mervyn Le Roy, Gower Champion, Marge Champion, Jack, Louella Parsons, and Jack Warner at a party in the 1950s.

Jack and George Burns portray a couple of Roman statues on a Benny special, in 1974. *NBC photo*.

Jack as Hamlet in *To Be or Not to Be*.

Jack, Alexis Smith, and Guy Kibbee in scene from *Horn Blows at Midnigh*

Jack in scene from the Twentieth Century-Fox production *Charley's Aunt*, 1941.

Jack as an Indian for TV show.

Jack Benny as Ab coln's father for TV s

Jack Benny with Harry Truman at one of the former President's famous birthday lunches in Kansas City.

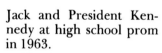

Jack and President Kennedy at high school prom in 1963.

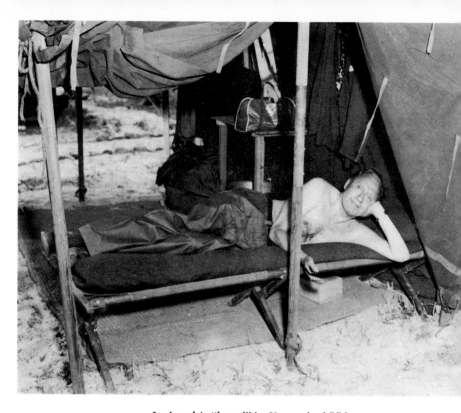

Jack at his "hotel" in Korea in 1951.

Entertaining the troops in Nuremberg Stadium, July 4, 1945.

At a Friars Dinner in the 1940s. Left to right: George Jessel, Jack, Eddie Cantor, Bob Hope, George Burns, Al Jolson, and Kay Kyser.

Phil Harris and Marilyn Maxwell with Jack. They went to the Palladium in 1948.

Jack and Mervyn Le Roy at a geisha house in Tokyo in 1959.

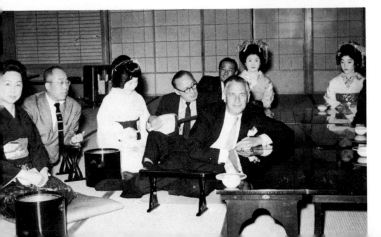

Old lady band, part of Jack's act at Harrah's Club, Lake Tahoe.

Jack Benny slot machine in Fla-
migo Hotel, Las Vegas. *Photo:
Las Vegas News Bureau*

With Lucille Ball and Mary on
Twentieth Anniversary Special.

Jack and Pablo Casals in a duet while visiting Casals in Puerto Rico.

Queen Elizabeth II, Shirley Bassey, Tony Bennett, and Jack.

Jack and the author at a concert in Nashville. *Nashville* Banner *photo by Owen Cartwright*

Jack and Zubin Mehta at Lo Angeles Philharmonic rehea sal.

Jack playing with the London Philharmonic in 1968, with conductor John Pritchard.

Dean Martin and Jack in a
Benny comedy special,
1973. *NBC photo*

Liberace rehearses with
Jack for Benny's TV show.
CBS photo by Gabor Rona

Jack getting honorary degree at Jacksonville University in 1972 with
Bob Hope.

Photo: Roddy McDowall

One of Jack's proudest achieve-
ments was having a junior high
school named after him. *Photo:
Waukegan* News-Sun

Jack confronted with one million dollars in cash on one of his
TV specials. *NBC photo.*

Dinah Shore, who starred
on Jack Benny's first TV
show, with Jack on a 1974
special. *NBC photo.*

Jack and an admirer at an RCA press party
before his *First Farewell Special* in 1973.

Joseph Nee, president of March
of Dimes, Jack, Johnny Carson,
and Bob Hope when Jack Benny was named "Man of the
Year" by the charity in 1974.
Photo: Atkinson.

With one line about a thrift situation, he could get a bigger laugh than other comics could with long, involved jokes.

When Jack was vacationing with Mary in the south of France, Aristotle Onassis invited them to visit his 195-foot yacht one afternoon. That night Jack was a guest at a gala at the Monte Carlo Casino, where Tony Martin was performing for the European jet set. He called on Jack to say a few words. Jack said, "I was on Onassis' yacht this afternoon, and it's the most lavish thing I've ever seen. It must have cost at least thirty or forty thousand dollars."

That's all he needed to be a great success that night.

We often publicized the fact that in order to counteract the "tightwad" character, it cost Jack $7,500 a year more than everyone else because he had to tip much more to prove he wasn't really cheap. He was forever yelling at me because I didn't give the porter or cabdriver a big enough tip to suit him. Where most people would leave $1, I would give a porter $2 for a couple of bags, and Jack would always insist I give him $5.

The frugality of his character was a subject wherever he went. One time he gave a hatcheck girl a $1 tip for his hat and she handed the dollar back and said, "Please, Mr. Benny, leave me some illusions."

We were rushing to NBC one day, and when we got out of the cab, we both sped to the door, he thinking I had paid the driver and I, thinking of the problems we were rushing to, having forgotten. As we reached the door, the unpaid cabby called, "So, it's true about you, Mr. Benny!"

Jack thought that was so funny he gave the man a $10 bill for the $4 ride.

Jack once took a Las Vegas cab for a short seventy-five-cent ride and felt guilty because the driver had lost his place in line for such a short haul. So he gave the man $5 and told him to keep the change. The fellow said, "Gee, I wish you hadn't tipped me, Jack."

When asked why, he answered, "Because then I could have told my wife that you really are a cheap guy."

So Jack said, "Okay, then give me back four twenty-five and you can tell your wife."

The driver thought better of it and kept the $5.

Jack went to a hospital every year for his annual checkup

because he found that he could get a good rest while going through all the dull tests. One time when he checked in, having just gone to the bathroom, the nurse handed him that little bottle and asked him for a urine sample. He had a difficult time and finally managed to deliver just a few drops. When the nurse came to collect it, she looked at the bottle with a disdainful face and said, "You never give anything away, do you, Mr. Benny?"

This gave Jack the idea for a routine that he did with great success in nightclubs and theaters:

"I went to my doctor for a checkup before playing this engagement, and my doctor said, 'Jack, I can't understand why you're playing these two weeks in Las Vegas. Surely, it can't be the money.' [Long Benny stare] Now, there's a brilliant surgeon, but the minute you take off his rubber gloves, he's an idiot. So I said to my *new* doctor—and incidentally, these surgeons really hold you up for money. No wonder they all wear masks. So he sent me to the hospital for a checkup. Five boring days. And it's *so* expensive. You have to have a morning nurse, an afternoon nurse, a night nurse . . . that runs into a lot of dough . . . they give you three enemas a day . . . and *they're* sixty cents apiece. That's one dollar eighty cents right there. [pause] Two dollars with the tip. Now who do you tip in a case like that?"

One of the best "stingy" bits he ever did on a program was a sketch in which he and Jimmy Stewart were having lunch. When the check came, Jack made a halfhearted try for it, but Stewart said, "Please, Jack, I'd feel much better if you'd let me pay the check."

"All right, Jimmy, if your health is concerned."

A true story that really happened concerning his miserly image occurred when we were leaving San Francisco one morning to fly back to Los Angeles. We had decided to check out of our rooms at the Fairmont Hotel before breakfast so we could leave for the airport immediately after the meal. After breakfast we had a few minutes to wait for our car and Jack went downstairs from the lobby to use the men's room in which there were ten-cent toilets. By the time he returned to the lobby I had the bags in the limo, and off we started for the airport. A few blocks away from the hotel, Jack reached into his pants pocket and discovered that his wallet was missing. He thought he might have packed the wallet in his bag by mistake, or maybe it fell out of his pants pocket in the men's room at the Fairmont. The driver immediately turned back to the hotel, and when we got there, Jack dashed downstairs to the men's room, while I hurriedly opened his bag and searched it. In a few minutes Jack came running to the car, waving the wallet in his hand and a great big smile on his face. As we sped to the airport, he laughingly told me, "You'll never guess what happened. I went to the stall I had used and looked under the door, and sure enough, there was my wallet lying on the floor. It was a little too far for me to reach, and I didn't have a dime to open the door. By the time I could run upstairs to get change I thought we might miss the plane, and since no one else was in the men's room, I got down on my hands and knees and started to crawl under the door. Just then a man entered the room, saw me, took a double take, started to laugh and said, 'So, it's true about you after all, Jack.' I reached under, grabbed my wallet, and rushed out of there. I didn't have time to explain it, so I just didn't say anything."

Jack's devotees in Ireland were perhaps as vociferous and adoring as any he had, which accounted for the fact that for a time his TV program was number one there. One year my wife and I went with him to London when he was a guest star on a Liberace show taped there. After our commitment in London we decided to return to the States by way of Dublin, where the three of us had never been. Jack was very excited about that trip because he knew what a hit his program had been.

Sure enough, it seemed that every cabdriver, truck driver and newsboy in Dublin knew him, and all day we heard "Hello, Jack" and "Hi, Jocko" called from all sides as we walked the streets.

The Book of Kells is on permanent exhibition at Trinity College, and several times each day we passed the entrance to that famous old college when we'd walk from our hotel to the downtown area of Dublin. Each time we would suggest to Jack that we'd like to go in and see it, but no sightseer he, Jack always made some excuse and said we'd see it later. On our last afternoon in Dublin, as we passed Trinity College, we again tried to persuade him to go in with us to see the

Book of Kells. While we were trying to convince him that it would be a shame to miss seeing this world-famous manuscript, a uniformed guard was standing at attention about fifteen feet from us in front of the college gates, motionless with his eyes staring forward and face expressionless. After about five minutes of cajoling, with Jack very reluctant, the immobile sentry suddenly said in a heavy Irish brogue, "You might as well go in, Mr. Benny. It's free!"

Jack's roar of approval at that line from the silent guard was the one push he needed to make him go.

Dublin loved Benny, and he loved Dublin, so Jack insisted on coming back to play a week at one of their theaters, even though their admission prices were so low that our expenses would be greater than our profits. So the following year we played one week at the old, charming Gaity Theatre and broke the hundred-year record of that theater.

People always used to ask the "where there's smoke, there's fire" question: Is Jack really cheap? I invariably pointed out his very generous qualities, and believe me, he was a very generous man. He would contribute $25,000 to the United Jewish Appeal or $25,000 to the Los Angeles Music Center without blinking an eye. He gave thousands of dollars to the Symphony Fund, the Art Museum, and scores of other charities. He would think very little of giving $1,000 or $5,000 for any good cause because it merely meant calling to ask me to have our bookkeeper write out a check. But for some enigmatic reason, it would bother him to reach into his pocket and pay cash for anything, even dinner or a gift. If he could sign a check or charge it, somehow, he felt he wasn't actually paying it; the girl at the office was.

For years he carried a $100 bill at all times. I don't know if it was the same one, but whenever the check came, he would pull out the $100 bill and ask if anyone could change it. Naturally, no one would let him break it for a $12 check, so someone else always ended up paying the bill for lunch or drinks or whatever. When we were on the road and I paid the check, which was most of the time, he knew that it would be on my expense account and he would end up paying it anyway, but the fact that he didn't have to reach into his pocket seemed to make him happy. We ribbed him about the $100 bill all the time, but he let it slide right off his back.

One time, however, when we were playing a theater in

Phoenix, he gave his money to me to hold for him while he was on stage. Right on top of the roll was that $100 bill. Mary's brother, Hilliard Marks, was in the dressing room with me, and we decided to play a joke on Jack. We took the bill out of the money clip and wrote on it: "Thanks for entertaining the troops." And we signed underneath that: "Abraham Lincoln."

We thought it was hysterical, and when Jack came off stage, we showed it to him expecting a big laugh, but all we got was a nod.

In the spring of 1974 we went on a Canadian concert tour, and one stop was Winnipeg, where Jack was to play with the Winnipeg Symphony Orchestra. The night before the concert we went to dinner at a new Japanese restaurant as the guests of the owner, Nat Hart, a friend who had run dining rooms in Las Vegas. Naturally, we were guests at a most lavish meal. When we went to get our coats, Nat was starting to tip the hatcheck girl when Jack made the magnanimous gesture of being allowed to pay her tip. He pulled out his $100 bill and asked if anyone could change it. Before Jack knew what was happening, a man standing behind us quickly stepped forward and pulled out a roll of small bills, counted out a hundred in fives and tens, shoved them into Jack's hand, and grabbed that $100 bill and walked away.

Although Jack was not a big gambler, he enjoyed betting on the baseball games with Al Gordon, one of our writers, the bets usually being $50 or $100. Jack would sweat out those bets as intensely as any million-dollar deal he might be waiting to hear about. Once he bet a bookie $1,000 on a World Series, and when his team won the first game, he began to hedge his bet by taking odds on the other team and then betting individual games, resulting in the possibility of his either winning about $200 or breaking even. Then he sat back and relaxed about the Series.

Jack loved to shoot craps, and in the old days in Las Vegas he would play often, always betting $5 at a time, and when he was way ahead, he would sometimes bet as much as $25. But in later years he was embarrassed to go to the crap tables with his $5 bets, when standing alongside him sometimes were gamblers in torn shoes and cheap sport shirts who were betting $50 or $100 on each number.

One time Glenn MacCarthy, the Texas oilman, walked

over to Jack in Las Vegas, asked for $500, and told Jack they'd be partners at craps. Jack couldn't think of an excuse, so he gave him the $500. Two minutes later Glenn was back and said, "Well, we blew it." And then he walked away.

Jack didn't say a word, but he was very pale for several minutes.

When we played Harrah's Club at Lake Tahoe, they put a one-cent slot machine in the center of the lobby with a big sign that read: EXCLUSIVELY FOR JACK BENNY. We did the same gag in Las Vegas, and it was not far off the truth. Jack did spend many of his gambling hours just playing the quarter and fifty-cent slot machines, limiting himself to $50 a day while he worked in the showrooms there for $50,000 a week.

Like all the other comedians, Jack used to do gambling jokes, but his were generally on the "cheap" side: "The only way I'll ever get hurt in the casino is if there's an earthquake and a slot machine falls on my foot. . . . I gambled at the crap table all night and finally lost $8, but during that time the house gave me four drinks and two cigars, so it was still a lot cheaper than renting a room."

32

THE Jack Bennys lived in their Beverly Hills home for nearly thirty years, selling it in 1966 to move to an apartment. It was a beautiful two-story fourteen room Georgian house on Roxbury Drive, with a swimming pool that had an octopus design inlaid at the bottom and a large pool house. The Bennys lived an extravagant life-style with a large staff of servants to care for Jack, Mary, and daughter, Joan. A charming Englishwoman named Julia Vallance, who started as nurse and governess when Joan was four years old, remained with them as housekeeper and secretary to Mary until 1970, when she retired to La Jolla, California.

The elegant way of life, the fine furnishings, the butlers, cooks, upstairs and downstairs maids, were the creation and desire of Mary, who loved to enjoy all the comforts and grace that she could afford. As for Jack, in many ways he seemed oblivious to such indulgence, often bewildered by a new face opening the door for him as the maids and butlers were changed from time to time.

Joan once characterized Jack, when asked to describe her father in one word, as a "simple" man. He surely had the capacity to enjoy the comfortable life he earned, but he wouldn't have minded living in a small home with one servant.

Early in our association we were stranded in Dallas when every hotel in town had been booked by conventions, making it impossible for us to get a suite or room, even for Jack Benny. Finally, the airline was able to produce one room for us to share in a tiny hotel near the airport. That room was so small—the kind that comedians joke about—that we couldn't unpack our bags at the same time. I thought that Jack would be very unhappy with such meager accommodations, but he seemed perfectly content, insisting he could sleep just as well there as in a larger room.

The first time we went to New York on a train together, we could get only one compartment for the two of us. When it was time for bed, he suggested we toss a coin for the lower berth, which I naturally refused to do, even though he kept insisting.

My wife and I shared two-room hotel suites with him countless times, and he would always offer us the larger bedroom, saying that there were two of us and only one of him. It took a great deal of argument to convince him to take the better bedroom. One time, however, he prevailed, much to our embarrassment. It was in Victoria, British Columbia, where Jack was violin guest soloist with their symphony orchestra. We were given the Empress Hotel's vice-regal suite, which is their counterpart to a presidential suite. That suite was one of the largest and most beautiful we had ever seen and had recently been occupied by Queen Elizabeth and Prince Philip on their goodwill tour. Naturally, Jack was ushered into the royal suite adjoining a gigantic living room, while my bags were placed in the bedroom adjoining a full-sized dining room. When Jack saw the setup, he insisted that we take the royal rooms and that he would be very comfortable in the smaller sitting-room-bedroom. We had a long discussion that amazed the symphony committee members standing by, but Jack picked up his own bag, took it into the smaller room, and began to unpack, thereby calling finis to the whole thing.

In our travels around the United States Jack always professed to prefer the older luxurious hotels and complained bitterly whenever it was more convenient for us to stay at the more modern ones. One year when we played an engagement in Warwick, Rhode Island, we stayed at a beautiful modern hotel near the theater. During that week Jack went to Providence to have lunch with a friend, and when he returned, he was very unhappy that we were not staying at the hotel to which his friend had taken him. He extolled the charms of the quaint lobby, the rich woods, excellent dining rooms, and the New England aura. So the following year when we returned to Providence to do a concert with the Rhode Island Symphony, I specifically reserved the old hotel for our party, knowing how delighted Jack would be.

In preparation for his arrival, the hotel repainted his entire suite, and during the two days we were there, Jack couldn't open the closet doors and the bureau drawers or raise the old-fashioned windows. The first night he could not open the door to his room, which was so tightly stuck with the new paint that he had to wait in the hall for thirty minutes while the one maintenance man worked to release it. In addition, he couldn't get a decent reading light for his nightstand, and the bathroom plumbing was sluggish and noisy. When he grumbled about the suite, all I remarked was, "Jack, you always said you wanted to stay at old hotels."

He was very happy in his bedroom, spending most of his time at home in that room. He always had breakfast in bed, and if they were alone, Jack and Mary usually had dinner served in his bedroom so they could watch television while they ate. His bedroom was where he would meet with his agent, his writers, his secretary, and it was the room in which he enjoyed practicing his violin until Mary put a stop to that when the sounds awakened her from her nap or disturbed her while she read or watched television. So he moved his music stand to his bathroom, which was soundproof, and there he would practice to his heart's content, although it looked very peculiar to visitors who might wander into the bathroom during a meeting.

168

Jack, who could be so sagacious about a distasteful line in a script, was frequently insensitive to the feelings of people around him without realizing it. His lack of delicacy of feeling was unintentional, and he would have been distraught had he been aware of some of the comments he unwittingly made.

Shortly after I came with his company, he had occasion to come to my Beverly Hills home, which, although not as luxurious as the Bennys', was a beautiful one-story house with a lovely flower garden. On the day when Jack came to see me for the first time, he looked around the rooms admiringly, and then, impressed by the sun-filled garden as he looked at it through the picture window in my den, he exclaimed, "My, isn't California marvelous! Imagine! Even a publicity man can own a house like this!"

He would drop by my home often and each time, if my wife would greet him at the door, he'd ask, "Is Irving upstairs?"

And each time my wife would explain that I couldn't be upstairs because we had a one-story house. But Jack, who always had his mind on his next performance, would promptly forget and ask the same "upstairs" question every time.

Jack was not one to putter around the house fixing things because he had no conception of anything mechanical. He once complained to George S. Kaufman that he was the champion dumbbell when it came to anything electrical or mechanical, but Kaufman said he thought he had him beat because, Kaufman said, "I still can't understand the principle of the hammer."

One time the writers were working at Jack's house because he had a little cold. The room was chilly, and after a time one of the writers asked Jack if he could put on some heat, but Jack said he couldn't because the butler was off. Now Jack had lived in that house for fifteen years at that time and had visions inherited from his childhood in the Midwest of having to go down to the cellar to shovel coal into the furnace to generate heat for the house. The writer merely walked over to the wall, pressed a button that controlled the unit heat, two lights went on, and he sat down again. Jack couldn't get over that newfangled invention.

Another time when he was having a working session with

169

his writers in his bedroom, the door kept opening. When one of the writers closed it, it opened again in a minute or two. After this happened several times, Jack told the writer not to bother closing the door because it had been opening like that for years. The writer took a dime out of his pocket, tightened a screw in the door with the dime, closed the door, and it stayed closed. Jack was astounded at this ingeniousness.

Jack always had three or four books on his nightstand, but very rarely, if ever, did he finish any of them. But the books represented the learning for which he forever hungered. His major regret in life was that he had very little education, and he continually spoke of taking courses in English and other subjects. When I first joined him, he told me that he was planning to take some courses at UCLA, and being an eager press agent then, I encouraged him. I had visions of this famous man sitting in a class with college students and thought of all the exciting space such a story would get. But he never seemed to find the time, or, possibly, the real inclination.

He told me he had carried a copy of *Gone with the Wind* on two of his tours entertaining the troops, lugging that large volume practically all over the world and then giving it away half read. He carried three or four books on every trip we made, and I can't remember any that he ever finished. He confessed to Bill Davidson, as reported in Davidson's *Saturday Evening Post* piece in 1964:

> "I feel a terrible loss about not having had an education. I have developed a good vocabulary but I never use it. I know too much about show business but not enough about everything else. I've lived in the same house for 25 years and I still don't know where things are or how to fix a loose screw. I don't know what's going on in the world. I try to read at night to educate myself, but I'm so tired from working so hard that I fall asleep."

Jack adored Mary, and Mary loved gifts, especially jewelry, and over the years he gave her rings and pins and bracelets every birthday and anniversary until her collection reached large proportions. He finally bought her a huge diamond ring, but in 1963 she was held up in her suite in the Pierre Hotel in New York, and the holdup man made off with her prize diamond ring. Jack, in the meantime, was on a plane in flight to Pittsburgh, and when he arrived, the reporters told him about the robbery. In shock, he called Mary, but she was out. When he finally reached her and asked where she had been, she told him she had been at Harry Winston's, the jeweler, looking for another diamond ring.

"What!" exclaimed Jack. "At a time like this you're looking at another diamond?"

"Sure," answered Mary. "Like when you fall off a horse, you've got to get right back on if you're ever going to ride again."

However, when Jack returned from his overseas trips, instead of the jewels she cherished, he often brought back bizarre gifts, sometimes ethnic in style, especially from Africa and Persia. Even though Jack was excited about those gifts, Mary usually shuttled them to the basement without telling him. After the war was over, the Bob Hopes came to dinner one evening and in discussing gifts, Dolores Hope asked Mary, "Did Jack, like Bob, bring you those awful snakeskins, the terrible shoes with the pointed toes, and those scruffy rugs?"

The Benny home was not a "drop-in" place, but they did give a great many parties that always featured good food, danceable music, and the most notable stars in Hollywood. The guests might entertain, but Jack was not a comedian in his own home. While another comic friend would be doing his routine for the convivial group, Jack would stand on the sidelines quietly. His big bit would be to go upstairs, change into patent leather evening shoes, formal shirt, white tie, white vest, tailcoat and top hat, and come down the stairway with no pants on playing his violin.

Lucille Ball and her husband Gary Morton moved next door to the Bennys, and Jack would drop over to their house from time to time. The Mortons had a dinner party for eighteen people one night, and when Jack heard about it, he put a bandana on his head and strolled over as a Gypsy violinist, walked around the table playing a Gypsy tune, and then strolled right out. But as he was crossing the lawn to his own home, still playing the fiddle, an excursion bus on a tour of the homes of the movie stars pulled up in front. When the fans saw the comedian, they began to yell, and Jack, embarrassed, ran quickly for his side door.

Perhaps he didn't get many laughs at home, but at his barbershop and at his dentist's office he was always a smash. Charles Pincus, who was his dentist from 1936, once asked Jack if the bridge he was making for his mouth was too high.

"Well," responded Jack, "I won't say it's too high, but if you left it this way, I'd look as if I was yawning all the time."

One day he arrived for an early morning dental appointment without having had breakfast and he told Dr. Pincus that he really would like some doughnuts and coffee. Dr. Pincus replied, "I'll be happy to send out for breakfast, but I want you to have eggs instead of the doughnut because it has fewer calories and more protein."

"A fine restaurant this is," Jack complained. "I can't even get what I order."

When he finished his breakfast of eggs and coffee, the nurse asked Jack if he wanted another cup of coffee.

"No," said Jack, "because then I'd want a doughnut to go with it, and Charlie would get mad at me and wouldn't put in my bridge. It's too risky."

Jack was a customer of Harry Drucker's barbershop for almost thirty years. It is an informal shop where he could relax and enjoy the company of friends, clients, and barbers alike. The first three years he went there, he always said "Hello" to the owner of the shop, but then he began to say "Hello, schmuck" to him every time he came in, and that worried Drucker. When he asked Mervyn Le Roy about it, Mervyn answered, "Now he likes you."

Drucker and one of his barbers, Steve, were commenting on Jack's youthful appearance one day, and Steve said, "You look like a million, Mr. Benny."

"Before or after taxes?" inquired Jack.

"When our shop was having its twentieth anniversary," Drucker recalled, "I mentioned it to him, and he surprised us on that day by walking into the shop with his violin and playing 'The Anniversary Waltz' as he walked up and down the chairs where the men were all lathered or getting haircuts. And as casually as he walked in, he walked out. All the customers applauded, and just as if it were a stage, he reentered the shop, played a little encore, and walked out again."

Drucker used to make Jack laugh a lot, and the last laugh he got from the comedian was on one of Jack's last visits. Jack told him, "I used to get a lot of change from a ten-dollar bill thirty years ago. Now I get nothing back from a twenty."

172

"Give me back thirty years," Drucker answered, "and I'll give you the works for nothing!"

One last violin gag he pulled occurred on a flight from Los Angeles to Lake Tahoe. Since there were a few people on the plane he knew, Jack wasn't self-conscious about doing something he'd been thinking about. We had the captain of the plane announce on the public address system, "Please fasten your seat belts. Jack Benny is going to play his violin."

We then walked up the aisle of the plane, Jack playing the fiddle and I offering a hat for contributions. Everyone went along with the gag and dropped in quarters and dollar bills, which we announced we were keeping—and we did.

33

IT was difficult to be the daughter of two celebrated people, but Joan Benny managed very well for an only child in a home where the daily visitors were Robert Taylor and Barbara Stanwyck, Van Johnson, Frank Sinatra, or any one of the movie 400 who might drop by. She was graduated from the El Rodeo grade school in Beverly Hills as valedictorian of her class and was one of the top students at the Chadwick School in Palos Verdes before entering Stanford University.

During the Christmas holidays in 1953, in the middle of her junior year at Stanford, Joan visited friends in New York City and met Seth Baker, a young, handsome stockbroker. After a weeklong, whirlwind courtship, they decided to get married, and all the persuasion from her parents went unheeded. When the Bennys met the young man a few weeks later, they reluctantly agreed to an early wedding, and so it was set for the middle of March, 1954.

It was decided to make a big event of the wedding so that Joan would have her day in the sun. I worked hard publicizing it so that as the day approached, it became a lavish, glamorous, star-studded affair. Jack told Mary to shoot the works as far as expense was concerned, and that was all the encouragement she needed.

Six hundred guests were invited to the Crystal Room of the Beverly Hills Hotel and the newspapers reported that every important celebrity and executive in town attended. The top society orchestra was hired to play for dancing, and a few days before the wedding the leader of a ten-man violin group playing at the hotel came to see me. He wanted to perform with his group, but I told him we had already hired a band. He then asked if he could come during dinner and serenade Jack and guests, but I told him that the orchestra would take care of all the music. He finally said it would be a privilege to serenade Jack with his theme song, "Love in Bloom," and offered this as his contribution to the wedding. In the end I told him he could surprise Jack with that one number during the dinner if he wanted to do it just for the publicity, and he agreed.

Life magazine reported, with an accompanying page of pictures:

> Jack Benny . . . threw Hollywood's most expensive wedding in years. He sent a Hollywood designer to Paris to oversee the weaving of the bride's $2,500 gown and flew in white lilacs from Holland to adorn the Beverly Hills Hotel. With such incidentals as $2,750 for 700 pounds of boned breast of squab, $5,100 for 35 cases of champagne and $500 for a 200-pound five-tier wedding cake, the bill added up to a grand $50,000.

That was at 1954 prices, too! The wedding went beautifully with no unforeseen developments. Joan and Seth were a handsome couple in a real-life storybook setting. Even the violin serenaders did their surprise number to the delight of the father of the bride, who couldn't resist grabbing one of the fiddles and playing a solo. Bob Hope had the funny line of the night when he told Jack, "You're not gaining a son, you're losing a deduction."

The next morning the wedding party was the lead front-page story in both morning papers, both with eight-column banner headlines. The Los Angeles *Examiner*'s headline read: BENNY WEDDING COST $ 50,000; the Los Angeles *Times*' headline read: BENNY WEDDING COST $60,000. Eddie Cantor immediately telephoned Jack and advised him:

"Jack, just read the *Examiner*. You'll save ten thousand dollars." The topper to the affair came a few days later when I received a bill from the violin leader for a few hundred dollars. I phoned him at once and raised hell about it.

"Well," he said, "I figured that since Jack had such a good time with the fiddle. . . ."

A particular pet of Jack's who couldn't come to the wedding was Phil Silvers, who was in New York working on the Sergeant Bilko television show. Jack had first seen Phil work in burlesque, and when Phil came to Hollywood and made all those movies in which he was the leading man's pal, Jack and Phil spent much time together. When Phil was starring in *Top Banana* on Broadway, Jack fell in love with him. As Phil tells it:

"Jack saw *Top Banana* twice in New York and each time came backstage to tell me how great I was. And I loved it, especially coming from him. When we were on the road with the show, playing in San Francisco before coming to Los Angeles, Jack called me there and asked me to get him four good seats for the Bennys and George and Gracie. A few days later he called for more seats for his writers, and by the time I came to Los Angeles he had the entire second row. Now I'm a very nervous fellow, and opening night before all the stars, producers, and studio executives can be a frightening thing, especially for me. As we got closer to curtain time, I was sweating and shaking and didn't think I could go on. During the overture I was a zombie, but I managed to drag myself to the curtain and peek out. There was Jack, laughing at the overture in anticipation of what was coming, and when I saw him, I relaxed and gave one of the best performances I had ever done."

When Silvers was offered the lead in the Bilko TV show, he came to Jack for advice.

"Don't get into that TV trap," counseled Jack, who was one of the top stars in that "trap" at the time. "Stick to the Broadway stage. It has dignity, and you are one of the best in it."

Silvers didn't take Jack's suggestion and did the Bilko show, which was slotted opposite the Milton Berle program and soon surpassed it in the rating war. The following year Silvers was nominated opposite his mentor, Jack Benny, in practically every category in the Emmy Awards, and that was the year of Silvers and Bilko as they swept the coveted prizes. Jack then sent Phil a wire: YOU SON OF A BITCH. YOU WOULDN'T LISTEN TO ME.

"Many years later," Phil related, "I was offered the lead in the New York revival of *A Funny Thing Happened to Me on the Way to the Forum*. Again I asked Jack what he thought, and he advised against it. 'Look, Phil, what have you got to gain? Zero Mostel was fabulous in the original, and you'll have to suffer by comparison. The show ran for a long time, and the movie was no great shakes. So what can you gain by doing it again?' Well, I did do it, the reviews for me and show were as good or better than the original, and we were the hit of New York. Then Jack wired me, YOU STILL WON'T LISTEN TO ME."

Years later the two comedians were together on the Dick Cavett show, and Phil said to Jack, "I feel guilty about all the wonderful things you always said about me." When Jack asked, "Why?" Phil answered, "Because I never liked you."

Jack fell on the floor and started to pound it, and in front of the nationwide audience, he couldn't stop laughing.

34

JACK BENNY was not the world's greatest athlete. He was never very proficient at games, and golf was the only active sport at which he made a halfhearted attempt to be good. Although he played all his life and had thousands of lessons, he could never match the ability of the Bob Hopes and Bing Crosbys. Jack never broke eighty in golf and rarely broke ninety, even when he was younger and playing comparatively well. In his later years he was high in the hundreds and, as a result, would not enter the celebrity tournaments because he was embarrassed to have the big galleries see him duff the shots.

He was a bug on physical fitness, partly because of his health, but primarily because he realized that the better he looked, the longer his life span as a performer would be. He repeatedly said, "I can get away with all the thirty-nine-year old gags because I don't look my real age. If I did, most of those jokes wouldn't be funny."

His ideal weight was 151 pounds, and he would weigh himself every morning. As soon as his weight would go to 153, he would immediately diet down to 150 to allow himself a little margin to cheat. He liked to keep slim because he felt appearance was very important, even for a comedian. He was careful about his clothes, especially those he wore on the stage, and always looked meticulous when he made his entrance.

He hired a professional to work out with him, and when he was younger, they would jog for miles every morning before going through a series of exercises. In later years when Jack could no longer jog, the man would put him through a half hour of calisthenics and then give him a massage, and Jack would do the exercises regularly when he was traveling or when he was at home but his man was out of town.

Walking was a source of great enjoyment to him, and he could walk miles at a brisk pace. He had few friends who liked to walk as much as he did, which is one of the reasons he played golf so often. The true stories at golf clubs are usually very funny, and everyone seemed to have a story about Jack and golf. Jack was the only man at his club who would hire a caddie and a golf cart, then walk the eighteen holes and let the caddie ride. Danny Kaye could talk about Jack and golf for hours:

"For a time, I was very serious about golf," Danny reminisced, "and if I was playing well, I concentrated on my game, and if I was playing badly, I was so annoyed that I didn't talk. Once I was playing with Jack, and after nine holes he said, 'Please talk—it's so boring.' I then talked incessantly for the next three holes until in desperation Jack yelled, 'Oh, shut up!'

"We were going up to Pebble Beach to play golf for a few days. I picked him up and started driving north fairly fast, while Jack kept asking me to slow down. I continued at a pretty speedy clip with Jack telling me every five minutes that I was going too fast, and just as we reached Oxnard, about fifty miles from home, we heard a siren coming up behind us. 'See,' said Jack, 'you wouldn't listen to me. I told you a hundred times to slow up, but you were a wise guy.' The motorcycle cop pulled us over to the side of the road and said to me, 'Are you Danny Kaye?' I nodded. Then he turned to Jack. 'Are you Jack Benny?' When Jack said yes, the cop said, 'You took your wife's clubs by mistake, sir.' Mary had called someone when she discovered the mistake and whoever it was figured out that we had to pass Oxnard and so alerted the police there. We had to turn around and drive back for the clubs.

"One day, playing at Pebble Beach, I hit a beautiful second shot with a wedge, and it landed a few feet from the pin. Jack asked what club I had used, and I said in an accent, 'A vetch.' Jack thought that was so funny he fell on the green and couldn't play the rest of the day. A few weeks later we were playing at Hillcrest, and after the game we came into the clubhouse for a bite. When the waiter asked Jack what he wanted, he didn't know and wanted to know what I was going to have. I said I would have a pineapple soda, and with that, Jack fell on the table, pounding it with his fist in his characteristic fashion as he roared with laughter. I said, 'Jack, I didn't say anything funny,' and Jack replied, 'But I expected you to say it with an accent.'

"We were playing golf in Palm Springs with Bob Hope and his friend Charlie Resnick. I had been playing well up to that day, but for the first six holes, I couldn't make a decent shot and I was cursing the ball, the caddie, the golf club, and the whole world—using very filthy language. Jack tried to shut me up a few times, but I continued to curse every shot. When we came to the seventh hole, there were two little old ladies ahead of us, and we asked them if we could play through. With the two ladies sitting there, I got up to drive the ball, and Jack and the others watched me with worried looks as I hit a terrible shot. I looked around and said, 'Oh, dear!' and with that, Jack exploded and ran away from us about fifty feet, screaming with laughter, leaving the two women wondering what was so funny."

Producer Gary Morton, Lucille Ball's husband, was playing golf with Jack in Palm Springs, and Morton, a fine golfer, was hitting the ball exceptionally well that day, while Jack was flubbing nearly every shot. Finally, Jack drove the ball on the thirteenth hole, and Morton, trying to give him some encouragement, said, "That sounded good."

"I'm hitting a golf ball," snapped Jack. "I'm not giving a concert!"

Jack's friend Harry Tugend, the writer, played golf with him very often, and they'd bet a golf ball on the match. Tugend won the first day but never received a golf ball, nor did he ask for one. The next day Tugend won again, and again no golf ball was forthcoming from Benny. The third day Jack suggested they play for a golf ball again. Tugend won, and Jack left the club without mentioning the prize. On the fourth day, while Tugend was having his lunch at the club, Jack walked into the dining room and handed him a box with four dozen golf balls in it.

Judge Ben Landis, a close friend, once brought his fifteen-year-old son to join them for a game. The boy, a three-handicap player, shot a birdie, a par, and another birdie for the first three holes as Jack looked on in astonishment. Finally he said to the judge, "I hate that little son of a bitch."

The first time he played golf with his friend Jerry Lavin, Lavin took him out to the Tam O'Shanter Club in Chicago. While they were playing the first hole, the word spread around the club that Jack Benny was playing, and by the time they reached the first green a gallery of about 200 was waiting for the comedian. He had a ninety-foot putt, and as the gallery breathlessly watched, Jack stepped up, stroked the ball, and it rolled into the cup in one miraculous putt. As the crowd applauded, Jack loudly asked in feigned innocence, "Isn't that the way you're supposed to do it?"

Jack often used to go out to his club on the spur of the moment and play alone. He was telling Fred De Cordova one day that he had played nine holes by himself, and Fred said, "I don't belong to a club, and you know I love golf. Why would you play alone when it would be so easy to call me and I'd pick you up, drive you to the club, and you'd have company?"

A few weeks later Jack called him and asked him if he could be ready to play in half an hour.

"Sure," said Fred eagerly. "Where do you want me to pick you up?"

"I'm in Room Four Fifty-six at the Broadmoor Hotel in Colorado Springs," was Jack's answer as he hung up the phone.

As Jack got older, he played less often, played worse and

worse, and ended up disliking the game, although he wouldn't admit it. He continued playing because his doctor wanted him to get as much exercise as possible, but he cut down gradually on the number of holes and the number of days a week he'd play. Sometimes he would play only five holes; frequently he'd play only four. Our little gag with him was to suggest he go out and play one hole because it was such a lovely day. But in his later years the greatest golf day of all for Jack was when he had a date for a game and he'd awaken to see pouring rain.

35

THE television career of Jack Benny, although never reaching the greatness of his radio shows, did achieve a record of some sort. His half hour programs were on the networks for fifteen consecutive years, and when he ended that series, by mutual agreement, he continued to perform in specials for nine more years.

Since there was no cable to transmit coast-to-coast television, we had to fly to New York for the four programs in the 1950–51 season, as well as for the six in the 1951–52 season. The shows were telecast live for the East Coast, and kinescopes were made and telecast a week later on stations in the rest of the country.

For his first program, after the "I'd give a million dollars to know what I look like" line, his opening monologue followed with:

"Ladies and gentlemen, I must tell you why I decided to go into television at this time. You see, last year it got to be a little bit embarrassing. . . . So many of my fans kept asking me why I didn't get into this particular medium. They wanted to know if I was afraid of it. Well, of course, that's ridiculous—I wasn't afraid, it was my sponsor who didn't have the nerve.

"But one thing I must say about my sponsor. . . . When

he moves, he really plunges. Starting tonight, I go on once every eight weeks. . . . Yup, every eight weeks I'll be doing one of these shows. So don't expect to find my television show listed on the television page in the newspapers. . . . It probably will be marked on the calendar under 'full moon.'"

While doing the TV programs, for which CBS paid Jack a salary of $15,000 for each one, he continued to perform in his radio shows, cutting down from thirty-nine to thirty-five shows a season and receiving as his fee $10,000 per program. The radio shows continued for five years as Jack increased his TV schedule to nine programs the third year, then thirteen for a few years, and then sixteen, alternating with such shows as Ann Southern's *Private Secretary, Bachelor Father* with John Forsythe, and finally, *The George Gobel Show.*

Although he still did the toupee jokes, the cheap gags, the age routines, the vanity lines, the Maxwell, the vault, and all the other sketches from the radio shows, he added a "touch of class," and his programs had a more mature, literate quality about them than most of the others that were on the air at the time. As a result, many motion-picture stars, who had been terrified of the new medium, refused to appear as guests on any program until they were approached for the Benny show. Many of those celebrities had great faith in Jack and the quality of his program, and they realized he would protect them. As a matter of fact, some of the stars made their one and only comedic appearance on TV on the Benny show. Those who made their TV debuts on the Benny program included Helen Hayes, Humphrey Bogart, James Stewart, Barbara Stanwyck, Claudette Colbert, Fred MacMurray, Kirk Douglas, Irene Dunne, Bing Crosby, Marilyn Monroe, Gary Cooper, and Gregory Peck.

The first few TV shows were a nervous time for Jack, but soon he found his footing in the new medium and decided he liked it much better than radio. It was back to the stage again for him, and he could use his eyes, his pained expression, and his stares for laughs, something that was lacking in radio. After a time people began to say that all Jack had to do was stare at the audience and he could get laughs, but Jack would answer, "How long do you think I could stare after a lousy joke? The audience would stare right back at me."

Others would say that Jack didn't need writers. All he had

to do was read the telephone book, and with his stares and his timing he would get screams. Well, one day Louella Parsons printed a line about all Jack had to do was read the telephone book, and Jack told the audience on one of his programs about the Parsons line. He told them that he thought he really needed writers, but if Louella Parsons thought he could get laughs by reading the phone book, he'd try it. On camera he opened the phone book at random and read a name and phone number and then looked at the audience. Nothing happened. Then he said that it probably wasn't a very funny name and number, so he tried another name and number, and that brought only a few titters. Just as he was ready to give up, Ed Wynn, a guest star on that show, walked onstage and told Jack he *could* get laughs reading the phone book and asked him to try once more. When Jack read the next name, Ed cut off Jack's tie. For the next number he ripped Jack's coat up the back. And as Jack continued reading the phone book, Ed Wynn kept doing his crazy tricks on Jack's person to complete a very funny routine.

After the first two years in TV, our shows were produced at the new CBS Television City on Beverly Boulevard and Fairfax Avenue in Hollywood, right in the heart of a Jewish district. During rehearsals we often had lunch at Cantor's Delicatessen on Fairfax Avenue. On one occasion Jack and I and the writers were having lunch at Cantor's when we noticed what seemed to be more business than usual in the restaurant. When we walked out, we saw a sign in the window that read: JACK BENNY IS EATING INSIDE.

In searching for plots and ideas for television, Jack and his writers utilized every possible radio program that was adaptable to the new medium, and very successfully, too. One of the key shows they converted was his satire of the film *Gaslight,* which had starred Ingrid Bergman and Charles Boyer. After his wartime USO tour of Germany in 1945 with Ingrid Bergman, Jack persuaded the Swedish star to guest on his radio program, and they did a hilarious version of *Gaslight* with Jack in the Boyer role. For one of his early live TV programs he repeated the *Gaslight* satire, only this time with Barbara Stanwyck in the Bergman role. A few years later, when he started to film a few programs each year to intersperse with the "live" shows, he decided to film the *Gaslight* satire with Barbara Stanwyck, reasoning that there were so many more

TV sets in use by then that a new audience would see the show. However, MGM, the studio that had produced the film and owned all the rights to the play, always insisted that special plugs for new films they were producing be given on TV shows that satirized MGM properties. Jack decided to do it without their permission, planning to placate the studio after the telecast.

After the film was completed, MGM heard about it, raised hell because it hadn't been asked permission, and got an injunction against the running of the film. CBS, who owned the producing company at that time, having purchased Amusement Enterprises years before, went to court to remove the injunction, claiming the right of satire without permission. CBS lost the suit and appealed it all the way to the Supreme Court, a case that created much interest in the entertainment industry. Even though the Supreme Court recognized the right to satirize, the Justices agreed that the plot and dialogue of the Benny program was too close to the original and upheld MGM. By the time the suit was concluded all rights to the Benny programs had reverted to Benny and his new company (more on this later), and we bought the right to telecast *Gaslight* from MGM for $1,000 since they explained that they didn't want to hurt Jack but were just going on record for future satirical programs about MGM films.

Good ideas for programs were plentiful, and with the six creative writers spilling forth suggestions constantly and the backlog of funny radio shows that could be converted, the Benny series rolled along very smoothly. It seemed that guest stars were Jack's for the asking because each program was an event and the agents and studios were offering their biggest stars to Benny.

Johnny Carson was just beginning in television, doing a five-minute comedy program on CBS in a late-afternoon time slot, and Jack took a liking to his slow, easy type of humor which was similar to his own. In 1952 he used Johnny on his program, the first important guest star appearance the young comedian had ever made.

The writers came up with a funny routine for Carson. He told the star that he was Johnny's idol and had been his idol for the two years that he, Johnny, had been in the business. When Jack beamed with delight at the praise, Johnny then asked him if he'd mind if he, Johnny, made a few suggestions. He then proceeded to tell Jack that he spoke too slowly, that he stared at the audience too long, that he shouldn't put his hand to his cheek so often, and all the while Jack kept interrupting to ask him how long he had been in show business. It was such a good routine that years later we used it again on a filmed TV program with Bobby Rydell, and again the routine worked so successfully that we adapted it for personal appearances, rewriting it for Wayne Newton, Della Reese, Caterina Valente, and many other performers with whom Jack appeared in theaters and nightclubs all over the world.

For the half hour shows Jack always preferred to use his regular cast of supporting players: Mel Blanc, Frank Nelson, Herb Vigran, Bea Benaderat, Hy Averback, Sandra Gould, Benny Rubin, to name a few. Jack felt more secure with those professionals surrounding him and would often spend a great deal of extra money to use a regular rather than take a chance on a new actor or actress. Once, when I was producing the program years later, the writers had created a sketch in which only one word was written for Frank Nelson, the "nasty man" of our program who always insulted Jack. The culmination of that sequence ended with Jack dialing a phone number. After the ring, you heard Frank Nelson's voice saying, "Yeessssssss?" from offstage. Since Frank Nelson's fee was rather high for his appearances, which generally involved four days of rehearsal and taping, I phoned and asked him what he would charge to drop by the studio for an hour on the day of the taping to say that one word. He asked for his usual salary, which I thought was out of line under the circumstances. When I reported that to Jack, he said that Frank had a perfect right to ask for his regular fee, and we had the same right not to use him if we felt it was excessive. The writers, Jack and I discussed whether or not that one word would get a big enough laugh to merit the fee, we decided it would, and Frank Nelson received $750, the highest fee for one word in the history of television at that time.

Our executive producer-director for the first seven years of the television program was Ralph Levy, who was the bright young man in the industry at the time. Jack respected his talent, and they worked together beautifully. The producer was Jack's brother-in-law, Hilliard Marks, who worked

184

for the advertising agency, BBD&O, as contact man on our show.

The first argument that Jack and Ralph Levy ever had was when we did a program in which we satirized the Beverly Hills police department. The police station, on that program, was described as an elegant establishment with crystal chandeliers and French Provincial furniture. The jokes were all about the chichi way Beverly Hills ran its operations. The police department's having an unlisted number was only one of the dozens of gags along that line. The end of the show had the police officers all excited about a murder and the police captain yelling to his men, "We've got to track them down. Send out the dogs!"

Immediately, a pack of little, beautifully groomed French poodles scurried across the stage and exited.

To achieve a fresh look, Ralph Levy hired Lyle Talbot, the former motion-picture star, to play the role of the police captain, and he was supported by a cast of actors Jack had never used before to play the other roles. At the first rehearsal, when Jack saw the cast, he took Ralph aside and bawled him out for not using his regulars. He insisted that Ralph get rid of the entire troupe and recast it, but Ralph refused, explaining that the whole cast would have to be paid off, and it would look terrible to fire them for no apparent reason. Reluctantly, Jack agreed to go on with the rehearsal with this cast to see if it could work. Finally the show was done with them, and it turned out to be one of the best of that year. Immediately after the show, Jack called Ralph into his dressing room and said, "Ralph, I'm delighted I didn't have to say, 'I told you so.'"

36

WHEN Amusement Enterprises was acquired by CBS and the Jack Benny program moved to that network, I had the assistance of the CBS publicity and advertising staff in both

New York and on the Coast to help me in the handling of the show, which allowed me some free time. Gradually, CBS began to use me in publicizing some of their other programs, and before I knew it, I was named director of exploitation for the CBS radio network, a new field of promotion for them. Although my primary concentration was the Benny show, eventually I became director of public relations for the West Coast for CBS.

I had had several feelers from the New York executives about moving there, but no one wanted to incur the wrath of their number one star, so no definite proposition came along until one day when I was offered the post of vice-president in charge of four departments—press information, advertising, promotion, and sales promotion, with the understanding that it had to have the approval of Mr. Benny.

I went to Jack and explained the offer, telling him that I had gone as far as I could go on the Coast and the main opportunities were in New York where all the top executives were working and where the important advertisers and advertising agency heads were officed. I also told him that I could still keep an eye on his activities from New York, and we could easily be in touch by phone and visits from time to time.

Jack thought it over for a few moments and then told me that he couldn't stand in my way and wished me luck. We arranged for the man who was handling publicity for Edward R. Murrow to move from New York to California to take over my duties with the Benny program, and after a short breaking-in period in which he and I worked together, I left for my new job in December, 1955.

Meanwhile, Jack had gone to Taft Schreiber, his TV agent at MCA, with his problems and worries.

"Jack came to me sometime in 1955 with his concerns," Schreiber recalls. "Jack was making fifteen thousand per TV program, and he was just managing to take care of his obligations at that time. He had always lived lavishly in a home with many servants, and he was supporting Mary's parents and helping his sister in Chicago, and his daughter had just been divorced as well. Although he was earning a big salary at the time, he was only an employee of CBS, and he worried that should his rating go down, he would have to take a salary cut. In a nutshell, he wanted his own company so that he could start producing some other programs in order to have an income in case his own program was ever in trouble. So we organized a new company called J and M Productions, Inc., and made a new deal with CBS to produce the Benny shows for that network."

In the interim, I started to reorganize my departments at CBS in New York, and during this time, Jack would phone me at least two or three times each week to ask my advice about something or other or just to talk about nothing in particular. After I had been in New York for two months, he phoned one day, and in the course of the conversation he asked me how I liked living in New York. I told him I loved it, having been born there and having family and friends there. But for the next week he repeatedly asked if I was happy with New York and with my work there. I was always very affirmative in my replies, and then one day he asked if I would ever take a job back in California. I didn't think I would, I said, but told him that if something sensational ever came up, naturally I would consider it. Then he asked if I would like to work with him again, and when I said yes, he told me that Taft Schreiber was coming to New York the following week and had something to discuss with me.

Next week, to my surprise, Taft told me that Jack wanted me to be president of J and M Productions, and was prepared to offer me a good salary and 15 percent ownership of the stock of the corporation, of which Jack and Mary each owned 42 1/2 percent. Taft felt that I could develop enough outside activity in addition to the Benny show so that eventually it would be a very lucrative deal for me, as well as for the Bennys.

Since I had only been in New York a short while and CBS had invested a good deal of money moving me, my family, and furniture to New York, I felt guilty about leaving them. But I also felt that returning to Jack on the Coast was a better future for me, so I agreed to the offer but only with the understanding that CBS would have three months' notice from me.

Edgar Bergen, who was a good friend of Jack Benny's and mine, came to New York a few days after I made my new deal, and we had dinner together.

"I think you're making a great mistake," Edgar counseled. "I love Jack and want only the best for him. But on the other hand, I want you to make the most of your opportunities, too. I know they think the world of you here at CBS, and you might go far here, whereas when you think of Jack's age, you could be stepping into a temporary job—and then what? And this business is so uncertain, how do we know Jack's popularity will hold up and then where will you be?"

Eighteen years later when we were taping our last special at NBC, I ran into Edgar Bergen at the studio, and he said, "Jack tells me he's going to retire in a year or two. I told you it might be just a temporary job."

Shortly before I completed my last three months at CBS, Jack, Mary, and our production staff went to London to film four TV shows to be titled *Jack Benny in London, Jack Benny in Paris, Jack Benny in Venice,* and *Jack Benny in Rome.* Although location work was to be done for a few days in each of the other three cities, the principal photography and all interiors were to be shot in London. I took a week's leave of absence from CBS to fly over with the Bennys to London, where I helped get things started, and then I returned to CBS and went on to California, where I began my work as J and M president.

In order to save expenses, none of the regular Benny cast was sent to Europe, and the only recognizable name on the four shows was Maurice Chevalier, who came from France to guest-star in the Paris show. Ralph Levy cast the programs with the best stage actors he could find in London. Sean Connery was a complete unknown, and his first acting job was in the Rome show, on which he played an Italian porter with one line of dialogue.

Peter Sellers was a young actor who had been doing minor roles in British television. He was cast in the London show and was excellent. But after a few days of rehearsal Jack called Ralph Levy aside and told him he thought that Sellers was a fine actor but wrong to play against him because their deliveries were so similar and their tempos were identical and it would hurt the laugh reaction. So poor Sellers was paid off and dismissed, which was a big blow to him at that time.

After having worked in Hollywood, the slow pace of the technicians in London was a source of great consternation to the California staff as they waited for hours at times while the sets were lit and the props put into place. What had started out as a two-week schedule in London went on for what seemed an interminable four weeks, leaving Jack frustrated. At a London press conference he described his feelings about the time everything took and the slowness of the film crew by commenting, "If he had known the British were so slow, Paul Revere could have walked."

When this quote appeared in the newspapers, the entire crew walked off and threatened a strike. Jack had to apologize publicly to the film union in order to get them back on the set.

As the costs mounted on the first four films produced by his own company, J and M, Jack became more and more worried about losses and regretted ever having started his own company. He wrote to me in California recounting all that had been happening and mentioning that if he hadn't been responsible for taking me away from CBS, he would disband the corporation and let CBS again take on the responsibility of the financial end of the business.

When the four films were finally completed, the company ended up in Rome, where the Bennys decided to stay on for a rest. Mervyn Le Roy was directing the film spectacle *Quo Vadis?* in Rome at the time, and he spoke to me about Jack's Roman holiday:

"I was shooting the giant arena set for the MGM film, and there must have been three thousand extras on the set. It was costing us about fifteen thousand dollars an hour, and we were fighting time the whole day. You can imagine how long it took us to get the extras in the right positions for the big scene and keep them quiet, and just before one take, when I was finally able to create order out of chaos, I yelled through a megaphone, *'Silencio.'* The assistant director called out, 'Roll 'em,' to the cameras and sound crew, and suddenly, from the back I heard a familiar voice holler 'Moivyn,' which was his name for me. And through the crowd of extras came Jack, strolling in his slow, nonchalant manner, as if it didn't matter a bit how long he delayed this costly production. Naturally, I laughed, the extras started to talk to one another, and while I embraced Jack, the company broke for a ten-minute recess while the MGM production chief tore his hair. It was an hour before we started that shot again, and it was

189

estimated later that the simple word 'Moivyn' cost MGM twelve thousand dollars!"

That night, Mervyn took Jack to see *Madama Butterfly* at Rome's giant outdoor opera amphitheater, the Caracalla Baths. Their seats were so far back that they could scarcely see the stage, and in the scene in which Cio-Cio-San was singing to her mother, Jack asked which one was Cio-Cio-San. Mervyn answered, "From here, each could be Sophie Tucker as far as I can tell."

Jack laughed so hard and for so long that everyone nearby turned and stared, embarrassing the two into leaving the opera before the end.

Mervyn Le Roy is a very enthusiastic man, and he spent hours telling Jack about the beautiful shirts he had made in Rome with his initials on them. He urged Jack to have some made with his monogram handsomely embroidered. Jack insisted that he had plenty of shirts and wouldn't need any more for years, but Mervyn was persistent. One day he ran up to his rooms at the Grand Hotel and brought down a few of the shirts to show Jack how great they were. He again pointed out the initials and fine workmanship until finally he broke down Jack's resistance and the two of them went to Mervyn's shirtmaker to order a dozen shirts for Jack with the marvelous monogram. From California a month later, Jack wired Mervyn, who was still in Rome directing the picture: THE SHIRTS CAME. INITIALS PERFECT BUT SHIRTS DON'T FIT.

He had known Mervyn Le Roy ever since he started in vaudeville as "Le Roy and Cooper. . . . Two kids and a piano," and when Mervyn became a director, Jack always played little gags on him whenever he had the opportunity. When Le Roy was directing *Rose Marie,* the filmed operetta about the Royal Canadian Mounted Police, starring Jeanette MacDonald and Nelson Eddy, Jack went to much trouble for one laugh. Mervyn recalls:

"We were shooting at Mammoth Lake, California, and I was photographing a difficult sequence. It was the song 'Song of the Mounties,' the music and vocal having been prerecorded, and the scene called for forty Mounties riding over a hill singing the song. Jack had made all the arrangements with my wife in advance, and he and Irving Brecher, the writer-producer, drove up to the location. They were dressed in red Mountie uniforms and the makeup man put mustaches on them. The horsemen were hidden from the camera behind the hill, and I fired a gun to indicate the start of action. As the cameras rolled, the recording of the song was turned on and the horsemen emerged from over the hilltop, riding toward the cameras. The lineup wasn't very good, so I yelled, 'Cut.' Most of the horsemen stopped, but two of them continued to ride toward us. I kept yelling at them through the megaphone to stop, but they kept on coming, and I got really mad and told the assistant director to fire the two guys. And then I recognized Jack and Brecher, and there went the scene for a long break while I laughed."

Mervyn Le Roy was always a very secretive man, and practically everything he told anyone was a secret. He was, and still is, president of Hollywood Park Racetrack, and he knows a great deal about horses and jockeys. One day Jack Benny was at the track with Jack Warner, head of the Warner Brothers Studio, and Warner kept asking Le Roy for a good horse to bet on. Le Roy told him he had a horse in the eighth race but cautioned Warner about telling anyone about it. He even told Warner that he wouldn't tell him the name of the horse until just before the race. After the seventh race Warner met Le Roy, and Mervyn whispered the name of the horse to him, at the same time reminding him not to breathe this secret to a soul. Warner promised not to tell anyone, placed his bet, and then he and Jack, trying to avoid the heavy traffic, left the track. In the car homeward bound, they listened to the race results and heard that the "tip" horse Le Roy had given Warner finished last. Benny suggested a wire which Warner promptly sent to Le Roy: NOW CAN I TELL?

37

THE first office of J and M Productions was on Camden Drive in Beverly Hills, and my first effort as president was to try to keep the costs down. I operated with a very small staff, consisting of one bookkeeper, a secretary for me, and a secretary for Jack Benny. Since we were no longer writing the radio show, only four writers had been signed for the sixteen alternate week shows we were to produce that first season of our new corporation. Ralph Levy had an office at CBS, and Hilliard Marks was at the advertising agency.

Our comedian was a very informal man. Everyone called him Jack, including the girls in the office. He was used to disrupting any meeting by coming in and making a few of his little jokes. He would often interrupt my secretary while she was typing, put his feet up on her desk and tell her stories for an hour while the work she was trying to get out lay incomplete. In order to maintain a semblance of the dignity of a business office, I insisted that the bookkeeper and my secretary call me Mr. Fein. One day I was on an important phone call, and I needed Jack to answer a question. I asked my secretary please to have him come into my office right away. Jack was in his office in the midst of a meeting with the writers, and she interrupted by announcing, "Jack, Mr. Fein wants to see you right away."

The writers thought that was hilarious, but Jack never even noticed how she had referred to each of us.

The writers, Sam Perrin, George Balzer, Hal Goldman, and Al Gordon, worked exclusively on the Benny half hour programs. American Tobacco paid J and M $70,000 per program, the highest fee paid for a half hour show at that time, and J and M paid Jack $15,000 per show. At the same time, Jack Benny signed to star in a series of twenty one-hour spectaculars for Chrysler titled *The Shower of Stars,* which were to be produced over four years at the rate of five shows a year. CBS produced this series. At Jack's suggestion they hired his old team of Wedlock and Snyder to write those shows, and Jack received $35,000 for each show.

Jack's secretary, Bert Scott, had been with him since 1942 and ran his office as informally as his boss ran his. He was nearly Jack's age, was a dapper fellow, very thin, well dressed, and, like Jack, didn't look his age. Everyone liked Bert, and we used to joke with him that he should run for mayor of Beverly Hills because he had a speaking acquaintance with half the people he'd pass on Wilshire Boulevard. Like many people who are good-looking, Bert was too vain and would not wear the hearing aid he so badly needed until the last few years of his life. And Bert was hard of hearing. It was not unusual for Jack to yell for Bert to get Andy Devine on the phone and for Bert to ask, "Danny Thomas?" Not too many years ago Jack was playing an engagement at the Sahara Hotel at Lake Tahoe, and he dictated a telegram to Bert to send to General Omar Bradley, who was then living in Beverly Hills. Bert typed the wire, and when Jack read it over to okay it for transmission, he noticed the address Bert had typed: "General Bradley, Omaha, Nebraska."

Of the sixteen shows, we did eleven live programs and five on film. On one of his shows, Jack did a gag about this: "I do some shows live and some on film, and I asked my audience to write in and tell which way they liked me best—live or on film . . . and you'd be surprised at how many don't like me at all."

In 1956 I sold CBS Radio a two-year deal to repeat the old Benny radio programs, and they in turn sold the shows to an insurance company, which turned out to be a very lucrative deal for all of us. At the same time we had signed the well-known dance team of Marge and Gower Champion to a television contract, and I wrote a six-page outline of a situation comedy that would utilize their youthful enthusiasm, as well as their dancing abilities. MCA sold the show to the American Tobacco Company, and it decided to try out six programs in place of the *Private Secretary* show. Jack, who always spoke of wanting to be a producer, attended a meeting or two and then didn't pay any attention to the show, devoting all his time to his own activities. However, we did manage to produce some excellent scripts, written by Joe Connolly and Bob Mosher, a writing team that had written many of the Amos and Andy shows. A few days before our first live program, Gower Champion was in an automobile accident and broke his leg. With Gower in a thigh-high leg cast, we had quite a problem delivering a dancing show. At the last moment we substituted Dan Dailey and rewrote the script to show Gower in a wheelchair. It was no surprise that the show and the series didn't come off successfully. Although show business lost a possible TV star in Gower Champion, it gained a great musical comedy director.

In 1953 Jack played a three-week engagement at the Curran Theater in San Francisco. He surrounded himself with a group of fine performers, including the little known Sammy

193

Davis, Jr., who was then with his father and uncle in the Will Mastin Trio, and Gisele Mackenzie, a Canadian singer who had been performing in the United States for only a year. He took the same show out the following year to Dallas, Portland, Seattle, and Vancouver and, all during this time and afterward, sang the praises of Sammy and Gisele. As a matter of fact, Jack phoned his sponsor, who also sponsored *Hit Parade,* and suggested that they hire Gisele for that program, which they did. In the next two years she became one of the leading stars of that show and in demand everywhere.

Gisele was ready for her own TV series by 1957 and had had many offers to star in one, but she was very cautious and waited for just the right opportunity and format. Knowing the respect she had for Jack and his judgment, I wrote a television format for her and told our agents, MCA, also her agents, that I thought my idea was right for her and that Jack and I would like to produce the show for her.

She and her husband read the treatment, loved it, and we made a coproduction deal and sold the show to a sponsor for a full season to air at 9:30 P.M. Saturday nights on NBC. Because of Jack's admiration for Gisele, he was excited for a few weeks and made some suggestions. We had been looking for a theme song for the program, and Jack brought in his dear friend Phil Baker to write it. Phil wrote the music, and his old "man in the box," Sid Silvers, the fellow who had heckled him for years in his vaudeville act, wrote the lyrics to a catchy song called "Gisele."

Because of Jack's close association with the show, he didn't want to guest on her first program, but he did agree to go on the second one. We secured Art Linkletter for the first show, which we thought would bring a large audience since Art was then starring in the nighttime *People Are Funny* show, as well as the five-times-a-week kid show every noon. Charles Isaacs was the producer and head writer for Gisele, and he did a brilliant job with the script. Gisele was one of the hardest-working performers I had ever been associated with, and although we knew she was a marvelous vocalist, she surprised us with her sense of comedy, as well as her dancing talents. The first show went on without a hitch, and when it was over, the sponsors were hosts to the cast and press at a lavish party at Romanoff's restaurant. Everyone concerned loved the show and felt we had a great success. But when the first ratings came out, a surprise program opposite us, *Have Gun, Will Travel,* with an unknown actor named Richard Boone, trounced us. As the weeks went by, Boone became a big star as a result of the Western drama, and *Have Gun, Will Travel* sent Gisele traveling off NBC at the end of the season.

As a summer replacement show one year, we sold a show brought to us by producer Cece Barker and director Seymour Berns, the team that was doing the Red Skelton weekly shows. Their show starred two Canadian comics, Wayne and Schuster, who had done some funny appearances on the Ed Sullivan program. This show was done on film and was mildly funny and didn't create much interest in the industry or the sponsors, and the boys soon went packing back to Canada. We formed a coproduction deal with Connolly and Mosher on a show they created, *Ichabod,* but this farm-oriented comedy must have been ahead of its time, for it died a long time before *Beverly Hillbillies, Petticoat Junction,* and other shows of that type were born.

Finally, we bagged a winner in a coproduction deal with Universal on a detective program, *Checkmate,* which turned out to be successful and ran for three years on the network before it went into syndication.

All the while the Jack Benny show rolled on, never achieving the top position in the ratings, but always hovering above the mediocre shows and forever maintaining its style. William Saroyan was a big Benny fan and wrote a cover story on him for *Look* magazine, in which he said:

> Jack Benny had style from the beginning. He stood straight and walked kind of sideways as if he were being gently shoved by a touch of genius—and knew it, and you'd know it too, in a moment. . . . But I listened to all of the clowns, because they were always talking about me—and you too. And Benny has always been one of the best, week after week, year after year, and right now too. . . . He makes me laugh, as the saying is. I thank him. You do too, most likely.

In addition to taste, Jack had enough basic comedy intelligence to realize that the audiences were getting more and more sophisticated as they were exposed to a mélange of comedy from all over the dials, and he tried to keep pace with them. His cheap jokes had to be more sophisticated as the years rolled by, and gradually he started to drop elements of his program that had been overplayed and were now dated. The Maxwell was the first to go, and even though every once in a while one of the writers would come up with a funny Maxwell idea, Jack felt that he had passed that by a long time ago. The hair jokes fell by the wayside, too, and the craze for singing commercials was gone as well, and Jack felt that it was time to start phasing out the Sportsmen Quartet, of whom he once said, "I found two of the Sportsmen at the Flamingo Hotel in Las Vegas and two at the Sahara. That's making a four the hard way."

The comedian found himself a very busy man, working with his writers, rehearsing and then performing on his half hour programs, and then repeating the same process on his five one-hour *Shower of Stars* shows. He found himself spending most of his time in his Beverly Hills office or at CBS Television City. His two "new writers," Al Gordon and Hal Goldman, recall that one evening, after rehearsal, Jack suggested they go across the street to a Chinese restaurant for some dinner.

"While we were eating," remembers Gordon, "Jack suddenly looked up from his chop suey and announced that it was his birthday. We were too stunned to say anything, so the three of us just continued to eat after wishing him a soft 'Happy Birthday.'"

The same story was told by director Hy Averback.

"It was while I was an actor on the radio show," Hy remembered. "I hardly knew him and was surprised when he invited me out for a bite of dinner after a show. We went to the Beachcomber's because he always liked Chinese and Cantonese food, and while we were eating, he told me it was his birthday."

Hy also recalls another evening with Jack which describes a lonesome man. Hy was an actor on a Bob Hope TV program on which Jack was a guest star, and when they finished their sequence about seven thirty that evening, Jack suddenly asked him, "You live in the Valley here near NBC, don't you?"

When Hy told him he did, in a house in Toluca Lake, Jack

said he'd like to go over to the house with him because he wanted to see a TV program that was coming on soon on which his friend George Burns was guesting.

"I lived in a teeny, little house at that time, and I quickly phoned my wife and told her I was coming home soon with Jack Benny. My wife screamed because the house was a mess, her sister and aunt were over visiting, and my daughter wasn't dressed. She asked me to stall him as long as I could. Walking out of the studio with Jack, I tried to stop and talk to everyone I knew, and then I took the long way home. Just before I got to the house, I remembered that I needed cigarettes, and so I stopped for some, which gave my wife an extra ten minutes. Just as we arrived at my front door, I saw my sister-in-law and my wife's aunt scurry out of the house. My wife had swept all the junk into my daughter's room so that the living room looked fairly presentable, but as soon as we entered, my daughter fell in love with Jack and insisted on showing him her room. We died as they went in, but when Jack came out, he said, 'Nice room.' We watched the show, and then Jack insisted on taking my wife and me to dinner, and we ended up having a great, relaxed evening."

For Jack's regular TV programs, he interspersed shows with his regular cast in offbeat ideas, as well as utilized important guest stars, so that the audience never knew what they might be missing if they failed to see his program. And for his guests, he exchanged regularly with all the top stars in the business. As a result, Bob Hope, Danny Thomas, Lucille Ball, George Burns, and many others appeared with him time after time.

Another star with whom Jack exchanged guest shots was Bing Crosby, and it was on Bing that Jack pulled a much-quoted line. Bing's home in the San Fernando Valley, near his golf club, Lakeside, had burned down, and he moved to a home in Holmby Hills, adjoining the Los Angeles Country Club, one of the toniest in the city. Bing, however, used to drive over the mountain to play at his old club, Lakeside, until a member friend of his from the LA club suggested that he join there and proposed him for membership. At the time that club was not too kindly disposed toward actors, and it turned Bing down.

When Bing was a guest on our radio show, he told us all

the story about being turned down because he was an actor. Jack promptly asked him, "How would you like to be an actor *and* a Jew?"

But in their early years of television, Bing and Jack had a misunderstanding about a rerun of a Benny TV show on which Crosby was a guest. As a result, Jack, for many years, was annoyed with Bing, but never to the point of breaking their friendship. Jack once said to announcer Gene Wood, "I'm like Will Rogers. I never met a man I didn't like . . . well, Eichmann maybe."

38

SHORTLY after he started in television, Jack began winning Emmys for Best Comedian and Best Comedy Program, and before he was through, he and the program had won eight Emmys. He was also the recipient of the first trustees award of the Academy of Television Arts and Sciences in 1957, an award that read: "Jack Benny—For his significant contribution to the television industry as a showman. For the high standard for all to emulate, set by his personal skill and excellence as a performer. For the consistency, quality and good taste of his program through many years and many media."

Jack always gave much credit to his writers, and in his first six years in television, he extolled the praise of his director, Ralph Levy, sometimes going so far as to say he would quit television if he ever lost Ralph. But in 1957 Ralph took ill just before one of the *Shower of Stars* programs, and Ralph Nelson, who had won fame as a director of many *Studio One* programs, was hired by CBS to do the one show. Jack was extremely nervous without Ralph Levy, and poor Ralph Nelson, who had come in cold and didn't know all the likes and dislikes of CBS's comedy star, had Jack making entrances and exits that were different from what he had been doing. Finally, in exasperation, Jack yelled at him, "Dammit, we're not doing *Studio One* here!" There was an awkward hush in the entire rehearsal studio. Nelson, who became a top motion-picture director, didn't say a word for a minute and then called lunch. We managed to complete a fairly presentable show in spite of Jack's unhappiness with the director.

Ralph Levy returned to direct the next few half hour programs, but because of his health, he took a long leave of absence from the show and he never came back to our regular program.

The first show we did after that was another *Shower of Stars,* and we hired Red Skelton's director, Seymour Berns, to take Ralph Levy's place. Again Jack was a nervous wreck with a new director, and his fears were compounded when the night before the live telecast, our guest star, Nanette Fabray, was in an automobile accident and had to be replaced with Janis Paige. While Berns was trying to get Janis up on her performance in the few hours of rehearsal time they had, Jack was crying doom. Finally, Berns cornered him in his dressing room, and since he could be independent with his regular job with Red Skelton waiting for him, he said firmly to Jack, "Jack, you're a nervous old Jew, and you're making me one, too. Now relax and let's do a good show."

He waited for Jack to scream at him, but instead Jack thought it was very funny, and that changed the whole mood of the show. Jack told Berns, "I want you as my director," and then he rushed off to find me to sign him for our regular series.

When it came time to air the program, they hadn't yet rehearsed the "Mr. Wonderful" number, a song Jack had been doing with leading ladies for years on the stage. It involved the girl singing the love song to him while he reacted for comedy. Berns asked Jack if they should cut the number since he and Janis had never rehearsed it musically or on camera, but Jack told him just to photograph the two of them in a two-shot without any camera tricks, and Jack would react to make the spot work. He told the musical director to play the number straight and asked Janis to sing the song directly to him.

"I did just as Jack told me, and he did all his gag bits as Janis sang," Berns recalls. "And when the reviews came out, many of them said that the director was brilliant in the way he handled the 'Mr. Wonderful' number and made a great comedy performance out of a simple song number."

Seymour Berns directed the Benny series for two years

and did a fine job, but he was not so lucky on an Easter program we produced. On radio each Easter we usually did an Easter Parade show, with Jack walking down the street, singing the Irving Berlin song "Easter Parade" and stopping after each line as he ran into a member of his cast or some other character. We decided to tape a television version, a difficult task to do in a TV studio. We attempted it just before Jack was to leave for Japan and Hong Kong on a vacation trip with Mary. Seymour Berns came up with the idea of Jack and the cast walking in place with the scenery behind them moving, to simulate a picture of people walking down a street. I was against the whole idea. I felt that it wouldn't work and would look exactly like a man walking in place with the scenery moving, especially since Jack was terrible about all things mechanical or involving any synchronization with cameras and scenery. I argued that Jack couldn't even dial a phone while speaking his lines, but Berns persisted that he could make this work, and so I okayed the moving scenery idea.

We rehearsed the show, and it looked awful, but Berns insisted that it would be all right by showtime. When we taped the show, it still looked bad to me and to the writers, and after we finished Jack insisted on seeing the show run in the control room, even though he had to go home to pack for his trip. What he saw was a group of actors walking in place with the scenery moving behind them, and when it was over, he exploded with rage at all of us for allowing him to be made to look so foolish. In a final burst of anger, he yelled, "But *you* fellows are the ones stuck here to see the show two weeks from now when it goes on the air. Thank God I won't have to see it. . . . I'll be in Hong Kong!"

A sad experience that turned out well involved a guest appearance of Tallulah Bankhead. When she came to rehearsal and we sat around a table reading the script on the first day, she looked old and unattractive, quite different from the swinging woman called for in the script. To make matters worse, she questioned every line and every joke, and by the time we got through the reading, which took twice as long as usual, Jack was ready to drop her and try to replace her with another actress. But she had already been signed, and we all told him she'd be fine for the rest of the rehearsals. But she wasn't. She continued to question each sentence of dialogue, and on the third day of rehearsal two of the writers, Gordon and Goldman, met Jack as he rushed into the elevator.

"Where are you going?" Gordon asked.

"To the hospital," said Jack. "Then there'll be no problems with the show because they'll have to call it off and put another show on instead."

The boys told me about it, and I talked to Jack for a long time until he finally consented to go ahead with it. By the time Tallulah was made up, wigged, and dressed for the program, she looked smashing, and like a real professional, she was marvelous in every line. We ended up with one of our funniest programs, and I must give Jack the credit he deserved because he was the first one in Tallulah's dressing room to tell her how great she performed that evening.

About this time, 1958, Mary retired from show business, even though she hadn't been too active in television. The first few years in vaudeville, and the first year or two in radio, Mary was an amateur, and as such, she didn't seem to have a nervous bone in her body. But as the years went by, acting became a chore for her, and she would tighten up every time she had to perform in a radio show. Her performance on radio sounded so effortless and her laugh was so contagious no one could have dreamed that she was ready to faint every week. Finally, she became so upset that she refused to face the studio audience, but Jack devised a scheme to keep her on the show. Our script girl, Jeanette Eyman, would read Mary's part in front of the studio audience after Jack explained that Mary was at home with a cold. Then the engineers would go to the Benny home the next day, record Mary's lines, and edit them in place of the lines read by Jeanette, retaining the audience reactions.

When we started doing television, Mary wouldn't do the live shows and agreed to perform only in those on film, where there was no audience and where she felt little pressure since any mistakes could be reshot. Even though she did comparatively few films, each one was a problem for her, and then, when her friend Gracie Allen retired, that was all the incentive she needed to follow suit. Despite Jack's pleading, she insisted on retiring, and from then on she refused all our overtures except that she did do a short scene in the *Twentieth Anniversary Special.*

After fifteen years as sponsor of the Benny radio and television programs the American Tobacco Company decided to spread its money around in more one-minute TV spots and relinquished its sponsorship of our program. In two days the show was resold to State Farm Insurance Company. Shortly thereafter, Hilliard Marks left the program, and Seymour Berns was made producer-director, a position he held for two years until CBS felt that he couldn't do justice to the Red Skelton weekly program and direct the Benny show at the same time. He was replaced by Fred de Cordova, who had been directing feature films as well as television shows, his last being the George Gobel show. Fred became the producer-director of our show, and I became the executive producer.

We were still doing sixteen programs a year on an every-other-week basis, and at that time I started to work on Jack to do the show every week. Jack worried that it would be too much work at his age, but we decided on a plan to make his week very easy, and he finally agreed. We sold twenty-six weekly shows for the 1960–61 season which we started to shoot at Desilu Studios. We used the three-camera technique, a system that is almost like taping a live show and takes much less time for the performer than the regular one-camera film method.

In previous years we had usually produced only four or at the most five shows on film since Jack preferred live or tape shows in which he could do timely jokes and used the films only to give him breaks for vacations or personal appearances. But I realized that eventually we would want to sell our company, and films would be an asset. I told Jack I wanted to do twenty-two of our shows on film and only four on tape, but he objected strongly, as did the four writers. Obviously, it was easier to write the timely jokes for the live shows, and they argued, along with Jack, that without all the current and topical flavor, the show would lose some of its impact. I felt that there were too many comedy shows that were doing topical jokes, Bob Hope being a prime example, and we would simply have to be brighter and more inventive than the others and do shows that would be timely, not just at the moment, but year after year. Privately, I pointed out to Jack that doing it my way would mean quite a bit of money to him someday. He was finally persuaded, and we ended up producing twenty-three shows on film that year, twenty-two the next, and for the two years after that, we were signed for twenty-eight shows a year, of which twenty-six each year were done on film.

It proved a fortunate decision that we started to produce more and more films because when we ultimately sold our company, the backlog of films, plus those which were contracted for the future, gave us that many more salable assets.

39

JACK BENNY loved to fool around with his studio orchestra during rehearsals and made characters out of three of the musicians on his radio and television shows. Sammy Weiss, the drummer, and Wayne Songer, the sax and clarinet man, were so often the butts of his gags that the public came to know them well. Of Songer, who combed his hair straight up for the act they did, Jack used to remark, "Wayne looks like a guy who was pardoned ten seconds after they pulled the switch."

Frank Remley, the left-handed guitar player, became so famous on the Benny radio show that when Phil Harris started his own radio program with his wife, Alice Faye, the writers created the character of his sidekick Frankie Remley, and actor Elliot Lewis was cast in that role. Remley had the best laugh I've ever heard and was even a better audience than Jack. Jack loved to have him around because he made Jack and anyone else with any sense of humor feel like the greatest comedian in the world.

When Jack was young, he enjoyed taking long drives with a friend during his summer vacations, traveling through small towns, eating at diners along the way, and stopping at motels on the road. He often said it was his greatest pleasure and relaxation, and he would constantly be looking for a traveling buddy. Sometimes one of his writers or his brother-in-law would accompany him, and I made several trips with him and had fun each time. Jack always got a kick out of stopping at some small out-of-the-way diner in Oregon or Mississippi for lunch and then waiting with obvious pleasure as the people sitting nearby gradually realized as they stared and wondered if it could possibly be—then shake their heads—then, finally, tentatively come over and meekly ask if it really was he. Jack and I generally had the same argument when he suggested stopping at a café where the trucks were parked: he insisting that the truck drivers knew good food and I asking him why truck drivers were suddenly such gourmets.

The person Jack made the most number of summer driving trips with was Frank Remley, and the two would laugh from the time they started out until they returned. Once they decided to drive from California to New York City and return by way of Banff and Lake Louise in Canada. Jack picked up Remley at his home on the morning of their departure, and when they were ready to leave, Remley asked him if they should drive to New York first or go to Banff first and then on to New York. Jack answered, "Which way is the car facing, Rem?"

When Remley said it was facing north, Jack told him, "That does it. Let's go to Banff first because it's silly to turn the car around." That's all Remley needed to send him into a paroxysm of laughing, which put Jack in a great mood for the trip.

It was on one of their trips that Jack spotted a sign over a stand in a small town in Iowa. The sign read: MOM'S WORLD-FAMOUS APPLE PIE.

Jack ad-libbed an entire routine about all the people in Teheran and Paris talking about Mom's Apple Pie in Iowa near Sioux City. Remley became convulsed on the floor of the car while Jack continued about the apple pie. Jack brought that idea back to his writers, and they subsequently used it in one of his television monologues.

Although Jack could not send funny letters, at which he was extremely talented, to his writers or to me because he was self-conscious and insecure about his ability to be funny and was afraid we would analyze his humor, there were some people to whom he could write hilarious letters. Judy Garland was someone to whom he would write, often making up dirty lyrics to popular melodies which would send her into gales of laughter. But Frankie Remley was his favorite letter writee since Frank would scream at everything Jack did or said or wrote. Years ago he began sending Remley letters about some of Ripley's odd discoveries that he shared with the public by way of his famous "Believe It Or Not" articles. Jack would sometimes spend hours writing these letters, and through the years he wrote hundreds of them to Remley, some of which were truly brilliant comedy.

In the following letter he enclosed a Ripley item about a "Sally Eager, 1816–1905, of Harlan County, Kentucky, after losing her eyeglasses at the age of 90, could thread a needle without glasses for the remaining five years of her life."

DEAR REM:

When I first saw this Ripley item—about three months ago—I didn't give it much thought. But a few days later it began to bother me. I couldn't figure out one thing. . . . If this woman, Sally Eager, lost her eyeglasses at the age of ninety—and could still thread a needle for the remaining five years of her life—why did she need glasses in the first place?

Well anyway, one night I kept thinking about it. . . . I couldn't sleep, so I sent a letter to the public library in Harlan County, Kentucky, asking them to send me all the information they could about Sally Eager, who lived there between the years 1810 and 1905.

About a week later—or rather two weeks later—no—it was a week later—I received a letter from the secretary of this library, telling me that there was no Sally Eager living in Harlan County, Kentucky, at that time. There was a Sandy Eager, a Sarah Eager, a Saundra Eager, and a Tally Eager—but no Sally. So, I figured, Rem, that Ripley made a slight mistake, and I forgot about it.

About ten days later—or twelve days—I don't remember which—I got another letter from the Harlan County library telling me that even though there was no Sally Eager living there at that time, in checking the records further, they found out there was a Sally Burnbaum and a Sally Lipshitz—but there was no record of either one of these Sally's losing her eyeglasses. So I sent them back a letter thanking them for their information and hoped I hadn't put them to too much trouble.

Now, Rem, two more weeks went by (I had completely forgotten the incident) when I received another letter from the library telling me to disregard the first two letters, as in checking further, they discovered that there *was* a Sally Eager living in Harlan County, Kentucky. It seems that the Sally Burnbaum they mentioned in their letter two weeks ago married a fellow named Sam Eager and his wife, Sally, did lose her eyeglasses—but not at the age of ninety. When she lost her glasses—she was forty-nine years old—but could still thread a needle without them for the remaining forty-six years of her life. They also added that they were terribly sorry about the mistake they made in their previous letters.

So I had Bert answer their letter, thanking them again, and also telling them if I ever played a week in Harlan County, Kentucky, I would certainly visit the library. Now here's the payoff, Rem. . . . Last Saturday—or Friday rather—believe it or not—I got another letter from the secretary of this same library, telling me that they made one more mistake.

Sally Eager of Harlan County, Kentucky, did not lose her eyeglasses at the age of forty-nine. In fact, she didn't lose her glasses at all. What she actually lost was a hearing aid. She was nineteen years old at the time—but could still thread a needle for the rest of her life. She died at twenty-two.

Now how about that, Rem? This girl, Sally Eager, was killed crossing a railroad track. Even though she could see the train coming, she couldn't hear it.

Incidentally, she died with her glasses on.

Regards—

JACK

P.S. Bert Scott lost his glasses at the age of sixty-two—but that's another story.

J.

DEAR REM:

This is the kind of a "Ripley" that drives me nuts.

He says here—"The sea butterfly isn't a butterfly—it is a winged snail." Now, Rem, if a sea butterfly is a winged snail, why the hell isn't it called a "winged snail"? Doesn't that make sense? Here it is in black and white—"The sea butterfly isn't a butterfly." Well, if it isn't a butterfly, why call it a

206

butterfly? If it's a winged snail—for Christ sake—call it a winged snail.

That's like saying a left-handed guitar is not a guitar. It's a leg of lamb. Or . . . Sammy Weiss isn't a drummer—he's a pr——k. Now Ripley doesn't even know Sammy Weiss. He never met him in his life. So why would he call him a pr——k? Sammy Weiss is a drummer.

Now you and I and Songer know that he is a pr——k and even we could be wrong (although I doubt it). However, I don't think it is any of Ripley's business what Sammy is. Therefore, I repeat if a "sea butterfly is a winged snail" for God's sake call it that. And even though Sammy Weiss is a pr——k, he is still a drummer—and a damn good one.

Am I right or wrong?

JACK

DEAR REM:

I am enclosing an article by Elsie Hix which is not unlike Ripley.

It says here, quote "Mrs. D. R. Barrett and Mrs. L. R. Ballinger, sisters, both had baby daughters born at exactly 2:24 P.M. September 23, 1960—St. Vincent's Hospital, Los Angeles"—unquote.

Now there is certainly nothing unusual about this. It could happen to any two sisters. Mrs. Barrett and Mrs. Ballinger were probably married the same night—at exactly the same time. Naturally this being their wedding night, they both got to bed early. They were probably f——d at exactly the same time. So naturally their babies were *born* at exactly the same time. The fact that they had baby daughters is certainly not unusual and why shouldn't they go to St. Vincent's Hospital? Being sisters, they probably live in the same neighborhood.

I remember when Wayne Songer and Sammy Weiss both got the clap at exactly same time. What's so strange about that? The only odd thing about it is—Songer got it from a dame, and Sammy got it from Songer.

But again I say—this could happen to anybody. These are the kind of articles that drive me nuts.

All good wishes—JACK

In the following letter to Frank Remley, Jack enclosed a

207

Ripley that read: "This talisman, if worn for four weeks, is believed by the Chinese to have the power to assure promotion to a better job."

DEAR REM:

I happened to have a CHINESE TALISMAN and last year I made the mistake of giving it to Freddie De Cordova. He immediately got a better job with Screen Gems and left me flat. However, he returned the Chinese Talisman to me.

He was then fired by Screen Gems—so I gave him the Talisman again, thinking he would come back with me. Instead of that, he got a better job directing Bob Hope and he is still with him. So Freddie and his wife, Janet, can kiss my ass before they ever get this Talisman from me again.

Strangely enough, this Chinese Talisman doesn't always pay off. A long time ago I gave one to Sam Hearn, and he hasn't worked a day in five years.

I guess that's show business.

JACK

40

FRED DE CORDOVA and Jack Benny had been friends for a long time, but they became very close when Fred became the director for the Benny TV show. When Jack told him about some of the letters he had written to Frankie Remley, Fred asked Jack to send him copies, which Jack did for many years until Remley died in 1968. Then Jack started to send the letters to Fred, and Frank Sinatra asked to have the copies sent to him, which Jack proceeded to do very often.

An early letter he sent to Fred contained an item about a famous strong man: "Eugene Sandow, touring in vaudeville for four successive years, daily supported on his back his act's entire cast of twenty. He died in 1925 at the age of 58 while straining to lift an automobile out of a ditch."

DEAR FREDDIE:

Am sure you will remember this fellow in vaudeville. Now I happen to remember when he died in 1925 (BUT IT WAS NOT WHILE STRAINING TO LIFT AN AUTO OUT OF A DITCH).

He had no trouble at all getting the car out. He did it very easily. Then he decided to put the car with 4 people in it on his back with his entire cast of 20—making it 24 people and a car. He had no trouble with this either.

Then he added a gas station with 3 attendants—making it 27 people, a car, and a gas station with two pumps. This was a little bit tough for him, but it was a miraculous feat—and he did it every night to tremendous applause and a standing ovation.

But here, Freddie, was 'The Straw That Broke the Camel's Back.' On the last day of this particular engagement, he decided to put a cigarette machine in the gas station. This was too much for Mr. Sandow and he was crushed to the ground. However, in three weeks he was well enough to go back to his original act with just the entire cast of 20 on his back.

Strangely enough, while appearing in Winnipeg—during the month of November—he caught a bad cold (as he was only wearing a jockstrap) and he died of pneumonia.

This is the real story.

JACK

P.S. He was buried with the car, the gas station and the cigarette machine—but without the 27 people.

J.

With a Ripley that read: "The Turnstone of Hawaii is a bird that, in search of insects and worms, constantly turns over little stones," Jack wrote the following letter:

DEAR FREDDIE:

The reason I am sending *you* this letter is because I am so ashamed of myself that I wouldn't want Janet to read it.

This is the most embarrassing thing that has ever happened to me—or let me say—one of the most embarrassing things.

209

As you know, Freddie, I go to Honolulu quite often and I had always heard about a bird that exists in Hawaii that was constantly turning over little stones in search of insects and worms—but I never knew the name of it. So a few months ago—when I was playing in Honolulu—I asked quite a few people (some who have been living there all their lives) the name of the bird that constantly turns over little stones.

Strangely enough, not one person was able to tell me the name of the bird. I even went into bird shops and pet shops—including the Chamber of Commerce—but no one seemed to know. I couldn't even find it in the library. I even called the Bird Watchers Association—but to no avail. However, they *did* know about a bird that in search of insects and worms constantly turns over little stones.

Now here is the part that makes me feel like a shmuck. About two weeks ago I was doing some work in the office with Bert Scott. And out of the clear sky I happened to ask him if he knew anything about birds, and he said he did. So I said to him, "Bert, there is a bird in Hawaii that constantly turns over little stones in search of insects and worms. Do you happen to know the name of it?" And Bert said, "Well, I'm not positive—but I imagine it's called THE TURN-STONE." Then I asked him why. And he said, "Because it turns over little stones."

Well, Freddie, I got so goddamn mad that I just looked at Bert for about a half minute, and then I said, "You know, Bert, I think you are a fu——g idiot. Just because a bird keeps turning over little stones doesn't really mean that TURNSTONE is its name. You ought to have your head examined." So Bert said, "Well, look, Jack, there's no sense in getting angry about it and anyway it can't be that important. I still think the name of the bird is TURNSTONE."

By this time I was so infuriated I said, "F——k you, Bert, we'll finish our work tomorrow." And I walked out of the office. As I was leaving, Bert said, "Jack, for heaven's sake, there's no use getting upset about it." And I yelled, "OH, SHUT UP"—and I left.

Now, Freddie, you can imagine my embarrassment when I picked up last Sunday's *Herald-Examiner* and found the enclosed Ripley. I was ashamed to go to the office Monday for

210

fear that Bert had also seen the Ripley item. But then I
thought I might as well face him—apologize and get it over
with. At first I was going to fire him—but then I thought that
would be ridiculous.

Anyway, when I walked into the office, I said, "Hello,
Bert, how are you?" And Bert said, "Fine." Then I said,
"How's Ann?" And he said, "She's fine, thank you." Then I
waited about five minutes and I said, "Bert, I want to apologize for all the things I said to you the other day because you
were right. The name of that bird in Hawaii *is* TURN-
STONE. I'm sorry I was so insulting." And Bert said,
"That's all right, Jack—it's over with, but next time don't get
so goddamn irritable. Find out first whether I'm right or
wrong before you call me a f——g idiot." So I said, "I told
you I was sorry, Bert, and that's all I can say. Forgive me."
And Bert said, "Okay, let's drop it—but watch it next time."
Then he walked out of the office, and I didn't see him until
the next day. Believe me—that was some experience.

Love,
Jack

P.S. I just gave Bert a raise.

J.

In another letter he enclosed a column by Hank Grant
from the Hollywood *Reporter* and marked off an item in that
column that had the following information: "Wanna bet
Sammy Davis Jr. won't be renewing his warbling pact with
the Reprise label that ran out last month. Sammy has a better
deal with Motown prez Berry Gordy."

Dear Freddie:

If I told Hank Grant *once,* I told him a dozen times, I *don't
wanna bet him!* I spoke to Sammy Davis myself and asked him
if he was going to renew his warbling pact with the "Reprise"
label—and he told me he didn't know, so *why* would I take a
gamble like that? And another thing—Sammy told me he
was very happy with "Reprise Label." Well, for Christ's sake,
Freddie, Hank Grant could lose a bloody fortune making
bets like that. Evidently he thinks he's going to keep his job
forever!

If Sammy Davis wants to leave "Reprise Label" and go with Motown prez Berry Gordy—that's up to him—but I'll be goddamned if I'm going to bet on it. And believe me I've got more money than Hank Grant has!!

JACK

Another Ripley item said: "In 1820 President James Monroe ran for reelection without an opponent." The following note was sent to Freddie with that Ripley attached:

DEAR FREDDIE:
Even though President James Monroe had *no* opposition, the Chicago *Tribune* had a big headline saying that he lost.
They found out their mistake the next morning.

Love,
JACK

One day Freddie received a Ripley about "the Green Guy—of Bramshill, England, Henry Cope, 1714–1806, always dressed entirely in green, lived in a green house with green furniture, always rode in a green carriage and ate only green fruit and vegetables."

DEAR FREDDIE AND JANET:
Every now and then Ripley has a true item in his "BE-LIEVE IT OR NOT."
Now I went to the library (the one I usually go to for research) and found out that Henry Cope of Bramshill, England, was actually known as the GREEN GUY and as per the enclosed picture, he was always dressed in green—lived in a green house—with green furniture—always rode in a green carriage and ate only green fruit and vegetables. Unfortunately, he only lived to be 92 years of age.
I also discovered that there was a man in Auckland, New Zealand, by the name of Samuel Copeland who was known as THE YELLOW GUY. He always dressed in yellow—lived in a yellow house—with yellow furniture and ate only wax beans—summer squash—kumquats and bananas. He lived to be 47.
There was also a man in Windsor, Ontario, by the name of

212

Gregory Pecker who was known as the RED GUY, who always dressed in red—lived in a red house—with red furniture and always ate red beets—rare meats—radishes and tomatoes. He lived to be 51.

There was also a man by the name of Peter Fuch who lived in Perth, Australia, who was known as the BROWN GUY. He always dressed in brown—lived in a brown house—with brown furniture and ate nothing but chocolate—A-1 sauce and shit. He lived to be 17.

Love,
JACK

Ripley claimed that "at the age of 30 or so, a person shrinks in height."

DEAR JANET AND FREDDIE:

This Ripley is definitely true.

When Willie Shoemaker was 30 years old, little did he dream that he would ever be a jockey. He was six feet three inches at the time.

Of course, there's always an exception to the rule. When Jim Arness was 30, he was five feet one inch. So you see, you never can tell.

Love,
JACK

P.S. Mervyn Le Roy and Irving Lazar remained the same from birth.

J.

A Ripley "Crocodiles cry when they eat" elicited the following hilarious letter:

DEAR FREDDIE:

This is probably one of the silliest Ripleys that I have ever seen. The reason it's silly is because we all know it's true. He didn't have to give us this information.

Naturally crocodiles cry when they eat. So would you, Freddie, and so would Irving Lazar and Ronald Reagan if all you had to eat day after day was a lot of crap that they find in the water—or dead fish—or when they crawl up on the bank of the river and find a lot of leftovers . . . maybe by people who were on a picnic—or kids who have been eating a lot of hot dogs.

Let me tell you something, Freddie—and you know this as well as I do—you give a crocodile a nice piece of smoked salmon and a steak—or a lamb chop and a nice green salad—with any kind of dressing—except maybe Roquefort, (I understand crocodiles don't care for Roquefort). . . . Then maybe a nice dessert of maybe ice cream or pie or anything—I assure you a crocodile won't cry. . . . He would be very happy.

Have you ever seen a crocodile in Chasen's—or the Bistro—or Dominic's? You're goddamn right you haven't. That's my answer to Mr. Ripley!

Love,
JACK

P.S. No wonder they eat people.

J.

Another letter-provoking Ripley was: "Spiders and scorpions are not insects. They belong to another class of animals called Arachnids."

DEAR FREDDIE:

Once again I got into a big argument with Bert Scott, and as usual, I put myself in a most embarrassing position.

Several weeks ago Bert came into the office a little bit late and he had a Band-Aid on his forehead and I said to him, "What's the matter, Bert? What happened to your forehead?" And Bert said, "Oh, it doesn't amount to anything. I was home cleaning out the basement and I was bitten by an Arachnid." So I said, "Bert, what are you talking about?" And he said, "You asked me what happened to my forehead, and I told you I was bitten by an Arachnid." So I said, "Bert, for Christ sake, what the hell is an Arachnid?" And Bert said, "It's a spider. I was bitten by a spider. It's as simple as that."

Well, anyway, Freddie—you know my temper. I got mad as hell and I said, "Bert, what is all this shit about an Arachnid? If you were bitten by a spider, why the hell didn't you say so in the first place? You could have said—spider or insect—instead of that f——g word that you made up.

So Bert said, "Look, Jack, there's no use getting angry about it. In the first place, I have news for you. A spider is not an insect. It doesn't belong to the insect family at all. A spider is an Arachnid—and I'm surprised you didn't know it."

So I said, "Bert, you want to know something? You really give me a pain in the ass." And I walked out of the office and for about two days I couldn't even look at him.

Well, Freddie, wouldn't you know that yesterday I saw the enclosed item and I was so embarrassed that again (and as you know it has happened before) I had to walk into Bert's office and not only apologize—but I didn't know how to make up for my stupidity—so I gave him a raise in salary. And although he wasn't smiling—he thanked me.

Love,
Jack

P.S. Now get a load of this. This morning Bert walked into my office and with a smug look on his face said, "Jack, did you know that a scorpion is also an Arachnid?" And I said, "No, Bert—and I don't give a shit and it's the last raise you are going to get out of me."

J.

A Ripley that inspired Jack to compose another funny epistle was: "The Iron Man! Alexander Zass, a Polish strong man known as 'The Amazing Samson,' permitted himself to be run over by an automobile carrying 12 passengers."

Dear Freddie:
I keep going to a new library now in Westwood as it is closer to my home. I looked up this particular Ripley item and found out that it was absolutely true.

This man "The Amazing Samson" did permit himself to be run over by an automobile carrying twelve passengers. However, what Ripley fails to tell you is that immediately after this wonderful stunt, "The Amazing Samson" died. In fact, he lived just long enough to say, "Ouch."

The funeral was held the next day and was attended by eleven of the passengers in the car. His widow wouldn't attend because she was the twelfth passenger and was too grieved about it.

Love to you and Janet.

JACK

"A one-penny stamp issued by British Guiana in 1856 is now worth over $250,000." That Ripley caused the following message:

DEAR FREDDIE AND JANET:

This is the goddamnedest thing that ever happened to me.

About fifteen years ago Mary and I happened to be in British Guiana and somebody gave me one of their 1856 one-penny stamps. I thought it would be a nice souvenir, so I brought it home with me.

About three months ago I happened to be cleaning out my desk in my office and I found the one-penny British Guiana stamp. I had no particular use for it—so I gave it to Bert Scott.

Now I find out that f——g stamp is worth $250,000.00.

Naturally I was ashamed to ask Bert to give it back. But you know he is a helluva swell guy and he is going to split the money with me. We will each have $125,000.00.

I thought that was a very sweet gesture on his part.

Love,
JACK

P.S. Bert is also giving $10,000.00 to Mary.

J.

A Ripley item read: "A house in Masitisi, Basutoland, So. Africa, built inside a cave," and inspired Jack to further exposition:

DEAR FREDDIE:

This letter is not meant to be particularly funny, but it has something to do with some of my trips that I believe I have spoken to you about.

216

Many times you have heard me speak of South Africa and how I would like to visit there, or maybe work there for a season, or actually live there for a while. But for Christ's sake, Freddie, if I moved to South Africa it would certainly have to be a city like Johannesburg, Cape Town or Durban . . . not a f——g town like Masitisi, Basutoland. I've been there and I know what it's like—ask Larry Adler.

Another thing, Freddie, you know I like to work and there are certainly enough cities in South Africa that I could, but Jesus Christ, Freddie, there can't be over one or two agents in Masitisi and they must be up to their ass trying to take care of their other clients without looking for more.

I know one thing . . . Irving and Marion wouldn't go with me, no matter what I paid him!

Now, Freddie, let us assume that you and Janet and Mary and I wouldn't mind spending one year in Masitisi, Basutoland—just for a change—and let us further assume that we met and became close friends of couples with personalities like Billy and Audrey Wilder and Irving and Mary Lazar. Do you realize how far we would be living from each other? It's not like driving to the beach, you know, and I doubt that the Deutsches would join us.

And imagine, Freddie, just imagine trying to find a movie in Masitisi that you could run in your own home, even an old one. I know what I'm talking about—I've been there—ask Larry Adler.

So this Ripley has to put a picture of a home in Masitisi, Basutoland, built inside a cave yet. Now, Freddie, I would like to know one thing . . . just one f——g thing . . . why Ripley would bother showing us a house in a cave in Masitisi, Basutoland. *WHY!!!* Here's a town with a very small population, maybe four or five picture shows . . . not one massage parlor . . . they don't even know what a massage parlor is, for God's sake. I know, Freddie . . . I've been there—ask Larry Adler.

I'll tell you one thing, Freddie, if Mary and I ever go to South Africa and she wants to visit Masitisi, Basutoland, she'll have to make it on her own—*I'LL STAY IN CAPE TOWN.*

Incidentally, I forgot to mention that Mary and I were

217

sorry you and Johnny didn't win the Emmy. I was so Goddamn mad that when I went to bed that night, I wanted to
throw one of my Emmys out the window . . . but then I
wondered if you or Johnny Carson would ever do that for
me . . . so I thought, "f——k it, I'll keep all of mine."

Love to you both,

JACK

41

PRODUCING a weekly television program was almost easier
than doing the every-other-week show because when we
were on alternate weeks, each show took on such an air of
importance we felt we had to do something special. But as a
weekly program we were just one of many and didn't have to
try as hard. Jack always said, "I never try to top the program
I had last. I just try not to have a bad show."

Fred De Cordova and I had the weekly program running
so smoothly that Jack found himself working less and less.
We used his stand-in, Ned Miller, more and more, and we
finally figured out that Jack was only working about eight
hours a week as a performer and very little on the script since
the writers had been with him so long they knew exactly what
he wanted.

We continued to use fresh guest stars whenever possible.
Ann-Margret was then an unknown working in an act in Las
Vegas with George Burns when we saw her and hired her for
her TV debut on our show for $500. When Robert Goulet
made an impact after his role in *Camelot,* followed by big selling records, he appeared in one of our TV films before he
did any other guest spots. When Carol Burnett left the Garry
Moore show, she turned down all invitations to guest on
shows until we came up with the idea of her playing Jane to
Jack's Tarzan, which resulted in a marvelously funny program.

As I said before, we always tried to open a new season with

an unusual guest star, someone who might be a very important person but not necessarily on TV or in films. One year I read with great interest that Billy Graham was drawing 80,000 people a night to crusades in the Los Angeles Coliseum. I told Jack that I would like to make a pitch at the good reverend to be a guest star, and Jack thought I had lost my mind.

"You're crazy. What chance do you think you'd have of getting him on the show? Don't embarrass yourself by asking," was his opinion.

"I'm going to try," I said. "The worst he can say is no. We learned that with Truman, didn't we?"

"But this is different," argued Jack. "And you can kiss my ass."

The "kiss my ass" phrase was Jack's mark of affection, and he'd use it all the time to people he liked. When he would leave a room full of good friends, often he would turn with a parting comment: "I've got one more thing to say: kiss my ass."

In any event, I reached Billy Graham's manager and explained that I thought Graham would do well to appear on our opening program, which would be done with humor but in good taste, and I offered him a chance to do a two-minute inspirational message at the end of the show. Graham's manager told me to write a letter outlining all that and told me how to address it so that the reverend would be sure to see it.

A few days later my phone rang, and it was Graham himself, telling me he would be delighted to appear for us. When I told Jack, he was dumbfounded but elated. We brought the writers in to get out the script as quickly as possible so that we could have it approved by Graham before he changed his mind.

I arranged a luncheon with Graham at the Bel Air Hotel, where he was staying. Jack and I first went to his suite to go over the script with him. He loved every joke in it and approved it without a single change. As we left his suite for the dining room, he glanced up toward the darkening sky and asked, "Do you think it's going to rain?"

I looked skyward and then at him. *"You're* asking *us?"* I asked.

Graham was the first to laugh, but Jack joined in with one

of his thigh-slapping roars that was good for five minutes.

Fred De Cordova was getting along so famously with Jack that Jack was giving him the "kiss my ass" line all the time. The first Christmas of our weekly shows, he sent Fred a barrelful of liquor with a brass plaque on it that read: "Kiss my ass—Jack". A few days later Fred was visiting at the Benny home and Jack was moaning to him about a $600 vicuña coat he had had made in Hong Kong which was too large for him. When Fred noted that he was bigger than Jack and the coat might fit him, Jack brought it out and said to his director, "If it fits, you can have it."

Ten years later Fred was wearing the coat in New York, and Jack admired it, not remembering that it was once his.

"If it fits, you can have it," Fred told him.

Jack thought the words were familiar, and when he realized the switch, he really fell down howling.

Although Jack was usually very considerate of his audience, his cast, and his staff, he had his first argument with Fred on the set in front of all of us, including the audience. We were filming a scene between Jack and a hotel clerk, and Jack blew a line. Instead of stopping and retaking the scene, he kept talking, trying to ad-lib his way out of the mistake, but Fred yelled, "Cut."

"Why did you cut the scene?" asked Jack.

"I didn't think you could work your way out of the mistake," answered Fred.

Jack then turned to the audience and asked them if they noticed anything wrong with the way he had handled the lines, and they applauded approval for him. Jack then snapped at Fred, "From now on you will cut a scene when I tell you to cut."

"Usually we had a meeting of the staff after each show," Fred remembers, "but this time I went directly home after the last take. By the time I got home, Jack had already called and left a message for me to phone him, but I didn't. Soon thereafter an enormous bouquet of flowers arrived for my mother with a note that read: 'Please tell your son not to be angry with an old Jew.'"

George Burns had sold his company, and in 1961 we started to get nibbles from various sources about selling our company, too. Jack and Mary felt that it was the right time to sell because our program was doing very well in the ratings, we were contracted for a few more years, and our interest in *Checkmate* had a value, too. Our agency, MCA, had been producing television programs for many years, had just bought Universal Studios, and was looking for acquisitions. They began to negotiate with me to buy our company themselves, and after prolonged meetings with their president, Lew Wasserman, and Taft Schreiber, we concluded a deal whereby they purchased all the stock of J and M Productions for 45,000 shares of MCA stock, which, at that time, was worth about $3,000,000. Jack and I had contracts with J and M which had four more years to go so that even though we were only salaried employees for the next four years, we continued to produce the Benny shows in the same manner as we had before the deal was made.

Now that we were in the MCA family, they built a sound stage for us on the Universal lot that was designed to film the three-camera technique, and when it was completed, we moved over from Desilu to the Benny stage, as it was named. The shows continued at top quality, with everyone concerned enjoying the weekly filming schedule. Jack was a joy to work with, compared to.many of the stars who controlled their own shows. However, occasionally he would become depressed about something, and then there was gloom on the set. As he got older, of course he hated to look old, and he tried to stay away from any characterizations that would age him. But sometimes he would jump with excitement at an idea and urge us to do the show, but after he would see his makeup and wardrobe, usually too late to make a change, he would be depressed, not tell anyone why, and then pick on every little thing at rehearsal.

One of our sad days happened when we were doing a satire about the composer Stephen Foster with singer Connie Francis as Mrs. Foster. On the day of the show Jack told me and the entire staff how much he hated the show, nearly refusing to rehearse. The idea was a funny one with Jack as Foster trying to write a song while his wife was sewing and talking about her home: "Way down upon the Swanee River, far, far away."

"Shut up, will you," yells Foster. "Can't you see I'm trying to write a song?"

221

"That's where my heart is yearning ever, that's where the old folks stay."

"How do you expect me to ever get this song done if you keep yapping all the time?" says Foster.

That's the way the sketch went, and it was good, but Jack groused all through the day and threatened to cancel the show because it was so bad. Then he said he'd do it if we would ban the audience, but I told him that the ticket holders were already starting to line up and it would not be nice to cancel them at that late hour. We finally persuaded him to go through with the show, and although he didn't give his usual sparkling performance, the audience howled, and it turned out to be one of our better programs. He eventually admitted how good it was, but not until much later.

One summer we filmed a show with Mickey Rooney as guest in a satire of a modern prison. Jack felt that he didn't look good as a prisoner, but he wouldn't tell us that was the reason he was so unhappy with the show. He complained that he despised it and wanted it destroyed, but I wouldn't allow that and insisted that we could not afford to throw $70,000 down the drain. I also indicated that it was the opinion of the staff that the show was satisfactory. Finally, I persuaded him to let it go on as the last program of the season when the audience would be the smallest, and he agreed. After holding the program for eight months, we played it on the air, and Jack received so many calls telling him how good it was that he called to tell me he had been absolutely wrong and in looking at it again he realized what a good show it was.

The kind of program he loved was one we did with Dinah Shore as a guest. The closing sketch was introduced by Jack, who explained to the audience that he was going to show them how the Benny show would look twenty-five years in the future. The curtain went up to reveal Rochester in a gray wig, all bent over, hobbling on a cane to answer the doorbell. Don Wilson enters as a very old man, followed by Dennis Day looking about ninety years old. Then Dinah Shore makes her entrance with white hair and a granny shawl around stooped shoulders. The elderly group is now ready for rehearsal, and so Rochester calls up a stairway in the quavering voice of an old man to Jack, who answers, "Coming, coming!"

Jack comes bounding down the stairs, looking exactly as he

had in the first part of the program, the only one on the stage who hadn't aged a day.

Soon after Johnny Carson took over the *Tonight Show,* we had him fly out from New York to guest on our show. Jack was always impressed with the *Tonight* host, envying anyone who could handle a program nightly without a script except for his opening monologue. We also had Jack Paar on our show when he was at his height as host of the *Tonight Show,* and he and Jack became very good friends. As a matter of fact, when Paar and Ed Sullivan had their feud that erupted widely in the newspapers, Jack was instrumental in having them make up when he was a guest on the *Tonight Show.* He bawled Paar out for being childish, and speaking right into the camera, he told Ed Sullivan that he too was ridiculous.

"We want you both to make up and call off this silly feud," commanded Jack, and shortly after Paar and Sullivan reconciled their differences.

Impersonators often called Johnny Carson in New York, pretending to be Jimmy Stewart or Jimmy Cagney, and on Johnny's very first visit to the coast, Jack Benny called him at the Beverly Hills Hotel and told him, "Listen, Johnny, if you need me or if someone falls out on you at the last minute, call me, and I'll be happy to appear on your show."

Johnny was so certain that it was an impersonator, he coldly thanked him and hung up. Jack came into my office later that day and told me that he had called Carson, but Carson had been very unfriendly to him. I called Fred De Cordova, who by that time was producing the *Tonight Show* and asked him if Johnny was angry with Jack for any reason, and I told him about the phone call. He spoke to Johnny about it, and Johnny, who had always liked Jack and admired him, promptly phoned and invited him to be on the show the next night, explaining about his mistaken impression.

Talking about Jack, Johnny told me about one time that Jack appeared on his show in New York.

"We decided to go out to dinner together after the program," Johnny related, "and after debating for a while about which restaurant to go to, I suggested we go to my apartment for whatever I could find there and then we'd be able to watch the replay of the show. I had a typical bachelor apartment that had nothing in the fridge but a couple of seventy-nine-cent frozen spaghetti dinners. I was really ashamed to serve it to Jack, but while we had a drink, I put them in the oven to heat. Jack ate everything on his plate with relish, and when he finished, he announced, 'That was the greatest spaghetti I've ever eaten in my whole life.' For the first time I realized that all those George Burns stories were true!"

Dave Tebet, vice-president in charge of talent for NBC, repeatedly offered Jack the guest host spot on the *Tonight Show.*

"After urging him for a long, long time," says Tebet, "Jack finally confessed to me why he wouldn't ever host the show. He admitted he was scared. And you know who else told me the same thing? Bob Hope!"

42

WHEN he started television, even though it was much closer to the stage than to radio, Jack still missed the excitement of the theater and the live audiences. He used to say jokingly, "I miss the smell of greasepaint." Any time he had the opportunity he tried to make theater appearances between his radio and television activities. In the 1950's Las Vegas showrooms were beginning to attract the major stars, and though he had many offers, Jack consistently turned them all down, feeling that an appearance in a gambling hotel wasn't quite right for his image. However, when Maurice Chevalier played Las Vegas and then Noel Coward did a show there, Jack decided he shouldn't refuse any longer. As soon as he gave us the green light, he was booked into the Flamingo Hotel in 1957 for the record sum of $50,000 a week.

For that engagement he hired the dance team of Chiquita and Johnson, his hillbilly act consisting of five of his musicians and himself, and as guest star, Gisele Mackenzie. In addition to being a fine singer and pianist, Gisele was an excellent violinist, much better than Jack, and they worked up a double violin number to "Getting to Know You" in which Gisele outplayed Jack with extra cadenzas all through the number. Jack wrote a couplet which Gisele recited on a break in the middle of the second chorus:

> Roses are red, violets are blue,
> I'm beginning to sound like you.

On the next break, Jack recited in answer:

> Roses are red, carnations are white,
> You are fired as of tonight!

The violin number was one of the highlights of that show, which broke all records for the Flamingo. The hotel wanted Jack to return the following year, but in the meantime, Gisele's career had blossomed, and she wanted $12,500 a week for the three-week engagement, $5,000 more per week than the first year. Jack wanted her so badly that he agreed to her terms after the Flamingo increased its offer to $52,500 a week.

Jack Carter with his machine-gun style of joke telling followed the Benny Las Vegas engagement one year. We stayed over to see his act, and after the opening night show when we went backstage to Carter's dressing room, Benny said to him, "Jack, you've done more jokes in forty-five minutes than I've told in the last ten years!"

After Las Vegas we booked some small jobs that didn't pay Las Vegas prices, and we couldn't afford to hire Gisele. Instead, we used lesser known and, thus, less expensive girl singers, and even though our show was generally successful, Jack constantly bemoaned the fact that he was losing a great double-fiddle number. One day I suggested we find a little amateur girl violinist of about ten or twelve years old and do the act with her. I told Jack that we could have the child come out of the audience to ask for an autograph and work into the violin number from there. I put out a call for such a little girl to violin schools and teachers, and in a short time we interviewed several and chose an eleven-year-old girl named Toni Marcus. When Jack heard her, he fell for her and hired her immediately. Gisele wrote out the music for the counter-melody that she had played with Jack, and while Toni rehearsed it, Jack and the writers prepared some new jokes appropriate for him to do with a child.

That act proved to be a showstopper. Toni came out of the audience while Jack was playing "Rondo Capricioso," and she asked for his autograph. He handed her his fiddle while he signed her piece of paper, and she picked up the fiddle and played the "Rondo" even better than he. He then asked her to play a duet with him, but before the number they did some jokes. He asked her how long she had been playing, and when she answered, "three years," he asked if she played as he did. She answered, "I used to." After a few more lines in that vein, they dueted "Getting to Know You," Toni much more brilliant on the instrument than Jack. It was always the biggest hit of any show he ever did, never failing to receive bravos and standing ovations.

In the summer of 1962 we played three weeks at the Las Vegas Desert Inn with Jane Morgan as our guest singer, the Half Brothers, a superior juggling act, and little Toni Marcus. Jack used all his best bits in this show, and one of the biggest laugh getters, which he never missed doing in his stage shows, was a moment when he told the audience that he had had many requests to play the violin and, with their permission, would like to play a special number that night. The audience always applauded approval. Jack then looked off toward the wings and asked, "May I have my violin, please?"

From behind the side curtain, a violin flew through the air and landed with the sound of splintering wood at his feet. A moment later the bow came sailing out. This was such a shock to the audience that after a beat they'd roar with laughter and invariably burst into applause. We bought inexpensive secondhand fiddles and bows for this stunt for $10 or $15 each and through the years we purchased hundreds and hundreds of them since they used to break after a few throws.

Everyone was so enthusiastic about that show that Jack decided to take it to Broadway. Except for one week at the Roxy, Jack had not been seen by a New York audience since appearing in *Earl Carroll's Vanities* in 1931. He had talked about showing off for his friends in New York for years and couldn't wait to open and to see the New York rave reviews. He arranged to have lunch with Taft Schreiber as soon as we returned to Beverly Hills to get his opinion, and Taft remembers that when they met, Jack was laughing about something and showed him a page torn off from his date pad which had names written on it to phone. Jack had written: "Eisenhower–Kennedy–Taft."

Taft thought the idea a good one and suggested that we join up with the Theatre Guild to present Jack which would be rather impressive for a comedy revue. I made arrangements with the Theatre Guild, and we then met with Billy Rose, who owned the Ziegfeld Theater, to make the rental agreement for the theater for six weeks beginning the latter part of February, 1963. We signed the Clara Ward Singers to round out the show and booked two weeks at the O'Keefe Center in Toronto, Canada, to break in our show—just like a regular Broadway production.

Our first mail-order ad was breaking early in January, and just before the Sunday it was scheduled to run, there was a newspaper strike in New York City and all seven papers ceased publishing. It was predicted that the strike would last a short time, so at first we didn't worry about business. But when it continued, we placed ads in the papers in Newark, Jersey City, Brooklyn, and Long Island and in the *Wall Street Journal* and implemented them with one-sheet posters and heralds around New York City.

We went to Toronto via New York to do some radio and TV interviews to plug the engagement, and at the same time we saw a performance by Maurice Chevalier who was doing a one-man show preceding us at the Ziegfeld Theater.

Our opening in Toronto went very well, and Jack invited Billy Rose to fly up and see it since he thought Billy might have some helpful suggestions. After Billy saw the show, he, Jack, and I went back to Jack's suite at our hotel to hear Billy's comments. Billy, a shrewd man when it came to finances, had only one suggestion: "That blue curtain you're using behind the jugglers is all wrong. Now I have a beautiful black curtain that I used in *Seven Deadly Sins*, and I'll let you have that real cheap. It'll help the act."

"I'm surprised at you, Billy," I interrupted. "In the first place, the blue curtain is bright and sparkling and is perfect for the act. And in any event, the black curtain is the one you've rented to Chevalier, the only one he uses in his show, and wouldn't that look awful if we followed two days later with a new show and the same old curtain?"

"Oh, I forgot you saw the Chevalier show," was Billy's only comment, and he dropped that suggestion then and there.

"Is there anything else?" Jack asked.

Billy looked at him for a moment, as if in deep thought, and then said, "Yes, Jack. Your ticket sales are terrible. The show's a bomb, we've only sold a few seats, and you're opening in a week and a half."

Jack turned white.

"What can we do?" he asked in a terror-stricken voice.

"I'm a rich man," Billy said, "and you're a rich man, Jack. At this stage of the game, money is unimportant. What's important is to be successful in what we do, isn't that right?"

"Of course," Jack answered. "But how can we sell the tickets?" Jack asked, imagining headlines like BENNY BOMBS in *Variety.*

"I'll tell you what we should do. Let's spend whatever it takes to make this show a box-office success. Let's spend whatever it takes for a big radio spot campaign, over and beyond our regular budget, and I'll tell you what I'm willing to do. I'll split with you fifty-fifty, anything we spend over the twelve thousand five hundred we allocated for advertising."

Jack looked at me imploringly, and as I quickly agreed, Jack relaxed for the first time that evening.

We did two benefit previews in New York and opened the show at a dazzling premiere with a theaterful of stars and social figures and all the theatrical critics, even though the newspaper strike was still on. The show went without a hitch and ended with standing ovations and bravos.

At the party after the show in the private room at Sardi's restaurant, Jack delighted in the effusive praises from everyone, and we were certain we had a hit. When the reviews were phoned in, however, there were a few raves, a few good ones, and a few raps about the old jokes, but all lauded Jack for his performance. For the rest of his life Jack bemoaned the fact that there had been no newspapers for the readers to see the notices for themselves. He repeatedly complained, "Seven rave reviews. Can you imagine—seven great reviews, and I had to be there during a newspaper strike so that no one could ever read them."

The first week we played in New York we were loaded with theater parties, so business was fairly good. Jack reveled in the acclaim from friends and fans who came backstage after the performances to visit in his dressing room. He loved to sit there in his dressing gown and receive people, rehashing with everyone the various bits and gags in the show. When everyone had gone and it was time to take off his makeup, dress, and go home or out for a little supper, he very reluctantly left the theater and the "smell of greasepaint."

On some nights, when he would be advised that good friends or celebrities were in the audience, he would wait expectantly for them to come back after the show. There seems to be no business like show business in which compliments from peers is so important. Other nights not a soul would come, and he would wait for the longest time before he'd start to dress, sadly wondering why that particular friend didn't come back to see him. In almost every case the friend who failed to visit backstage was a considerate person who felt he'd be intruding in a dressing room full of people. But Jack would usually have gloomy thoughts and worry that perhaps his friends didn't like the show and didn't want to have to tell him how they felt.

Although Mary seldom traveled with Jack on business trips, she would sometimes accompany him to New York or London if he went for any length of time and usually to Las Vegas because she enjoyed gambling. Mary was a very important part of his life, and her involvement with show business did not stop when she retired; but even though her interest was there, she was not, choosing more often to stay at home than to go with Jack. In spite of making it very lonely for Jack, he constantly defended her right to stay at home, explaining that since she liked to bring her personal maid and sometimes her hairdresser and more than enough clothes for every possible occasion, it was too much of a hassle for her to go to all that trouble for short trips. In the old days when we traveled by train, Mary's maid would bring her own fine sheets and pillowcases in order to make her train berth as comfortable as possible.

Another advantage for the Bennys of being in New York was that their friend psychiatrist Sam Ehre spent a great deal of time with them, although not as a psychiatrist, but was always available for a flu shot or a vitamin B12 shot and would take care of them if they took ill. When Mary and the maid were along, the maid did Jack's shirts, but when Jack was alone, there was always a problem about laundering the shirts to his satisfaction. As Jo Ehre tells it: "No laundry in New York did his dress shirts to suit him. Too starchy, they bothered the violin playing—too soft, they wilted. So regularly Sam took Jack's shirts home in his medical bag, and our maid, Louise, did them perfectly. Thereafter, Jack used to introduce Sam as 'my New York doctor. I don't know how good a doctor he is, but he does great laundry.'"

By the second week of our six-week engagement, business started to be very slow, as the newspaper strike continued, but we felt that the excellent word of mouth would get around and soon we would be turning them away at the box office. By the third week it was awful; a sea of empty seats faced Jack at every performance. In the theater of almost 1,700 seats, sometimes we would only have 500 sold for an evening performance and 250 for a Wednesday matinee. In order to make the house look good so that we could get an enthusiastic performance from Jack, I would distribute hundreds of complimentary tickets for every performance to everyone and anyone I could reach. Some of my close friends became my distributors, and I would give each of them as many as fifty tickets to hand out. I was the most popular man in town, unfortunately, with all the employees at my hotel, my friends at the networks and advertising agencies, and the clerks in the department stores.

Despite the passes, the theater still did not look good, and Jack was at an emotional low point in his career. He was convinced that the public didn't want him anymore, and he kept saying that he was going to quit a business that was so fickle. He used to quote a line that Ed Wynn had told him when Wynn, one of the great comedians of all time, couldn't get a job in comedy any longer and ended up as a dramatic actor in motion pictures.

"There's something radically wrong," Ed told Jack, "when they hire me to make people cry and Perry Como to make people laugh."

About the fourth week of the engagement, most of the advertising costs came in, including the giant radio campaign

230

we did, and Billy Rose refused to pay any more than his share up to $12,500, as per contract. I raged into his office and reminded him of our conversation in Toronto when he offered to split with Jack all the excess ad costs, but he conveniently chose to forget all about it. I threatened to bring Jack in to confront him, and then he relented and made a settlement, the details of which I cannot remember at this writing. But I can remember that although we did get something from him, it was certainly not the fifty-fifty deal we had agreed on.

We all told Jack week after week that the word of mouth about the show would suddenly have an effect on the ticket sales soon, but it never did, and even though the news strike was settled in our fifth week and we placed ads immediately, it was too late to help, and we ended up weakly.

We flew directly home after our closing, and a few days later I received a gag wire from one of the Theatre Guild's producers, on the day Danny Kaye, the following attraction, opened at the Ziegfeld. He wired: THE WORD OF MOUTH FINALLY CAUGHT ON. THERE WAS A LONG LINE AT THE BOX OFFICE THIS MORNING.

Another engagement that was memorable for Jack, one he would talk about for the rest of his life, was our trip to Australia to play theaters in Sydney and Melbourne. Ever since Jack had visited Sydney during World War II for a few days of rest in 1944, he talked of the wonderful, friendly people there and how pretty the girls were, especially a particular one who had been assigned to drive him around.

Melbourne was known as a sophisticated city where the people appreciated theater and enjoyed show business, whereas Sydney was supposed to be a problem. We planned to play two weeks in Melbourne first so that the publicity resulting from that engagement would help generate business in Sydney. Somehow, however, we couldn't arrange the theaters in that order, and we had to open at the Theatre Royal in Sydney first.

We hired one of Australia's top singers, Lorrae Desmond, and the Elvis Presley of Down Under, Johnny O'Keefe. Since Jack wanted to do the same show we did at the Ziegfeld and the Half Brothers were not available, we hired a team of jugglers, the Rudenko Brothers, from the United States. We were going to do the little girl violinist act also, and Jack wanted to bring Toni Marcus to Australia with us, but I showed him that it was impractical financially because of fares, hotels, and expenses for the little girl and her mother. I assured him that we could find a girl in Sydney and I had some of the theater people auditioning kids in music schools before we arrived. We settled on a lovely young lady named Cynthia O'Brian, who was the concertmaster in a television station orchestra. The only problem was that she was twenty-two years old. Fortunately, she was only four feet eleven inches tall and weighed less than one hundred pounds, and when she dressed in flat shoes and girlish dresses, she passed for fifteen and was an enormous hit.

Years later, when we were going to Dublin and wanted to do that same act, Jack, always the pessimist, was positive we wouldn't be able to find just the right little girl there and wanted to take Doris Dodge, the girl we had used from the time Toni Marcus outgrew the role. But again I convinced him to take the gamble of finding an Irish girl, and we found a beauty in Dublin in the person of eleven-year-old Claire Crehan, who not only played the violin very well, but spoke her lines in the sweetest Irish brogue, completely capturing the hearts of the audience.

In Australia Jack used the same script as the New York show except that he changed the name of the hotel and streets to local names. The only new joke he did was a switch on the Onassis-yacht line when he commented that everyone in Sydney was talking about their opera house which was supposed to have been completed years before and was only half finished and millions of dollars over their cost estimate by the time we arrived. Jack said, "I've just been over to see your new opera house this afternoon. I don't think it'll be finished for five or six weeks yet."

A line I gave him which he credited as being the best in the show was said by Jack as he closed the evening: "I deserve a medal of some sort. I've done a whole evening and haven't told one joke about a kangaroo."

Jack's television shows had always been popular over there, but even he didn't realize how important he was in Australia. When we arrived in Sydney, there were at least fifty photographers waiting for him at the airport, and we had the greatest photo session I had ever seen. One of the newspapermen told me it was a larger press contingent than had turned out for Winston Churchill when he visited Sydney.

The publicity was perfect, and the ticket sales exceeded our fondest hopes, and after the excellent opening night reviews we were a sellout every night of the two-week engagement, breaking the 100-year record of the theater. Naturally, Jack was in his glory and loved every minute of his stay. The lord mayor, Harry Jensen, met Jack soon after our arrival and developed a great fondness for him. During our stay we were entertained by him all over town, and we experienced such warm hospitality that Jack was ready to move to Sydney.

The only damper on the Sydney trip, which I kept from Jack, was that surprisingly, the tickets were going slowly in Melbourne. However, I thought that by the time we would get to Melbourne the excitement of our Sydney engagement would help sell us out in Melbourne too.

Jack kept asking everyone he met if he knew the pretty girl who drove him around in 1944. I can't recall her name now, but Jack assumed she had married and knew only her maiden name. His inquiries seemed fruitless until just before we left Sydney when he told a radio announcer, who related the story of Jack's quest for the girl on his news show. He asked the girl, if she was listening in, to get in touch with Jack at the theater in Melbourne.

When we arrived in Melbourne, there were at least 5,000 people at the airport to meet our star, three uniformed bands and a girl baton-twirling team. Unfortunately, that many people didn't buy tickets, and that theater engagement, where we expected great success, turned out to be very weak.

The bright spot of this booking was a call from the woman for whom Jack had been searching. She had married and was living with her husband on a sheep farm a hundred miles from Sydney and was thrilled when Jack invited her and her husband to have dinner in Sydney with him when we were to return there to tape a televised version of our stage show for Australian TV.

So often we remember things from years past as being much better than they really were. On the night they were

233

coming to have dinner with us at the Menzies Hotel in Sydney, Jack started to get nervous. He had raved so much about her, extolling her charm and beauty, and now, twenty years later, she might be a dream turned sour. He was preparing himself to be embarrassed before me about the whole thing when they arrived. What we both saw was a beautiful, elegant lady who would stand out in any crowd and who was just as delightful as Jack had described her. Jack couldn't get over it.

"Was I right?" he kept repeating. "Didn't I tell you how beautiful she is?"

Jack's love affair with Australia continued for the rest of his life, and he kept after me to arrange another tour. I was working on a plan for him to play with five or six of their symphony orchestras, but it never materialized. When the Sydney Opera House finally opened, I received a call from Australia offering a good fee, fares, and expenses for Jack to fly to Sydney to be guest violin soloist at the symphony's initial performance in the new opera house. Sadly, we were in the midst of preparations for our TV special and it would have been impossible to get there in time, which was one of his greatest regrets.

43

WHENEVER he was asked what were the most memorable experiences of his life, Jack would without exception include command performances at which he appeared in London and having a high school named after him in Waukegan.

The first time he was invited to appear at a variety command performance was in 1951, and we flew to London with Dinah Shore for a four-day trip. The prospect of entertaining and meeting the king and queen of England was an exciting honor, but Jack and I agreed that since they were not our king and queen, we couldn't feel too emotional or awestruck about it. But the night of the performance at the Palladium,

234

sitting backstage with all the greatest stars of the English theater, we began to sense a reverent thrill in the air, especially when we peeked out of the curtains and saw the elegant audience arriving, the men in white tie and tails and the women beautifully gowned.

The stage manager took Jack, Dinah, and me to the corner of the orchestra pit so we could have a good vantage point to see the entrance of the royal family. After a short wait the conductor held up his baton, and the orchestra struck the opening bars of "God Save the King," and as the spotlight hit the royal box, King George VI, Queen Mary, and the Princesses Elizabeth and Margaret Rose made their appearance. We could feel the electric excitement as the audience rose and applauded and the royal family bowed, and as we watched, we were bedazzled by the pomp and circumstance of the occasion. Though we hadn't thought it would happen, we did feel that spine tingle that only occurs under rare circumstances.

A few years later Jack was invited again, and this time the two of us flew to England alone. For that show, which was held at the Prince of Wales Theatre, Jack decided to do the violin-throwing bit in his portion of the show, and I carried a prop fiddle all the way to London with us. That evening I made a very good throw when Jack asked for his violin, and it landed right at his feet without breaking apart. At the conclusion of the performance, even though I thought it was in perfect condition, I decided not to carry the fiddle all the way back to the States, and I gave it to a stagehand who had been helpful to us. After the show Jack and I went to a few parties and we didn't get back to the Dorchester Hotel until four in the morning. The man at the hotel reception desk told us that Scotland Yard was waiting for Jack to call on a matter of great urgency. I returned the call for him, and the detective who answered told me that we could rest easy as they had apprehended the man who had stolen Mr. Benny's Stradivarius. For a moment I was nonplussed. Jack anxiously opened his violin case where we found the Strad nestled safely, and then I suddenly remembered the stagehand. I explained his mistake to the detective, who embarrassedly apologized to the poor stagehand, who had been held in jail for five hours waiting for corroboration of his story.

The next time Jack went to a command performance, George Burns came with us and they did their "Burns and Allen" routine. This was an act they first prepared for a Friars Frolic at the Shrine Auditorium many years before, in which Jack donned women's clothes and high heels and played Gracie to George, doing the character as close to Gracie as he could and ending with the little dance with which George and Gracie always ended their act.

Since that number was originally done for charity, Harry Cohn, then the head of Columbia Pictures, had Jack outfitted at the studio and gave him the black, sequined suit that Rita Hayworth had worn in *Gilda*. To complete the costume, he bought a pair of black high-heeled evening shoes, and since he had nicely shaped thin legs that looked well in women's shoes, he cut a classy figure as a female. Jack used to laugh at himself when he told the story of wearing the Gracie outfit one night for a benefit when Ann Sheridan came backstage to see him.

"'You have beautiful legs,' Ann said to me, and like an idiot, I answered, 'Thank you.'"

The George Burns-Gracie Benny act was so successful at benefit performances that eventually Jack incorporated the act in his TV show. After Gracie died, however, they never did that routine again.

On the day they were to do the act for the command performance, George, Jack, and I had lunch at the Caprice Restaurant and decided to walk down Piccadilly to our hotel, the Dorchester. It was a very cold day, and as we passed the Ritz Hotel, we decided to go into the bar for a drink and to warm up. It was midafternoon and there wasn't a soul in the bar except us and the Cockney bartender. George thought that this was a good chance to rehearse their little dance and, despite Jack's objections, pulled him to his feet and made him go through the steps. Jack was embarrassed and kept missing his steps, so George got the bartender, who was watching those two crazy Americans, from behind the bar and started to show him the steps, all the time admonishing Jack, "Look here, Jack. See how simple it is. Even the bartender can do it with one lesson."

Soon the bartender was into the spirit of the act and danced along with abandon while George continued his patter of put-downs to Jack, who was rolling on the floor of the Ritz Bar by that time.

One of Jack's saddest regrets was that Mary traveled so seldom with him that she missed some of the outstanding performing times in his career, including many honors he received, some important symphony concerts, and his command performances. So when he was invited for the fourth time, he persuaded Mary to come to London with us, and she finally saw her husband do a command show and met the members of the royal family.

I had once tried to convince Mary how foolish it was to travel to London with a maid from home, explaining that for the maid's salary she could hire two English maids around the clock and in addition save a fortune in extra fares and hotel rooms—but was unsuccessful. Jack used to gag about it: "After all, the maid knows just how I like my shirts, and these hotel laundries are *so* expensive."

The Bennys often saved money like that. One year I remember they were living in the Oliver Messel suite of the Dorchester Hotel, one of the most beautiful and most expensive suites in London. They were paying an exorbitant rate per day, and Mary discovered a fellow who sent her a case of soda and tonic water at *wholesale* cost. She pointed out to all of us how much money they were saving as compared to what room service charged for soda and tonic water.

Mary's well-known love for shopping and spending was often good material for Jack. When Mary would be in the audience on opening night, he would introduce her. She would stand up and take a bow, and he'd comment, "Now I can deduct the dress. If you'd wave your hand, doll, I could deduct the ring, too!"

"Doll" was Jack's term of endearment for Mary, and he always called her that.

Another highlight of Jack's life was having his hometown, Waukegan, name a new junior high school after him. Jack flew back to Waukegan for the ground-breaking ceremonies and the parade that followed, and when the Jack Benny Junior High School was completed, we brought the entire cast and staff of the TV show there and taped a Jack Benny program to dedicate the new school.

He had always regretted his lack of formal higher education and having a school named after him was a tremendous compliment, he felt.

"What a great honor," Jack said afterward in many of his personal appearances, "having a school named after me. Can you imagine? The Jack Benny Junior High School! There are three schools in Waukegan—the Thomas Jefferson, the Alexander Hamilton, and the Jack Benny. That's some parlay."

He was very proud of his affiliation with the school and felt it was his duty to visit there every time he was in Chicago, which he did, speaking to the students at an assembly whenever he came. Ten years after the school opened, he was addressing a class of twelve-year-olds and at the conclusion of his speech, he asked if there were any questions. One little boy raised his hand, stood up and asked, "Mr. Benny, why did they name *you* after our school?"

44

OUR weekly TV program, which had been moved to the Tuesday 9:30–10 P.M. EST time spot on CBS following the *Red Skelton Hour*, was doing very well. Red Skelton was one of the top three programs on the air, and although the Benny rating dropped several points below Skelton's, it was still high enough to give us a respectable position on the list.

Our smooth operation was suddenly jolted when Fred De Cordova came to me in the middle of the 1962–63 season with the news that he had a fine offer of an executive position at Screen Gems and he wanted his release. Because of his close friendship with Jack and Mary and not wanting an unhappy producer-director, we couldn't stand in his way. However, I was worried that it would be a long time before a new director would have Jack's confidence to a point where we could operate as well as before.

Norman Abbott had directed two Benny shows in 1958 and had done a good job, so with Jack's acquiesence, I signed him as producer-director for the remainder of the season. It was fortunate that the first few programs he directed turned out well and he got along harmoniously with our star, so that in no time our show was back on track. Norman adored Jack and had only one complaint. Jack never knew Norman's wife's name, and for years he would phone Norman at home and when she would answer, he would call her "dear" or "sweetheart" or "honey." One day she complained to him: "Jack, I've been with you so often and you still don't know my name."

"Of course I do, honey," said Jack, and then he paused.

"You don't know my name is Ann, do you?" she asked.

"Sure, Ann, I knew it all the time," he blustered.

That same day Jack called for *Ann* eight times, and when Norman answered the phone, Jack would say, "I don't want to talk to you, Norman. I want to speak to *Ann*."

Like many people as they get older, Jack found it very difficult to remember names of the new people he met. He never could remember the names of most of the people who worked on our film sets, even though they were around for years. Nor could he remember names of the TV executives assigned to our show. One network vice-president, who was around us for five years, was terrified that Jack wouldn't know him if his boss ever brought his name up in conversation.

But Jack was an elephant when it came to the name of the doorman at a vaudeville house in Boston or the assistant manager of a Kansas City theater in 1922 or the woman who ran the boardinghouse where he stayed in Pittsburgh.

A crisis on our TV show occurred while we were in New York playing the Ziegfeld Theater. We had brought the writers back to New York to see the show and to work on a number of scripts to film for the 1963–64 season when we received the news that CBS officially confirmed that a new country show, *Petticoat Junction*, would be programmed in a time slot between Red Skelton and Jack Benny on Tuesday nights. Red Skelton would start the evening from 8 to 9 P.M. and be followed by *Petticoat Junction*, which was produced by the same company that was making the number one show, *Beverly Hillbillies*, while our program would go on at 9:30 to 10 P.M.

Jack was livid when he heard the news. He felt it was a great affront to him, and while working with his writers in his suite at the Pierre Hotel, he kept raging about the move.

"If they just had the courtesy to tell me about it before they did it," he raved, "it wouldn't have been so awful. But after all I've done for CBS all these years, why would they split Red and me? We were such a good combination, and now both of us could be hurt. Why didn't they at least explain their reasoning?"

The writers agreed with Jack, and he steamed and steamed until finally he had the script girl put in a call to James Aubrey, president of CBS. He was out. Then Jack fumed, "I'm going to call Bill Paley and raise hell with him. After all, he brought me over here in the first place."

The script girl put in the call to William S. Paley, but he was out, too. Jack continued working with the boys, all the while complaining and grumbling. When the phone rang and it was finally Paley returning Jack's call, Jack blanched, and his bravado started to fade. He hesitated for a moment and then told the girl to say he was out. A half hour later Paley called again, but Jack refused to speak to him.

Our contract with CBS had only one more year to run, and they had an option to renew but had to do it a year in advance. Before the season started, we sent them a wire reminding them that the option time was coming up and we wanted a yes or no answer by September 1, the date called for in the contract. They wanted to wait until the season started and the ratings were in, but after consultation with MCA, owners of our company, we decided to stand firm, and as soon as the option had expired, we signed a one-year contract with NBC for the 1964–65 season.

As it happened, we guessed wrong, because on our last season on CBS, *Petticoat Junction* became a giant hit, and following it, our rating was the highest it had been in years.

When we moved over to NBC, they scheduled us on Friday evenings, and although no one expected it, that turned out to be their weakest night of the week. We didn't worry before the season started because our competition was a new show called *Gomer Pyle* which starred one of Andy Griffith's supporting players, Jim Nabors.

As always, we wanted to kick off with strength, and we

240

signed the Marquis Chimps for our opening show. The three chimps had caused a sensation many years earlier when they worked with Jack on one of our hour specials, the critics having called their spot with Jack a "comedy classic." The chimps and Jack Benny notwithstanding, *Gomer Pyle* swamped us in the ratings and immediately caught on with the viewers to become the comedy hit of the year, while with our shows as bright and fresh as ever we floundered badly in the ratings.

By midseason Jack decided to write finis to a weekly program at the end of that season, and he told NBC he only wanted to appear in two specials the following season, to which they quickly agreed. I strongly suspect that Jack, although he didn't say anything, even to me, felt that he was going to be fired as a weekly program and was beating them to the punch. In my opinion, we could have sold a weekly Benny show again, but I too thought that he would be better off at the age of seventy-one to cut down on such a time-consuming schedule and allow himself more time for relaxation and other activities.

When we completed our last season of weekly programs in April, 1965, we also completed our contracts with MCA, and for the first time in his professional life, Jack found himself all alone, even without an agent or business manager. His business manager, Myrt Blum, had died a few years earlier and had never been replaced, perhaps because of Jack's unhappiness with Blum. Either because he never had too much cash to play with owing to the extravagant way in which the Bennys lived or because of his own conservative bent, Blum had never bought land or apartment houses or any of the many available investments in a rapidly booming Southern California. Instead, he settled for safe, certain security such as annuities.

"We were handled by Myrt Blum, too," says George Burns, "and one day Jack and I were driving past the corner where the Beverly Hilton now stands. There was a nursery on the property, and we took Myrt over to see it, but he didn't think it was a good buy. Another time some fellow came to us at our golf club with a map of a large piece of land that we could buy for $350 an acre. Jack, Harpo Marx, and I were all excited about it and told Blum, but nothing happened. Today that's the city of Lakewood."

One day Jack and George were in Palm Springs and Jack said, "George, we ought to have a ranch. Everyone else seems to have one."

They mentioned this to Leonard Firestone, of the rubber family, who told them he had a ranch in Indio near Palm Springs and there was land next to his for sale. He said that if they liked it, he would join them in buying it.

Jack and George drove out to look at the property, and when they got there, Jack looked out the car window and said, "I see nothing but sand."

"You're looking out the wrong side," said George, and when Jack turned, he still saw nothing but sand. After Jack finished laughing, they decided to buy it with Firestone. They planted grapefruit trees and cotton, and eventually they sold it many years later for a handsome profit.

But when Jack found himself all alone in the business world, he asked me to be his manager and to handle all his affairs and engagements, as well as the business matters. And although I had never had the title before, I had been doing a great deal of his career managing anyway. I debated going on to other things, but after eighteen years with him, I couldn't have possibly left him at that time of his life. I signed a contract with him giving each of us the right to terminate on ninety days' notice, and that is the way we operated for the rest of his life. At the same time, we set up a corporation, J.B. Productions, to produce our one-hour TV specials, this time with Jack as president and me as executive vice-president and executive producer of the TV specials.

I did not want to take the entire responsibility for Jack's career, which was at a low ebb, and after discussing it with his lawyer, Don Rosenfeld, I decided to engage an agent. I called George Chasin, a former top MCA agent who had formed an agency with two other ex-MCA agents, Arthur Park and Herman Citron, and I offered him Jack Benny as a client. They had a small stable of very important stars which was the reason we chose them, and when George listened to my offer, he said he'd like to discuss it with his partners and would get back to me. Several days later he phoned and regretfully turned us down. He and his partners felt that at Jack's age he didn't have too many more fruitful years, and they wanted younger people who they could build into five-

242

and ten-year relationships. I never told Jack about this turn-down, and ironically, in the next nine years of Jack's life, he earned more than $12,000,000 and would have been one of that agency's most lucrative clients.

Several months later, while in New York, I arranged a luncheon in the private dining room of Ashley-Famous Agency with their president, Ted Ashley, and the vice-president in charge of TV, Gerald Leider. Ashley-Famous had some of the biggest stars in the entertainment business and had recently bought a large British agency that brought many young British motion-picture stars to their bulging client list.

At lunch I told them I'd like them to represent Jack, but not if they were merely going to put his name on their list and then sit back and wait for offers. I wanted to be sure they were excited about him as a client and would go out and work for him. Ted Ashley, a very charming fellow, said, "I can't think of anyone I'd want as a client more than Jack Benny. Let me tell you a story. My father was a poor tailor, and we always lived over the store or in a small apartment nearby. He was forever going broke, and we had to move continually while he opened tailor shop after tailor shop. He's retired now and lives in Miami Beach, but when he comes up to New York once or twice a year and visits my offices and knows I have hundreds of employees, he's always worrying that I'll never be able to meet my payroll and pay the rent. I tell him the names of some of the stars I represent, but that's meaningless since he's never heard of most of them, and he's certain I'll go bankrupt soon. But if I call my father and tell him I've signed Jack Benny as a client, he'll relax for the first time since I opened my own office."

I told him that if he'd tell that story to Jack, he'd get him as a client. The next morning Ted and Jerry Leider came over to our hotel to have breakfast with Jack, and Ted told Jack the same story. When we finished breakfast, Jack took me into the next room and asked me what I thought. I felt he should sign with them, and he did so.

Jack was under contract to Ashley-Famous for about eight months and during that time they got him only one job, an engagement at the newly opened Caesar's Palace in Las Vegas for $42,500, less money than he had ever received in Las

Vegas before. Jack was not happy with his representation after that and asked me to get him out of the contract. From then on, he refused to sign with any other agent, insisting that I take care of all future negotiations for television, theaters, and all his other activities.

45

THE violin was Jack's great love, and he regretted that he didn't continue to practice after he reached the age of twelve. From the time he started to play in the pit of the Barrison Theater in Waukegan, he used the fiddle only to play popular music, and eventually he played no more than a few scratchy bars of "Love in Bloom" or a jazz medley. But fine violinists often would comment on his "excellent bow arm," and Jack would proudly relate his bow arm reviews to anyone who would listen.

In the presence of famous concert violinists, he felt awestruck, and his frustration at his own mediocrity would show. When Isaac Stern first guested on our television program, Isaac asked Jack what number he would like him to do as his solo. Jack suggested that he play three or four numbers, and then he would decide. We sat around for an hour during the rehearsal while Isaac played, and when he finished and asked Jack which one he wanted him to do, Jack told him to choose whatever he liked. In actuality, Jack simply had wanted to listen to him play.

I noticed that no matter how angry or disturbed he might be, whenever he played his fiddle, he would seem to forget all about his anxieties and relax completely. I always made it a point to suggest that he go to his dressing room and practice whenever any problems occurred around our show.

In 1955 Jack had a good idea for his TV show. He decided to do a scene in his dressing room in which he would be interviewed by a reporter. In the interview he would say that he would much rather have been a concert violinist, playing in front of large symphony orchestras, than have all the success he had achieved as a comedian. When the reporter leaves, Jack would take a nap, and as he dozes off, he would keep mumbling about his dream of being a concert violinist. We would then dissolve into a scene of a big symphony orchestra and Jack coming onstage in white tie and tails playing a serious, classical number with laugh breaks in between the notes.

The writers started to prepare the script along those lines, and our musical director, Mahlon Merrick, arranged the number "Zigeunerweisen" (Gypsy Airs) by Sarasate, with a "Love in Bloom" break in the middle of it. The only problem was that Jack really had not played the violin for forty-nine years, and he felt that the satire of the symphony violinist wouldn't be funny if he could play only poorly; it had to have some semblance of proficiency to make the idea humorous.

It was then, at the age of sixty-one, that he started to take violin lessons again. He began to study with Larry Kurdjie, a violinist in the studio orchestra who was also a violin teacher, and he found that his poor fingers were stiff and the lessons were a painful chore. He struggled for four weeks and managed to learn the number well enough to play it on the program. That show turned out very well, and he got more satisfaction from doing it than from anything he had done in years.

His spoof of the concert violinist created a great deal of talk in musical circles, and the following spring when New York's Carnegie Hall was to be torn down, a committee came to me to help them save the concert hall. Lawrence Tibbett, the Metropolitan Opera star was cochairman of the Committee to Save Carnegie Hall, and he asked me if Jack would consider appearing as violin soloist with members of the New York Philharmonic for a big benefit performance. I asked Mr. Tibbett why he didn't ask Jascha Heifetz or some of the other great concert artists, and he answered, "Heifetz and the others could only bring ten dollars a ticket, but Jack Benny, as a concert soloist, would get us one hundred dollars a ticket."

When I approached Jack with the idea, he jumped at the opportunity but insisted that the proceeds be split with the Retarded Children's Society, of which he was honorary chairman at the time. He refused to make his symphony debut in New York without a break-in date, so he scheduled a concert with the Oklahoma City Symphony for April 28, 1956, with those proceeds also to be split between the Symphony Fund and the Retarded Children.

He enlisted Alfred Wallenstein as his conductor and then spent months of practice on his program which consisted of "Zigeunerweisen," the first movement of the Mendelssohn Violin Concerto, *Capriccio Espagnol* by Rimsky-Korsakov, a number in which he acted as concertmaster, and "The Bee." As an encore he played his jazz medley, which, as he would tell the audience, one would rarely hear in a symphony hall.

The concert in Oklahoma City went very well, and $66,000 was raised, a record sum for that city. He could hardly wait to get to Carnegie Hall. He began taking two lessons a week and practicing at least an hour a day and sometimes for three or more hours, and he loved every minute of it. Up until that time Jack had not been much of a concertgoer, but he became very interested and from then on he attended whenever he had the opportunity, especially to hear violinists and occasionally to hear a noted pianist.

He was driving through Denver with Frank Remley one year, and after checking into the Brown Palace Hotel and looking through the papers to see what was playing, he read that Oscar Levant, a very nervous, talented friend, was giving a piano concert that evening. Jack, delighted, called Oscar and asked him to leave two tickets for him at the box office, but Oscar pleaded with him: "Please, Jack, please don't come to my concert. If you do, I will not play. I'll walk off the stage if I see you there because I'd be too nervous to play in front of you."

Jack and Frankie went to a terrible movie instead, and the next morning, as they were checking out of the hotel, they ran into Levant. "Oh, I wish you had been there last night. I was sensational. Never played better. You missed a wonderful concert."

The concert at Carnegie Hall was on October 2, 1956, with Wallenstein again conducting for Jack. When he arrived at the hall for rehearsal, there was a gift waiting from his friend Jackie Gleason. It was a barrelful of resin, enough for the whole violin section of the New York Philharmonic for their

246

lifetimes. When Jack finished his rehearsal with the symphony, he rushed back to his hotel to spend the afternoon practicing as he was still insecure about his violin playing. He also could not tune his violin very well, and at one point he broke the tension of the day by putting in a transatlantic call to Gisele Mackenzie in London where she was appearing. Gisele had perfect pitch, and when Jack got her on the phone, he asked her to hum an A. She did. Jack tuned his fiddle to her hum, said, "Thank you," and hung up.

The concert raised $50,000 and created a great deal of attention in the New York press. The next day the reviews were everything Jack hoped for, the critics all coming through with excellent notices. In fact, from then on, in the eighteen years of his concerts, he never received a bad notice because the critics realized what Isaac Stern said, "He never made fun of music, only of himself."

The New York *Herald Tribune* critic said, "It was a performance one is not likely to forget in some time—a wondrous evening—hilarious, tasteful and surprisingly touching." The *World-Telegram*: "One of the happiest nights in the history of Carnegie Hall." The New York *Times*: "Music was not the food of love, but the food of laughter, and Mr. Benny dishes it out in great, heaping doses."

The money raised for that concert was not nearly enough to save Carnegie Hall, but Jack's friend Isaac Stern then started what became practically a one-man campaign to save the historic hall which culminated in a CBS network program called *Carnegie Hall Salutes Jack Benny*, in which many of the notables of the concert and musical worlds appeared gratis to raise the money necessary to save Carnegie Hall. Eugene Ormandy and the Philadelphia Orchestra accompanied Isaac and Jack in their inimitable version of the Bach Double Concerto, which was the highlight of the evening.

The reception Jack received in his first concerts gave him the impetus to do as many as he could, and he honed his performance down to such a fine point that it became one of the best things he ever did on any stage. Jack said many times, "Where else can I get the laughs of Charlie Chaplin and the applause of a great violinist like Isaac Stern?"

On the other hand, Isaac Stern used to kid him with lines like: "When Jack Benny walks out in tails in front of ninety great musicians, he looks like the world's greatest violinist. It's a shame he has to play."

Eventually, Jack gave charity concerts with almost one hundred symphonies in the United States, Canada, England, and Israel, and the money raised from those endeavors totaled $5,901,000.

When Jack would play with a symphony, he would be advertised as violin soloist in the same way any of the leading guest soloists might be advertised. As a result, the local audience never really knew what to expect when they came to a Benny concert. Some thought he couldn't play very well except for a few scratchy notes and were surprised when he played better than they expected. On the other hand, many people thought he was a fine violinist and was just fooling around, trying very hard to play poorly. In actuality, Jack was a fair violinist, not good enough to play second fiddle in an average symphony. But because of his great comedy reputation and his many loyal fans throughout the world, he did attract patrons who had never seen a concert and who were surprised to find how much they enjoyed music. Leonard Bernstein once said, "Benny has done more than raise millions of dollars to erase operating deficits of major orchestras. He has brought multitudes of people who would not otherwise be there into the concert halls to prove that music can be entertaining and rewarding."

Jack's concert routine was a delight. Usually the first half of the program was serious symphonic music, with Jack making his appearance in the second half after an intermission. He would make his entrance looking every bit the magnificent virtuoso in his beautiful suit of tails and invariably receive a standing ovation. When the audience was finally seated in quiet anticipation, he would ask the conductor to give him an A, and the clarinetist would do so. With a flourish Jack would then bring his violin to his chin, raise his bow arm, only to discover that he had forgotten his bow. He would then walk off the stage in apologetic embarrassment to get his bow, and that opening bit of humor would set the tone for the kind of concert he was going to do.

His opening number was generally "Zigeunerweisen" which he would play as well as he could, which was not good enough, and at the first difficult passage, the concertmaster would play it so beautifully, taking it completely away from him, while Jack would look on in frustration. At the next complicated part the concertmaster, having got away with it the first time, would stand up as though he were the soloist and play the passage, while Jack would stare in pretended anger. In the midst of the classical number the orchestra would break into "Love in Bloom," which was always a surprise and a big laugh with a round of applause. In that portion the cymbalist would do a few solo strikes, causing Jack to turn and stare at him, too. When the number was over, Jack would whisper something to the conductor, who then would banish the concertmaster from the stage, and after that laugh, Jack would indicate with a point of his bow that the cymbalist must leave, too. During the second number, the Mendelssohn, the assistant concertmaster, who at that point had moved over to take the place of the banished concertmaster, would take another solo spot away from Jack. At the end of the assistant's lovely cadenza, accompanied by a burst of applause from the audience, the assistant would sit down for just a beat, then rise and leave the stage without being told since he would know that he'd be ordered off at the end of the selection anyway. During one passage of Mendelssohn which required a mute, Jack would stop the music to ask if anyone had a mute as he had misplaced his. One of the violinists would step forward with an extra one. Jack would finish that part of the number and then deliberately remove the mute and put it into his pocket. While the entire orchestra would play on, the violinist who "lent" the mute would get up from his seat, walk over to Jack, who would be energetically bowing, put his hand in Jack's pocket to retrieve his mute, walk back to his seat, and continue playing, Jack, all the while, never missing a beat and never noticing.

Until this point in the concert, no words were spoken except for the request of the mute and the few whispers into the conductor's ear. However, after the second number Jack would take the microphone and say to the audience:

"This is really my instrument. I must say in all my concerts, the critics have been wonderful to me. The New York *Times* critic said, 'Like Heifetz, Jack Benny held the violin under his chin.' Now where the hell else would you hold it, unless you were Raquel Welch? The critic for the New York *Post* said,

'Last night Jack Benny played Mendelssohn. . . . Mendelssohn lost.' Now in Philadelphia I am known as the Van Gogh of the violinists . . . yes, the Van Gogh of them all . . . because in the middle of the Beethoven Concerto, a lady in the third row stood up and yelled, 'My God, he's lost his ear.' Last time I got a standing ovation was in England when I played with the London Philharmonic. I played the Wieniawski Concerto, and when I finished, the whole audience stood up—and walked out! Now when I give concerts, the tickets sell for five dollars to one hundred dollars, but for my concerts the five-dollar seats are down in front . . . the further back you go, the more you have to pay. The hundred-dollar seats are the last two rows . . . and those tickets go like hotcakes! In fact, if you pay two hundred dollars you don't have to come at all."

Now that he was a concert violinist, Jack had to buy a good violin. The first one he bought was a Pressenda, which cost $5,000, at that time a sizable sum. Then he decided that he should have a Stradivarius because the thought of a comedian playing a Strad would add to the humor. For eighteen thousand dollars he purchased a Strad made in 1729, and although that was a rather large investment, in a short time his Strad had doubled in value. Many of these famous violins have names, and one time Jack wondered if his would ever become the "Benny Strad." He used to joke about his fiddle: "It's a real Strad, you know. If it isn't, I'm out one hundred and ten dollars. The reason I got it so cheap is that it's one of the few Strads made in Japan."

Or sometimes he'd describe it: "This is a genuine Stradivarius. You can always tell because it has the name of the maker inside. Here it is right here. 'Antonio Stradivari, area code 213.'"

He often told concert audiences about the time in Las Vegas when during his nightclub act he told the audience that his violin was a genuine Strad made in 1729 and a drunk at a front table called out, "Did you buy it new?"

After Carnegie Hall his next concert was with the Philadelphia Orchestra at the Academy of Music there, and again he had the assurance of Alfred Wallenstein conducting for him. At that concert $86,000 was raised, and that money was used to furnish seats for the Mann Auditorium in Tel Aviv.

250

Alfred Wallenstein conducted for him again with the Los Angeles Philharmonic when they raised $100,000 for the Cedars of Lebanon Hospital. During the promotion for that concert, his daughter, Joan, was asked on a panel show how well her father played the violin.

"Well, let me put it this way. He doesn't play as well as Jascha Heifetz—but then, who does?"

The first concert he did without Alfred Wallenstein conducting was for Bonds for Israel with the Toronto Symphony and Walter Susskind conducting. At that concert we raised a record $1,200,000, but when I broke the story to the press, I announced the sum of $992,000. When Jack saw that total in the papers the following day, he came rushing to me wondering who had made the mistake. I told him that I had purposely understated the amount because I didn't think anyone would believe we could possibly take in more than $1,000,000.

His next concert with the Chicago Symphony raised $108,000 for the City of Hope, and then when he performed with Harry Truman for the Kansas City Symphony on March 22, 1958, he realized that most symphonies were in the red and needed help. He decided then that from that time on he would only do his concerts for the benefit of the symphony fund or the orchestra pension fund; he could still help the other charities by appearing at dinners and theaters.

Before he was done, Jack had played with every major symphony orchestra in the United States and under the baton of all the leading conductors. In addition, he performed for many of the smaller symphonies like the Fargo-Moorhead Symphony and the Palm Springs Desert Symphony.

Leonard Bernstein invited him to come back to Carnegie Hall in 1959 for the Symphony Fund, and in connection with this concert the distinguished music critic Irving Kolodin said, "Had he been more gifted, he might have been sitting, conventionally, in one of the chairs to Leonard Bernstein's right, rather than standing, unconventionally, beside him."

Of that concert, the *Journal-American* commented: "He came, he sawed, he conquered."

On November 4, 1960, Jack was scheduled to solo with the Cleveland Orchestra under the baton of the late, feared George Szell, one of the world's great conductors and a man who was famed for his Germanic discipline. Jack was nervous before meeting Szell, but at rehearsal Szell was a pussycat and insisted on rehearsing all the comedy business over and over, even after Jack was satisfied with his acting. At the post-concert dinner for the symphony board and the city's notables, Cleveland's Mayor Anthony Celebrezze opened the speechmaking by saying, "George Szell has been one of our illustrious citizens for the past sixteen years, and this is the first time I've ever seen him laugh."

After four years in the world of symphony Jack found himself embraced in the life of a concert artist. His friendship with Isaac Stern ripened, and he spent more and more time with concert violinists in Los Angeles and New York. He then conceived an idea for a concerto which he called "Kreutzcerto." It had a story theme running throughout the number concerning a young boy taking violin lessons and playing the Kreutzer exercises at which he got better and better until he could play a concerto. But the boy was never good enough to make it in the concert world and ends up in a jazz band. Jack gave this idea to the late composer Jacques Belasco, who wrote it with Jack and made the symphony arrangement.

The number was successfully introduced at a Promenade Concert of the Los Angeles Philharmonic under the direction of Jack's good friend, now called John Green. When the Philadelphia Orchestra asked Jack to return for a Pension Fund concert at Robin Hood Dell, in order to present a new program, Jack played the "Kreutzcerto" with John Green conducting again. Green had his first unpleasant moment with Jack at this concert. He recalls:

"In the 'Kreutzcerto,' Jack had written in a very funny spot in which he hits a G natural on the fiddle and I yell at him impatiently, 'G sharp,' and he switches the note right after I shout at him. This got a big laugh when we did it in Los Angeles. At Robin Hood Dell I was waiting in my dressing room for Jack after the concert, but he never came in and when I went into his room, I noticed that he was angry. 'What's wrong?' I asked him, and he stormed at me, 'You didn't give me the G sharp line!' 'That's because you hit it correctly,' I told him, and when he realized it for the first time that night, he threw his arms around me and kissed me."

After the Los Angeles Music Center was built, Jack did a concert with the Los Angeles Philharmonic with Zubin Mehta conducting which was televised and released in a rather extraordinary way. In order to raise funds for the Music Center, the seven Los Angeles television stations cooperated and each donated one hour of their time during one week so that every night in that week, Jack Benny, Zubin Mehta, and the Los Angeles Philharmonic could be seen and heard in concert. Naturally, there were subtle pitches made for contributions. That endeavor was so successful that it was often credited with giving the Music Center its real start.

For the first few years of his symphony concerts many of the more austere symphonies shied away from inviting him to play with their orchestras, even though he was getting no fee and raising very large amounts of money for the orchestras. But soon word of the good taste and proficiency of his performance spread throughout the country and every orchestra began pleading for his services, especially since most of them were in need of money to cover their deficits.

Isaac Stern became our ex-officio agent, and he was constantly being approached by symphony orchestra managers who knew of his friendship with Jack to have him help get Jack for them. One such call came from the Hartt Symphony Orchestra to raise money to build a new music building for the Hartt College of Music at the University of Hartford in Connecticut. Mr. Fuller of the Fuller Brush Company had offered to donate $400,000 if the city could raise a matching amount. Isaac said that they felt Jack was the only one who could do it for them.

We agreed, and by the time we arrived for the concert they had raised $438,000, which, with Fuller's $400,000, gave them enough money to start the new school. At the conclusion of the concert, Jack told the audience the financial story, and then he introduced Mr. Fuller, who was sitting in the side section of the theater with his wife. Jack commented, "Pretty lousy seats for $400,000."

We had a similar experience when he played with the Jacksonville Symphony. Jack was near to having raised $5,000,000 from his benefit concerts, and we were doing the Jacksonville and St. Petersburg symphonies in one week. I figured out that if we could raise $75,000 in Jacksonville and

$60,000 in St. Petersburg, we would pass the $5,000,000 mark that week. I telephoned the chairman of the Jacksonville concert and asked him if he could possibly get up to the $75,000 figure for their concert. He asked me if they raised the entire $135,000, would Jacksonville get all the credit for that record sum, and I happily said yes.

In a short time he called with the news that a wealthy anonymous woman had donated $100,000, and it would be matched by twenty Jacksonville men, who would each give $5,000 to assure the figure we wanted. Jack and I were delighted, and by the day of the concert we had $268,000, a sum greater than had ever been raised in the state of Florida for any charitable show. I asked the chairman, who shall be nameless here, who the $100,000 donor was, and he admitted that it was he, but pledged me to secrecy as he didn't want to become a target for all the other fund-raising drives in town.

Edgar Kaiser once called for Jack to play with the Oakland Symphony, and he raised $121,000 net in a thousand-seat auditorium. A few years later he called me to have Jack come back for their Pension Fund, but I told him we had too many symphonies we hadn't played with yet. He guaranteed to raise at least $200,000 if we returned, and that was too big to turn down. Jack agreed, and for that second concert $210,000 was raised.

Early in his concert career, after playing with the Philadelphia Orchestra, we went to a party of concert artists and patrons. Gregor Piatagorsky, one of the world's great cellists, told a story which we all loved. It seems that when Mischa Elman was considered the world's greatest violinist, a young man named Jascha Heifetz was starting to make a name for himself, and after a great amount of attention in the musical world, he was finally scheduled to give a concert at Carnegie Hall. Everyone in the profession went to hear this new musical genius make his debut, and Mischa Elman went with Arthur Rubinstein, the pianist, and sat in the first box. Heifetz began to play brilliantly, and soon Mischa Elman was wiping his brow with his handkerchief. He turned to Rubinstein and said, "It's hot in here, isn't it?"

"Not for pianists," was Rubinstein's quick rejoinder.

Jack screamed at that story and told it many times along

with others in his rapidly building stock of classical music stories.

Fifteen years later we were giving a concert with the Boston Symphony, Erich Leinsdorf conducting, and while waiting backstage to make his entrance, Jack asked me if it wasn't very hot. I quickly answered, "Not for managers," and luckily he wasn't due to go on for about ten minutes because he ran into his dressing room and collapsed with laughter.

Actually, Jack always did get nervous before every concert, and although it was true, he would admit it humorously to the audience, "I'm never nervous when I'm doing my regular stage show or my television show, but when I do concerts, I am always nervous. And I don't know why, either . . . especially because I do them for nothing . . . honest to God! Maybe that's what makes me so nervous."

46

AFTER our last disastrous season of weekly programs, we produced our first one-hour special for J.B. Productions with guest stars Bob Hope, Elke Sommer, and the Beach Boys. Since that show was very important for Jack at that time, I agreed to let him and Ralph Levy, who returned as producer-director, have their heads and go as wild as they wished with sets, costumes, and budget, resulting in our losing money on the show. Also, we had no theme for that program, and unfortunately, it didn't rate too well. As a consequence, NBC found themselves in the position of having contracted for a second show from us that season with no sponsor interest.

We were asked to postpone our second program until the following season, and after we reluctantly agreed, they finally secured a sponsor, American Motors, for the following fall. For that show I gave our two "new writers," Al Gordon and Hal Goldman, the opportunity to turn producers with me as executive producer, and together we planned a show that would have commercial appeal. For years we had been pressing to do a satire of the Miss America contests, and we finally persuaded Jack into letting us use that as our theme. We hired the Smothers Brothers, Phyllis Diller, and Trini Lopez, and then auditioned hundreds of beautiful girls in Hollywood, and we chose the ten most outstanding, most of them former beauty contest winners.

Jack was at a low point in his career since the demise of his weekly show and the mediocre rating of his first special, and so even though the script was very good, he was very insecure about it. He hated the idea of the ten most beautiful girls, didn't quite understand it, and continually repeated how awful the show would be. When we were ready for the first reading of the script, he predicted doom for the show, detesting the comedy, especially the Phyllis Diller spot. I pleaded with him to go to rehearsal with some enthusiasm in order to spark the rest of the cast. I reasoned that after all it was his show and anything he didn't like could be corrected later. But as soon as we sat around the table to read, Jack told Phyllis that he hated her spot. She looked at him with surprise and told him that she had read it and thought it was very funny. We read it, and it was funny.

By the time we got to the final rehearsal, the night before the show was taped, our director, Bob Henry, was having difficulty getting Jack to rehearse. The representatives of Benton and Bowles advertising agency were out from New York, as were the executives of American Motors, and they watched in horrified disbelief as Jack told the entire group how much he disliked the show they were investing a fortune in. I did my best to get him on his feet to rehearse, but he was firm in his refusal, and finally Bob Henry had to play Jack's role for the rehearsal, asking Jack to study his moves for the camera. However, Jack was too busy complaining and bemoaning the fate of the show to notice anything that was happening.

After the rehearsal the agency men grabbed me and said they were worried about the show, but I tried to reassure them by telling them that some of our shows that turned out best looked this way in rehearsal.

I had been with Jack for many years, but I had never seen him as nervous or insecure as on that show. The next day our

dress rehearsal before an audience was sloppy because of
Jack's lack of preparation, and at the same time we were too
long by four minutes. As soon as the dress was over, I told
the writers, director, and producers that I would get Jack
and we would meet in the script room with them for cuts. We
had only a half hour before the new audience would enter
for the taping session, and so it was necessary to work speedi-
ly and efficiently. I rushed to Jack's dressing room, where I
found him standing before the mirror staring at himself. I
told him to hurry with me to the script room for the cuts, but
he simply continued to look in the mirror, not even turning
to acknowledge me. I told him we had to cut four minutes,
but he didn't answer. In exasperation, I said that we would
cut without him, and I left for the script room. Just then, Al
Gordon walked into Jack's dressing room, and Jack turned
on him.

"After this I'll never be able to get another special. You've
ruined me," Jack ranted. "You'll never work for me again as
long as I live."

Al came to the script room and told us what happened. We
cut the script, and then we all went back to Jack's dressing
room. I acted as if nothing had happened and had Bob Henry give him the cuts we had made. Jack accepted the cuts
glumly, all the while forecasting his ruination from this show.

Immediately after the show Jack and I were to leave for
New York for a short trip. Everyone on the program was
sympathizing with me for a tough three days ahead since I
would be sharing a suite with Jack in the terrible mood he
was in. We taped the show and Jack, surprisingly, having
learned his lines and moves at the dress rehearsal, gave a fine
performance. The script cuts all worked, the audience responded soundly to the comedy, laughing and applauding
all through the show, and we finished right on the button.

After it was over, I could see that Jack had spent his rage
and, begrudgingly, liked the show. When Al Gordon came
by the dressing room later, Jack managed to tell him he was
sorry he had yelled and said the things he did, and he admitted the show came off satisfactorily, which was as far as he
went that night. On the plane to New York, I didn't mention
the show, but I could see that it was on his mind. Finally, he
blurted out, "Well, it was lucky that I raised hell about that

257

show because the cuts we made in the script made all the difference between a good show and a lousy one."

The show was bright and fresh and the publicity featuring the ten bathing beauties assisted in giving us a top rating, as well as excellent reviews, and helped sell our next special.

I hammered away at the importance of finding a theme for the program and surrounding Jack with a strong cast. Jack resisted both those ideas strongly. He didn't think a commercial theme had any significance, much preferring a straight revue-type show. And he was embarrassed with the star names we assembled for the shows since he considered that an indication to the world that he couldn't carry the ball alone. As often as we explained to him that all the variety shows featured many star names, he still felt that people would think he was slipping if he had too many guest stars on his programs.

"What's wrong with just giving them a very funny show?" he would ask. "If it's funny, they'll look, and if it isn't funny, they won't," he would say.

For years Jack tried to sell the idea of doing a "one-man show" as a one-hour TV special, advertising it that way but actually using a lot of stars in the show. His idea was to bring in the guests by having each one interrupt to tell him that he couldn't possibly do it alone and offering to help. A comic would offer some gags; the singer would suggest the kind of song he or she could do on the show to help him; the dancers could do a great number. Actually, it was a very good idea, but unfortunately, no sponsor would go for it unless we advertised the names of the guests and Jack insisted that the only way he would do the show was if it was publicized as a one-man show.

We brought back Fred De Cordova as producer-director of the third special which was called *Carnival Nights*. We had as guest stars Lucille Ball, Johnny Carson, Ben Blue, and Paul Revere and the Raiders and cameos by George Burns, Don Drysdale, Bob Hope, Dean Martin, the Smothers Brothers, and Danny Thomas. It was such a strong show that we rated in the top ten of all the special programs produced that year, and from then on we maintained this high rating for the rest of our specials.

258

Jack Benny's Bag was the title of our fourth special, and it was designed to be very contemporary. We brought Norman Abbott in as producer-director for that one and we decided to do a satirical version of *The Graduate*, the hit picture of the year. When the idea was first suggested, Jack insisted that we must get Anne Bancroft to play the role she created in the picture while he play the Dustin Hoffman part, but her schedule made her appearance impossible. We then tried for Lauren Bacall, who was also unable to make it, and finally, for Melina Mercouri, and when she too was unavailable because of a European commitment, Jack wanted to call the satire idea off. Then we thought of Phyllis Diller, and when we finally taped the show, we realized that it was the best casting of all. She played the role in her usual crazy, hilarious fashion, making the satire all the funnier, especially opposite the ridiculous young college graduate as portrayed by Jack. Eddie Fisher and Lou Rawls bound the sketch together with their singing of special lyrics to the song "Mrs. Robinson," and to add to the surprises and star values, cameos were supplied by Jack Lemmon, Walter Matthau, Dick Clark, Rochester, and Rowan and Martin.

Jack Benny's Bag was the first of two TV shows we produced for Texaco in a tie-up we made for the programs and for Jack Benny's endorsement for which they paid us more than $1,000,000. In addition to the TV programs, they used Jack as their salesman in TV and radio commercials and newspaper and magazine ads. The idea of the campaign, which turned out to be very successful for them and kept Jack's name and face before the public every day for a year, was for Jack to drive into a Texaco station, ask the attendant a series of questions about the gasoline, and after being given a strong selling pitch, ask for "one gallon, please." The "one gallon" theme became their trademark, and soon Jack was being ribbed about it everywhere he went.

The second program we produced for Texaco was *Jack Benny's Birthday Party* with guest stars Lucille Ball, Lawrence Welk, Dan Blocker, Rouvan, Dennis Day, and Don Wilson. There were also cameo performances by Jerry Lewis and Ann-Margret.

For our sixth special program, we tried to think of all the

stars who had never been on TV before, hoping to find someone who would really make ours a special show. We decided on Gregory Peck, reasoning that if we could get him to do "Goldie, Fields and Glide," an old-fashioned vaudeville number, with Jack and George Burns, it would be a sensation. I asked Jack to try to get him, but Jack said it would be impossible. I pointed out to him that we had been successful in similar situations before, citing Harry Truman as a perfect example, and the worst Peck could do was turn us down. Jack finally asked him to drop by the office, and when we told him about the song-and-dance routine as well as an opportunity to do a vocal solo for laughs, he agreed enthusiastically. We then added Nancy Sinatra, Rochester, and Gary Puckett and the Union Gap to the cast. Gregory Peck seemed to have more fun and worked harder than anyone else at rehearsals. When Norman Abbott, the director, would dismiss the trio each day, Peck insisted on staying after hours to go over his dance steps and solo song, "The Shadow of Your Smile." When the show was over—and it proved to be the sensation we expected—Gregory Peck thanked us all profusely, maintaining that he never had more fun in his entire life and saying that he would be a song-and-dance man any time we needed him.

Jack Benny's Twentieth Anniversary Special was our seventh show, and it was a real blockbuster. The guest stars were Frank Sinatra, Bob Hope, Dinah Shore (who had been our very first guest twenty years earlier), Mary Livingstone, Dennis Day, Rochester, and Don Wilson, with Red Skelton and Lucille Ball doing cameos. We featured a series of film clips of most of the guest stars who had appeared on the Benny programs over the twenty years, including Billy Graham, Helen Hayes, Martin and Lewis, Marilyn Monroe, Humphrey Bogart, Irene Dunne, President Truman, Carol Burnett, and Gary Cooper, and the clips turned out to be the highlight of the program. For Frank Sinatra's song, "Fly Me to the Moon," director Stan Harris brought a large helicopter to the set which he had lowered to the stage by wires with Sinatra then stepping out of it to sing the song and do some jokes with Jack. Just before the first rehearsal, I asked Stan to tape the rehearsal so that we could intercut any usable material with the regular taping later. As Sinatra was getting into the helicopter, I whispered to him that we were taping the rehearsal, too, and not to fool around because we might be able to use portions of the rehearsal tape. As I expected, the first rehearsal went beautifully in every department; the camera work was excellent, the music and Sinatra's voice were great, and the comedy went off without a hitch. I told Sinatra it was terrific, and now if we could just repeat it on tape just like the rehearsal, but "one-take Sinatra" insisted that we couldn't get a better one and went back to his dressing room to see the rest of the football game on TV. I don't know if we could have done a better take or not, but we used the rehearsal tape and it was perfect.

Our eighth show was titled *Everything You Always Wanted to Know About Jack Benny But Were Afraid to Ask* and was produced when the Dr. David Reuben book was at the zenith of its popularity. We featured Dr. Reuben on the show, along with guest stars Lucille Ball, John Wayne, Dionne Warwick, and George Burns.

For the tag of that program, which had questions and answers about Jack's life, a question came from the audience: "Can you really play the violin?" That led into an idea Jack adapted from his stage shows when he played motion-picture theaters. He told the studio audience that he would demonstrate that he could really play by doing "Zigeunerweisen" for them, and as he began to play, the camera caught a few people in the audience getting up and leaving, and little by little the rest of the audience started up and out. As he continued to play, the camera cut back to Jack's unhappy face, and the credits started to roll. When the credits ended, the camera went back to Jack, alone on the stage playing to a completely empty theater, to end the program—a very funny idea.

Jack Benny's First Farewell Special was probably the most successful of the ten specials we produced under the banner of J.B. Productions, and it was rated as one of the best of the year. The cast was very impressive: Johnny Carson, Bob Hope, Flip Wilson, Joey Heatherton, Dean Martin, Isaac Hayes, George Burns, Lee Trevino, and Ronald Reagan. The idea of that show was that each guest came on to wish

261

Jack well on his farewell to television, with Jack exclaiming over and over again, "This is *not* my *farewell* show. It's my *first* farewell show. Next year I'll do my second farewell, and then I'll do my third . . . and then my fourth!"

Finally, at the tag of the program, Ronald Reagan had a big surprise for Jack. He started to wish Jack luck on his farewell, and when Jack tried to interrupt him, Reagan stopped him by asking to have the curtain raised. There on the stage was a beautiful "farewell" gift for Jack, a $50,000 Rolls-Royce with every imaginable expensive extra on it. As Reagan held up the gold keys to the car and rhapsodized about Jack's farewell and the beauty of the car, Jack, in obvious dilemma, looked from the car to the keys to the audience. Should he insist that it was not his farewell or should he quit the business and take the $50,000 car? As he looked back and forth undecidedly, the credits began to roll on the screen, and that's the way the show ended.

When it came time to prepare our tenth special for telecasting in January, 1974, we met with Jack many times trying to get an exciting idea. Norman Abbott, the writers, and I threw various ideas in for consideration, but Jack rejected all of them because he wanted to call it *Jack Benny's Second Farewell Special*. I felt that we had done that joke with the first show, and the second one would simply be repetitious, but he was definite and finally insisted that we go with that title. Our guests were Johnny Carson, Redd Foxx, George Burns, Dinah Shore, and the De Francos, with cameos by Jack Webb, Harry Morgan, and Don Rickles.

Redd Foxx was our prize star for that show as his *Sanford and Son* was one of the two top shows on the air then and he hadn't been a guest on anyone's TV show for quite some time.

Ironically, when Jack completed his weekly TV series, Harry Ackerman, an executive producer at Screen Gems, brought us to the studio to see two episodes of the British TV hit *Steptoe and Son* and wanted Jack to play the role of the junk dealer, but Jack refused to go into a series of any kind. When the Screen Gems option expired, Norman Lear and Bud Yorkin bought the show, rewrote it for two black leads, and the show became an instant success.

The writers came through with a good sketch idea for

262

Redd in which Jack goes to visit him expecting to find him living in the broken-down junk house of his TV show, but instead finds him in a lavish home with a butler, elegant silver service, and beautiful clothes. However, when Jack stays for lunch, he discovers that some things never change when they are served soul food.

Redd had refused to appear on a Bob Hope show after they had announced him as a guest because he didn't like the material. Jack was worried that we might lose him, too, so he asked me to be certain that Redd cleared everything well in advance. I set up a meeting with him, and Norman Abbott and Gayle Maffeo, our associate producer, and I went to his office at NBC. I told them I would read the script to Foxx and that they should be sure to laugh it up to help him appreciate the humor. I sat across from him and read his and Jack's lines from the script, trying my best to deliver the jokes with authority, and although Gayle and Norman were rolling on the floor and reacting to every little laugh line, Redd just sat there, looking at me impassively without the slightest trace of any emotion. I finally came to the finish, with the meal of soul food being served and Jack had a line, "What is this, Redd?"

"Some things never change, Mr. Benny. It's ham hocks and turnip greens."

I ended with the best flourish I could muster, not being a performer, and waited nervously. When there was no reaction from him, I thought we were in bad script trouble.

"Well, how did you like it, Redd?" I asked, trying to sound confident. "Any suggestions or changes you'd like?"

"Yeah," he answered, "I gotta change. Turnip greens don't go with ham hocks. That should be black-eyed peas."

"Gayle, change that to ham hocks and black-eyed peas," I quickly ordered, and we gathered up our scripts, thanked him profusely, and scampered out of the office.

Evidently, we must have been right about the *Second Farewell* being too much a replay of the first one because not enough people tuned in and our rating was not as high as it had been for the last number of years. And unfortunately, since he died before we could tape another show, that really was *Jack Benny's Farewell Special.*

47

WHEN I became his manager in 1965, Jack owed the City National Bank in Beverly Hills more than $700,000. Of this $500,000 was money he had borrowed to buy the building and land for a Zody's Department Store, a very good investment suggested by his friend and former agent MCA's Taft Schreiber. The rest was money needed to sustain his life-style and to pay his large income taxes. Jack had no conception of business matters and would always comment during any discussion of such things, "All I know is 'A funny thing happened to me on the way to the theater . . . '!"

That was the beginning of an old vaudeville joke, and although Jack would make the remark in jest, there was truth in it. He worried about the bank loan constantly and in his naïveté, I knew he was imagining that one day a man from the bank might demand the money immediately, and if he couldn't pay off on the spot, he would be forced into bankruptcy. No matter how much I assured him that the loan would not be pressed and that eventually he would be able to take care of it, he was still uneasy, and I determined to do everything possible to ease him out of debt.

Since he was only doing one Benny special TV program a year, and since he wanted to limit the number of guest appearances he made on other TV shows, his only way of making money was to go on the road to play theaters, nightclubs, state fairs, and special one-night functions.

In October, 1966, Jack played Caesar's Palace a few months after the hotel opened. On the show was John Davidson and Aliza Kashi, and on opening night, although our contract called for an hour and a half show, we ran over two hours. Dave Victorson, the entertainment director of the hotel, came storming backstage and raged that the overtime had cost the casino a fortune since the gamblers were in the showroom instead of gambling, and we had to cut the show for the next performance. I told Jack he had to cut, but he would only take out a joke or two and wanted the singers to do less time. John Davidson cut a song, as did Aliza Kashi and with a few less jokes from Jack, the second show that night ran one hour and fifty-four minutes, still much too long. Again Victorson came back, and this time he was livid.

"You cost the casino over one hundred thousand dollars tonight, and if this show isn't cut by tomorrow, Jack will never work here again."

Victorson agreed to trim the opening production number by six minutes, and I asked Jack if he'd please meet me at the swimming pool the next day to discuss the show. I told Mary's brother, Hilliard Marks, the whole story and asked him to be at the pool the following day to help me get Jack to cut some material. Promptly at noon the next day, Marks and I were lying on lounges and as Jack settled down beside us, I explained the situation and gave him my suggested time cuts, turning to Hilliard for affirmation. And as I turned, Hilliard sprang up, dived into the pool and swam away leaving me a team of one! I finally got the show down to an hour and forty-five minutes, and although we did great business, I don't know whether or not the time problem was the reason, but Jack was never asked to play there again.

He played at Harrah's at Lake Tahoe every year until 1967, and then we made a deal with the Sahara Hotel in Las Vegas where Jack worked four to six weeks a year for seven years. During that time we switched to the Sahara Hotel in Lake Tahoe and played there for many years, too. Meanwhile, we were booked into theaters all over the United States, and I discovered that the most lucrative engagements were in the new theaters-in-the-round that were springing up in the East. But Jack, who had been performing from a stage for too many years, insisted that he couldn't work in the round because in order to appreciate his humor the audience had to see his face and watch his frustrated looks. Then two friends of ours, Sammy Lewis and Danny Dare, built two theaters-in-the-round near Los Angeles, and I booked Christmas week through New Year's Eve in 1965 at their Carousel Theater in West Covina. I persuaded Jack to try the engagement, promising that if he didn't like it, we would forget playing in-the-round from then on. Jack was worried that he would not turn during the evening and that a part of the audience would not see his face, and for the first few minutes of his opening night, he was a little stiff. But after the first big laughs he eased up and ended loving the intimacy of playing in-the-round.

As a result of the success of that engagement, we booked ten weeks during the summer of 1966, most of those dates being at theaters-in-the-round. On that tour Wayne Newton was Jack's guest star, and just as Jack had the audience in the palm of his hand, Wayne, who was only nineteen at the time, was a dynamic performer, who even then had the ability to capture the audience until they would stand and yell for more at the end of his performance.

In 1964 on our Australian trip I had received a cable in Sydney from a Hollywood agent, Bobby Burns, asking me to be certain to see a young singer who was appearing at the Hilton there. I did, and I was so impressed with Wayne that I brought Jack in the following night after his own show. We both agreed that Wayne would someday be a leading performer. Until then Wayne had only worked in the lounges at Las Vegas, but the following year, when we needed a supporting act, I remembered him and signed him for an engagement at Harrah's—Tahoe. They loved him, too, and brought him back as a headliner. Later we used him as a guest star on our weekly TV show, and from then on he rose steadily to become a Las Vegas superstar, playing there thirty-two weeks a year.

On that summer tour with Wayne, who was already popular with the fans because of million-selling record hits like his "Danke Shein," we broke records in many of the theaters we played, while in some others we did poorly. Perhaps that is what makes show business so fascinating; sometimes there is no valid reason why you are a success in one place and a failure in another. In 1967 we played the Municipal Auditorium in Pittsburgh with Jack Jones, and we were embarrassed by the paucity of the audience in the gigantic theater, and yet just two weeks later, at the Montreal Expo '67, with the identical show, we broke the record for the season.

Another lucrative source of income came from one-night engagements for various organizations and commercial firms which paid excellent fees, yet had none of the headaches of the regular theater engagements where we had to generate publicity and worry about ticket sales. The club dates, as they are called, were played to a captive, sold-out, jubilant audience at every show. One of the most enjoyable of those was one Jack did at the Chicago Auditorium in 1966 for the fiftieth anniversary of Field Publications, publishers of World Book Encyclopedia. Bailey Howard, president of the company, had an exclusive publishing deal with the astronauts, which he shared with *Life* magazine, and every year he hosted a party in Houston for all the astronauts and the directors of the space program. Because no press or photographers were allowed, it was the one time they could let down their hair and have uninhibited fun.

Bailey asked Jack to surprise the boys at their party in October, 1966, and we worked out a scheme to do so. Jack and I flew to Houston arriving the morning of the party. We were picked up at the airport and quietly smuggled to our suite at the Shamrock Hotel where we had been preregistered as "Irving Fein and friend." We were kept hidden all day and that evening, and after everyone had been seated for dinner and the first course started, we were brought into the darkened dining room where the only light came from the candles on the tables. At the conclusion of the dinner, Bailey Howard went to the dance floor, made a short speech of welcome, introduced the officials and leading astronauts, and then announced a surprise visitor. The band struck up "Love in Bloom," and as Jack stepped to the center of the dance floor, the astronauts stood up as one and gave him one of the longest and warmest receptions he had ever had.

Jack performed for fifteen minutes, and every line was greeted with roars of laughter, and when he finished, most of the astronauts, including the famous ones who had already flown missions, lined up for autographs like kids outside a theater.

A few months later, while Jack was starring at Caesar's Palace in Las Vegas, Bailey Howard flew up to spend the evening with me, and when we met for cocktails, he asked if I minded having three astronauts as my guests, too. I was delighted to see Gus Grissom, Ed White, and Roger Chaffee, who had been in Los Angeles to train for the first three-man spaceflight to be made. After a few drinks, I persuaded them into staying over to see the Benny show. While we were having dinner, I went backstage and told Jack about our guests and wrote the three names down for him to introduce during the show.

When Jack introduced Roger Chaffee, after explaining

about the forthcoming three-man flight, Chaffee received an ovation as thunderous as any of the great stars who were usually in Las Vegas audiences. Ed White, the first man to walk in space, received even greater applause and brought the entire audience to its feet. And when Jack announced Gus Grissom, one of the seven original astronauts, a veteran of two previous spaceflights and the captain of the forthcoming one, the audience cheered and continued with such a long standing ovation that Jack had to plead with them to sit down and let the show go on. It was the greatest reception I had ever heard in a nightclub. Two months later at Cape Kennedy when their spaceship exploded at takeoff, a tragic accident which claimed the lives of those three men, we were especially distraught and saddened.

From time to time Jack would meet some of his astronaut friends and he was always very proud of his association with the group. One amusing incident happened on his seventy-eighth birthday which Jack loved to tell on himself, and it concerned an astronaut. We had been in Mexico City for a benefit performance for the blind children of Mexico City. It was Jack's first trip to Mexico City, and he fell in love with its beauty and sophistication. He was amazed that such a large, cosmopolitan city was perched some 7,000 feet above sea level and kept remarking about that fact. The morning after the benefit Jack left us to fly to Palm Springs, where Frank Sinatra was giving a party for him. Among the guests was Alan Shepard, the first man to fly in space, and Jack told him all about his wonderful four days in Mexico City.

"Just imagine, Alan, the city is seven thousand feet above sea level," marveled Jack. "Have you ever been up that high?"

There was a moment of silence, and when Jack realized what he had said, he roared with laughter and couldn't wait to tell everyone at the party the ridiculous remark he had made, and when he returned to Beverly Hills, he repeated his thoughtless line to all his friends.

Striving to keep our costs down so that we could pay off his giant bank loan, I pared our office staff to a minimum, operating with a secretary for Jack, a secretary for me, and a bookkeeper. We maintained unpretentious, inexpensive offices, and since I was conducting matters without an agent or business manager, Jack's overhead was insignificant for his income. When we traveled on the road, we had been taking our longtime musical director, Mahlon Merrick, to conduct the theater orchestras, but in our new setup, we decided to have the local orchestra leaders conduct the Benny shows since his music was simple and our featured singers usually brought their own conductors with them anyway. In that way, we not only saved the $750-per-week salary, but the fare and expenses, too. Although I had no musical background, I had heard Jack's music so often I knew every note by heart and finally ended up doing all the rehearsals without Jack, humming his violin part and marking tempo with my foot, a feat which never failed to amaze him and amuse the orchestra. For the first year or two beginning in 1965, we also took a stage manager with us on all personal appearance shows to handle the lights and curtains, but after that, since I had to be along anyway, I took over this chore also. Our show generally surprised the promoters and theater operators when we arrived with so few people in our company.

On our theater tour in 1966, Mary's brother, Hilliard Marks, after having been in the real estate business for nearly seven years, came back with us to help Jack on the road. After a season, Jack put him on as a writer, and he helped write the monologues for the stage and nightclub shows. Before long, Jack asked Hugh Wedlock to work with Marks, now that Wedlock's longtime partner, Howard Snyder, had died. When we produced our special TV programs, we always hired top TV writers to work with Marks and Wedlock, and most of the time we used our "new writers," Hal Goldman and Al Gordon, requesting them to take time off one of the other shows they would be writing.

For a man in his seventies Jack worked very hard. As a matter of fact, he worked hard for a man of thirty-nine, and he surely deserved long vacations. But vacations were the biggest bore in the world to Jack, and he preferred to combine a vacation with some kind of performance. For that reason, for many years we booked a week at the Broadmoor Theater, which adjoins the Broadmoor Hotel in Colorado Springs. He considered that a week's vacation because although he worked each night, he could play golf and swim in the daytime. We also played places like Palm Beach and

269

Honolulu, and Jack always said about those jobs, "How about that? I get a week's vacation, have something to do every night instead of being bored, and I get paid for it!"

He appeared in just about every English-speaking country in the world but never went to Rhodesia or South Africa, two places he always desired to visit. I had arranged for a theater tour of Rhodesia, after which we were scheduled to play Johannesburg, Capetown, and Durban in South Africa in the spring of 1968. In the preceding February Jack caught a bad cold, and since we had a busy schedule before the African trip, he worried that he might become too run-down to make such an arduous tour, so we postponed the engagement until the following year. But a few months before we were scheduled to leave the second time, Jack received a letter from an anti-apartheid group in Washington, D.C., asking him not to perform in those countries. The letter was signed by many important legislators and entertainers, both black and white, and Jack became worried about possible repercussions should he make the tour. When I canceled that trip, the promoter from Johannesburg flew to California to try to convince us to fulfill our commitment since he had already invested a great deal of money in advertising and theater deposits. Jack, forever anxious about his image, remained firm about not playing, and we finally settled our obligation by paying the promoter $17,000 for his loss, and regrettably we never did make the trip.

Jack was an Anglophile from way back, probably because the London fans loved him so much, and he tried to get to England once a year if he could—and we usually could. I often managed to book a few television guest spots in London which paid all the expenses for our two-week trips, and Jack would have his "working vacation." His friend Johnny Green was in London in 1967, working on the music for the film *Oliver* when Jack was there, and he remembers how much Jack enjoyed his stay.

"I was living in a rented house," Johnny said, "and had no help, so we had installed what the British call an answering machine to take phone messages when we were out. Jack was so fascinated with this device that he used to call five times a day and leave funny messages, and when Bonnie [Mrs. Green] and I would come home at night, we would enjoy a

Benny performance by phone. One night when we turned on the answering machine, Jack played half of the Mendelssohn Concerto and then said, 'Serves you both right for not being home when I called!' "

An interesting side to Jack's idea of vacationing, especially in the city of London, was exposed one night in Chicago at a dinner with the columnist Irv Kupcinet, his wife, and Kup's lawyer, Arthur Morse, who was going to make his very first trip to London after conquering a fear of flying. Everyone at the dinner was throwing suggestions at him on how best to spend his five days and what were the "musts" for his sightseeing—the Tower of London, Westminster Abbey, Windsor Castle, the Tate Gallery, and so on. The advice came from all sides, everyone having his favorite place to recommend, but Jack just sat without offering a single contribution. Finally, he interrupted: "Listen, the one thing you really must see is the Palladium. Don't miss it! It's the greatest theater you've ever seen."

We looked at Jack, and then we all howled—but Jack didn't see why the remark was so funny to us.

Jack's last working trip to England was in 1973, when he played two concerts at the Palladium on a Sunday night before doing shows in Southend, Bournemouth, and Manchester. The Palladium concerts were complete sellouts, and Jack worked for weeks beforehand on his material, which ended up almost exactly like the material he had been doing in theaters and nightclubs for years. But he polished and repolished every sentence, and just as he had been before an opening for the last ten years of his life, he became more tense as the days came closer to the concert. He wandered around the lobby of the Dorchester Hotel, looking thin, worried, slightly frightened, and very tired. Two days before the concert a friend from California, Armand Deutsch, said he didn't see how Jack would be able to do the two shows, but I told him that Jack was like the old firehorse who came to life when the bell rang. When the orchestra would begin "Love in Bloom," Jack would straighten up, shed years before your eyes, stride out to the center of the stage in his well-tailored dinner jacket and full makeup, and look like a different person from the anxious, nervous man walking around the hotel lobby.

Sure enough, with an audience full of British and American stars and entertainment executives, as well as a roster of socialites, Jack was a triumph that night with reviews that were ecstatic. The next morning I met Armand Deutsch in the lobby, and he admitted that he couldn't believe the man he saw on the stage the night before was the same man he had been seeing every day at the hotel.

Generally, once the opening night was over and the reviews were in, Jack's jitters disappeared. The pale, concerned façade would become replaced with the assurance of the trouper who had been around for so many years.

After our London visit, Jack and Mary usually went to Paris or Rome or both, but Jack was never happy in those cities because he was not a sightseer, he couldn't speak the language, and no one recognized him. The biggest kick he ever got out of Paris, he used to say, was once when he and Mary were walking along the Champs-Élysées and Mary saw a woman talking to her pet poodle, and Mary turned to him and said in perfect seriousness, "Isn't that amazing—that little dog understands French!"

In 1967, when he finished a London TV show, Jack went to visit his friend Norman Krasna, who was then, and still is, living in Switzerland, while Mary went to Paris for a shopping spree. Norman was not only a dear friend of Jack's, but he was grateful for past favors, especially when he married Earle Jolson, Al's widow in 1951.

"It had been a fast courtship," Krasna recalled, "and I really didn't know Earle that well when we married in Las Vegas. We went to Palm Springs for our honeymoon, and there at the airport to meet us was Jack Benny. I guess he sensed that I was still trying to impress Earle with my importance, so he made a big fuss over me and invited us to dinner at his house that night. Among other guests, he had Elizabeth Taylor and Jean Simmons, and Earle was properly taken with the whole thing, including me."

Without letting Jack in on it, Norman set up a most interesting few days for him in Switzerland. He met him at the airport, and on the way back to his home, he suggested that they drop by the Yul Brynners. There for lunch was a houseful of Jack's friends, all having homes nearby at the time, including Audrey Hepburn and Mel Ferrer, the Bill Holdens,

272

the Brian Ahernes, Noel Coward, Capucine, and the Peter Ustinovs. This had been set up in advance to make Jack think this kind of luncheon was a frequent happening. That night Krasna had a dinner party in Jack's honor, and again the same group attended, along with the Charlie Chaplins. They say that no one is as star-struck as a star himself, and Jack Benny was a perfect example of that. By the time that evening was ended Jack was so thrilled at the glamorous lifestyle of his friends that he began talking about moving to Switzerland, imagining that every day would be filled with the magical glitter of a totally theatrical world.

For the few days he was with the Krasnas, Jack slept in the guesthouse. His main concern was how he would be able to order his breakfast since the Krasna staff spoke only French. He also complained to Norman that he could only get Continental breakfasts in Europe and missed his usual cornflakes which he loved. Norman told him, "I have it all arranged for you, Jack. When you awaken in the morning, just pick up the phone, and when the maid answers, just say *Bonjour* and she will bring you cornflakes, toast, and coffee."

Jack followed those instructions and enjoyed his breakfast each morning, and when he was leaving, he told Krasna, "Now I can get cornflakes in every hotel I go to in Europe. All I have to do is say *Bonjour.*"

We traveled around the United States many times each year playing engagements and working hard to amass the money to pay off Jack's bank loan, and each year we brought it down somewhat. When we finished with the Texaco commercial tie-up, I consummated a deal with the Savings and Loan Foundation for Jack to appear in their radio and television commercials for $500,000 for the year, and with that additional income, we finally had enough cash to pay off the loan completely, thus allowing Jack to breathe a little more easily.

When we completed that campaign, we accidentally made an association that was the happiest and most lucrative of Jack's entire career. One day I received a long-distance call from someone I did not know, a Mr. Watson Powell, Jr., who asked if I could arrange for Jack to appear with the Des Moines Symphony for a benefit performance. I politely refused, explaining truthfully that we had too many symphonies that had put their requests in for Jack before Des Moines, some having waited patiently for five or ten years. He understood, and we had a pleasant chat, during which he told me that he was chairman of the board of the American Republic Life Insurance Company. Since we had no sponsor set for our forthcoming TV program, I asked if he'd be interested in sponsoring the show, but he declined, explaining that his company did only newspaper advertising. When I learned that American Republic handled low-cost insurance, I ad-libbed a campaign idea in which Jack could be their spokesman—who else could know a bargain in insurance better than our star? Watson was interested and said he would take the idea up with his agency. A month later we made a deal for Jack to help sell a new life insurance plan they put together, Americaire 39, for which Jack was to receive $500,000 per year for the use of his name and likeness in newspaper and magazine advertisements. The lead copy line WAS: LIFE INSURANCE AT JACK BENNY PRICES, and they also plugged away at 39 REASONS WHY AMERICAIRE 39 IS. . . .

Needless to say, our next concert was with the Des Moines Symphony, and what started as a business relationship grew into a close personal friendship with Watson Powell, his family, and his staff, as well as their advertising agency. Watson told Jack that their research showed that 97 percent of the people liked and respected Jack and that he doubted that anyone else in public life was so loved.

Jack's reply to that was: "What did I do to that three percent?"

American Republic Life Insurance Company set up an office for Jack on the executive floor of their building in Des Moines, and we sent plaques and photographs to decorate the walls. We estimated that Jack spent less than eight hours of his time a year posing for pictures for their ads, which we figured made Jack the highest-salaried man in the world, the $500,000 being for one day!

The job was so easy and the people we worked with so pleasant that we felt guilty taking all that money, and Jack found himself in the position of offering to do things over and beyond our contract terms. We went to Des Moines to attend a cocktail party for all the people who did business with the company, and we spent hours visiting the offices, talking to the employees and attending employee luncheons. Jack had such a good time that he often spoke of traveling to Des Moines regularly to spend time in "his office" and try to learn some of the workings of an insurance company, but something always came up to prevent that. When American Republic held its yearly convention in San Francisco, I called Watson and offered to have Jack perform for the gathering, which idea was gladly accepted.

At the end of our first two years at $500,000 per year, we negotiated a new two-year contract at $600,000 a year which, along with our other commercial activities, put Jack in the best financial position of his life. Since the insurance company had all the photographs they needed, there was very little work we had to do, so when the company was again having a convention, this time in Miami Beach, I called Watson and insisted that Jack be allowed to entertain the conventioneers again. Watson, who always treated Jack with great deference, felt that it would be an imposition to call on Jack again, but Jack was anxious to do as much as he could for them.

By the time of the fourth year of our association, insurance commissions in many states throughout the country were no longer allowing star endorsements, and since their advertising potential with Jack was being dissipated, it didn't look as if we would make a renewal for a fifth year. But we were never to find out because Jack died in the middle of the fourth year of the contract.

About the time we started the third year of the American Republic contract at $600,000 for the year, in 1973, the agency for the Wool Bureau approached me about using Jack for a seven-week TV campaign. I negotiated a deal for four thirty-second commercials for $200,000, and by using his stand-in, we estimated the four could be completed by Jack in two sessions of two hours each. The commercials were very clever and funny, but for some reason Jack was reluctant to do them. Because he couldn't very well turn down $200,00 for a minimum effort, he finally agreed. For months before we taped the commercials, he became angry every time mention of them was made and insinuated that he was being cheapened by such exposure. All my arguments were turned aside by his griping, and even when I pointed out that Bob Hope, Gregory Peck, Laurence Olivier, Bing Crosby, and many other leading personalities were doing similar commercials, he refused to give an inch about the forthcoming job. We taped the spots at the CBS television studios, and Jack questioned every word and every move until the poor director was beside himself. After we completed the first commercial, Jack took me aside and asked me to kill the deal. I told him it was too late as they had spent a good deal of money on sending the writers and the agency men on several trips to the Coast from New York, and if we backed out, they would be stuck with a large group of people, as well as the cost of the studio and crew. Jack petulantly offered to pay all the costs if he could get out of the contract, but he said that very hesitantly. When I said that their entire campaign, which was due on the air in a month, would be ruined and he might be liable in a lawsuit for a great amount of money, he begrudgingly agreed to continue, and in a few hours we completed the taping.

On the drive back to our office I pointed out to him that he had just spent four hours doing those commercials, would spend about two hours for the year for American Republic, and for that, a man who was just a few months short of eighty years of age, would earn $800,000—for about six hours of work. He listened to me and then said with a pout, "But I still didn't like the commercials, and I'm sorry I did them."

When the wool commercials started to break, they were very funny, and nearly all of Jack's friends phoned to tell him how much they liked them. He finally realized that they were really good commercials, and although he stopped complaining, he never admitted that he had created a great deal of chaos over what should have been a simple, pleasant half day of work.

48

WE were on the road about six months of every year playing theaters, nightclubs, concerts, and one-nighters and doing benefits, and Jack loved it, especially when the theaters were full and the audiences enthusiastic. The only unhappy note when we traveled was that he loved Mary so much he felt guilty about being away from her. On the road he would phone her several times a day, and her mood would be transmitted to him. Very often he would be feeling especially perky, go to his room to call Mary, and when we would pick him up a few minutes later, he would be depressed. He didn't confide in us too often at those times, but occasionally he would admit it was because Mary had complained about something or wasn't feeling good. On the other hand, she had the power to lift his spirits if she was feeling good when he phoned, and then he'd come away from the call full of fun and happy as could be.

When we were in town, Jack enjoyed visiting his daughter, Joan, and her four children. Joan is divorced and lives in a home in Beverly Hills close to the Bennys, and Jack would drop by often to play with the children. Joan's eldest son, Michael, came on the road with us a few times, and once Jack took him to Cape Canaveral for a space launching where they were guests of then Vice President Spiro Agnew. Unlike many children of famous stars who were raised in the lap of luxury, Joan grew into a bright, attractive young woman who contributes to civic work in her community and who is a good mother to four fine-looking, well-mannered children.

Although Jack missed Mary when he was away from her, as soon as he would come back to town, he was off with one of his cronies to a Dodger ball game, a concert, or a movie. Mary didn't like ball games or concerts, and since she was prone to fainting spells in crowds, she never cared to go to motion-picture theaters, preferring to run films in the privacy of their projection room at home when they had people over for dinner. Jack would attend a great many large civic and charity dinners without Mary. He was seen so often without her that typical of Hollywood gossip, many rumors flew around that Mary was an alcoholic, which was completely untrue as she very rarely has even one drink at dinner.

In 1966 Mary decided their Roxbury Drive house was much too big for them and she felt they should have an apartment, which would be cozier and need less help to operate. The Century Towers, an apartment across the street from their golf club, Hillcrest, had just been built, and we were fortunate to be able to rent the penthouse when there were only the four exterior walls up. Mary had her decorator, William Haines, lay out the apartment according to their needs, and the owners built it to their plans. Haines, a prominent interior decorator, did a magnificent job on the apartment, and when they moved in, Mary adored it, so naturally, Jack loved it too.

As soon as they were settled, they gave a series of small dinner parties to show off their new home, and most of their friends raved about it. For about eight months they were very happy they had made the move, but then, for some reason, Mary began to find things wrong: the air conditioning, the elevators, no garden, the lobby, and so on. She couldn't wait to move. Jack, as always, bent to her will, and they decided to go back into a house. It took nearly three years to find another home to Mary's liking, but they finally purchased one in Holmby Hills, a lovely residential area adjacent to Beverly Hills, and they subleased the apartment. Once again William Haines was recruited to work his magic in the new house, and after spending a great deal of money to renovate it, they moved into one of the most beautiful homes in town.

It may not have been Mary's habit to frequent any of the huge dinners or parties that so often mark the social scene of Beverly Hills, but she did enjoy the small dinners they regularly attended with their close circle of friends, and Jack was in heaven when they went out together since he not only was in love with her, but enjoyed her sense of humor too.

Jack enjoyed her offbeat humor just as he liked everything that wasn't strictly on the nose. He endeared himself to Harry Harris, who wrote more than two hundred songs for the late Joe E. Lewis, music with crazy lyrics that had saloon audiences laughing for many years. He wrote things like the Zipper Song:

> He took a shave, he washed his face,
> He neatly combed his hair in place,
> But like lots of us men do now and then,
> He forgot to zip the zipper on his pants.

When Joe E. Lewis introduced Jack to Harry Harris many years ago and told him Harris had written most of his songs, Jack said to him, "I just love your music. Those tunes are really lovely."

278

Of all the hundreds of compliments Harris had had about his lyrics, Jack was the only one who ever lauded his music.

Even for his own performances, Jack was always searching for that one line that was different. At the height of the run of *Fiddler on the Roof* in New York, starring Zero Mostel, Jack told a benefit audience, "I was offered the lead in *Fiddler on the Roof.* Not the Zero Mostel part. The *lead*—the part of the fiddler on the roof."

At "Broadway's Answer to Selma" benefit, Earl Wilson reported that Jack was the hit of the evening when he started to talk and then suddenly stopped and exclaimed, "My God, am I doing this for *nothing?*"

Buddy Hackett was a great admirer of Jack and his ability to do that one line or one word that would get a bigger scream than a whole routine.

"I do a pretty racy act," said Buddy, "and I use all the four-letter words and then some on the stage. One time I got sick and couldn't go on at the Sahara in Vegas, and I asked Jack to substitute for me. He was worried that his stuff might not go over with my audience, but he got to them right from the beginning when he said, 'Now I'm not going to say all the words Buddy says . . . but I'll start with one . . . affair.' "

Sometimes the great lines Jack did eventually became trite and were kicked around by every comic in the business. In the late twenties Goodman Ace gave Jack a line to do at a dinner in honor of Walter Winchell which was repeated endlessly after that: "I'm an old newspaperman myself, but I quit because I found there was no money in old newspapers."

One year when we were doing a show at the summer Starlight Musical Theater in Indianapolis, we had a complete sellout week in the 4,000-seat outdoor theater where even the stage was uncovered. On the Thursday evening performance, just as the audience was getting seated, a heavy rain started, but the people sat, covering their heads with umbrellas, pieces of plastic, or newspapers. When it looked as if we would have to cancel the show and refund the money, I asked the manager what we could do since we could not give them tickets to a later performance because we were all sold out. He said that if Jack would go on with the show, not too many people would leave and we might at least salvage something. We eliminated the strings and other perishable instruments from the band, leaving six brass and a piano covered with an oilcloth, and we outfitted Jack with a raincoat and rubber overshoes. Just before he went on, I gave him his opening line: "Good evening, ladies and gentlemen. Anyone else would have given you your money back—but not me!"

The audience screamed and were so appreciative that he was willing to perform under such circumstances that only four people left during the first half. The rain stopped as the intermission began, and the second half played under a full moon. Jack quoted that opening line from then on.

We were to play a one-nighter in Amarillo, Texas, a few days after a big newspaper story broke about the closing of Edna's Chicken Ranch, a famous bawdy house that had been in continuous business since 1884. Johnny Carson called and gave Jack his opening line for that show: "I came down for the closing since I was here for the opening . . . same girls."

Another line that Jack loved was done, but not in jest, by Tom May, head of the May Company in Los Angeles, the store where Mary had once worked in the hosiery department. The Bennys became good friends of the Mays, but May never acknowledged all the gratuitous plugs they gave the May Company on the radio shows through the years, mentions that would have cost millions of dollars in advertising. One day Mr. May called Jack a day before a broadcast and asked for four seats, but every ticket for the 300-seat radio studio had been already distributed, and Jack had to refuse him. May later told a friend of Jack's, "Can you imagine? He mentions the May Company all the time on his radio show, and when I called him for four tickets, he wouldn't give them to me!"

Just as Lucille Ball bought the RKO Studios, the studio where she once had worked as a chorus girl, and changed the name to Desilu, Mary Benny came full circle when their good friend Tom May announced that he was planning to sell his Palm Springs estate. The Bennys stepped in and bought it, and another Horatio Alger story was written.

Jack's sister, Florence, was his only close living relative, and since she was widowed and living in Chicago, Jack tried to visit her as often as he could, usually stopping off on his way to New York. When he did visit Chicago or worked there, Florence was with him every minute and always brought her friends and other relatives from the area to see the star. Just before his seventy-ninth birthday, we were in Birmingham, Alabama, for a symphony concert, and with five days free before meeting a commitment in New York, Jack decided to go to Chicago to spend the time with his sister while I went to New York. He asked me to book him on the train from Chicago back to New York because he really had a fear of flying and always professed to enjoy the train. For years he had asked that on cross-country trips between Los Angeles and New York we take a train, and I would argue with him the relative merits of the time lost against the relaxation of a train trip. But he would get very angry with me until I learned how to handle it. I would tell him that I'd fly and he could take the train and we'd meet in New York, and he always ended up flying with me. But at least we stopped the arguments. However, on this trip, he was to return to New York alone and said he was really looking forward to the train trip. We had no way of knowing that there would be a record snowstorm on the East Coast the night before Jack was to arrive. I sent a limousine to meet him at Penn Station, and when he arrived at the hotel, hours late, he was steaming.

"That was the worst trip I've ever made," he fumed. "It was bumpy and dirty and so slow. We had to stop in Pennsylvania and couldn't get started again because of the snow. The food was the worst I've ever eaten. I'm writing to the president of the company, and I'm really going to give him hell."

That was the last time he ever mentioned about preferring to travel by train.

When Jack Benny reached the age of seventy, the syndicated columnist Robert Peterson gave him his annual "Life Begins at 40" award, an honor he had previously given to President Truman, poet Robert Frost, and heart specialist Dr. Paul Dudley White. The inscription on the plaque read:

"To Jack Benny, whose vast popularity at threescore and ten attests to his genius as a comedian, and whose classic portrayal of a frustrated human clinging to youth has favorably influenced millions to laugh at their years and accept advancing age with humor and equanimity."

His audiences didn't seem to notice, nor did his friends, but the psychological fact of turning seventy did affect him, and I began to see a gradual diminution of his energy and ability to concentrate. Onstage he was a meticulous dresser, and offstage he had very good taste in clothes and always looked neat and well dressed. But he started to become careless about what he wore, sometimes putting on the same shirt two or three days without changing or wearing out-of-date sport jackets with slacks that didn't match. Mary and I would urge him to buy new clothes, and he was always meaning to, but he kept putting it off, claiming that there was nothing wrong with what he was wearing; all the while his newer clothes hung unworn in his closet.

He was blessed with good health, but as the years went by his hearing started to go, and he would become frustrated at the movies or a theater. He tried to use a hearing aid, but he was embarrassed to wear one in public and used one only in the office or at a movie. However, he was so unhandy that he never quite learned how to insert the little things in his ears, and finally the aid lay untouched in a bedroom drawer. The only physical ailment he had, which he diagnosed himself, was a slight case of diabetes. He was reading *Coronet* magazine one day and saw an article about ten symptoms of diabetes. The article stated that one might have some symptoms and be diabetic or have all the symptoms and not be at all. Jack felt that some of the clues applied to him, and so he asked his doctor to check him for it. It was discovered that he had, as the doctor said, a "touch" of diabetes. It was so slight that all he had to do was take Orinase tablets once or twice a day, and from then on, Jack cautioned whoever he was with to "remind me to take my Orinase." He not only often forgot to take his pills, but several times failed to bring them on a trip and we would have to scurry around to find a doctor to write a prescription for them. I was annoyed with him when we went to Australia because I had reminded him many times to bring his pills, and sure enough he forgot them. From Australia we had to phone his doctor in Beverly Hills and have him airmail a bottle of pills to us.

Although he was still a great star, he realized he wasn't the giant he had been years before when the whole show business world was at his feet, and he would feel frustrated when he saw other, younger comedians getting deals that he would want. Even though I pointed out to him that Ed Wynn, the man Jack thought was the funniest he had ever seen, was unwanted after the age of sixty-nine, he found no solace in the fact that he was in his late seventies and was still starring in theaters, nightclubs, concerts, and television. And yet, in his professional relationship with the other stars, Jack was always willing to let the other fellow take the top billing or the best position. When Barry Mirkin was producing the show for the Hillcrest Country Club's fiftieth anniversary, he was in a quandary about how to position the twenty stars on the bill, with most of them arguing about when they should go on. Jack solved all of Barry's headaches by offering to go on first.

His stature and rapport with his audiences became greater as the years went by until he really became "a legend in his own time." One critic said of him, "He seemed to have a love affair with his audience." Not only did he receive standing ovations at the conclusion of every show, but when he would make his entrance and say, "Good evening, ladies and gentlemen," he would more often than not be greeted by a roar of approval as the audience would rise to its feet. Sometimes, standing in the wings and listening to him tell jokes I'd heard for so many years, I'd be amazed at how he'd be received with such obvious adoration. He reached the point where he could do no wrong. In the last few years he would many times forget a routine right in the middle of it. He then simply asked the audience what he had been talking about, and after a prompt or two, he'd continue and end up getting a bigger laugh at the finish than if he had done it letter perfect. Those errors sometimes created the impression that he was just ad-libbing the whole routine, when in actuality it was carefully prepared and rehearsed.

Instead of being more secure and confident as he grew older, he became less and less certain of his success. Each engagement became a hurdle he had to get over if he were to continue as a star performer. He seemed like the man who had won the gold ring on the merry-go-round but never quite believed he had won a prize he could keep.

But then something would come along to give him confidence again. He had never been awarded an honorary degree until 1970, when Riverside University in California awarded him the degree of Doctor of Music. Then, in 1972,

Jacksonville University gave the degree of Doctor of Fine Arts to Jack and his friend Bob Hope on the same day. Jack was always a little in awe of Hope for his energy and comic ability, and to share the same platform and receive a degree together was a big thrill for Jack who was then seventy-eight years old. When Jack stepped forward to receive that honor, he said in part:

"If I knew I was going to wear a cap and gown today, I wouldn't have bought a new suit. . . . At Riverside University I received a Doctor of Music degree, and Jascha Heifetz nearly killed himself. . . . It's ironic that here I'm receiving a university degree, when I was thrown out of high school. At the time I was the most embarrassed twenty-year-old boy in Waukegan. . . . Bob Hope is surely one of the most dedicated and unselfish men in our industry. Each year Bob goes off entertaining our troops, while we sit home with our wives and loved ones. Who else but Bob, while the rest of us were at home, would unselfishly go off year after year with Jill St. John, Raquel Welch, Ann-Margret? . . . Bob was born in England but he came over here to entertain our troops at Valley Forge. He was sure we were going to win because he sent home for his golf clubs. . . ."

In Hope's speech, he had one funny line about Jack. He said, "Jack's a great musician, and I'm a great actor. It takes a great actor to say Jack Benny is a great musician."

During the last few years of his life, Jack's anxieties over his career would be reflected in many ways. Sometimes he would work with his writers for weeks before a theater or Las Vegas engagement, saying he wanted to do a completely new show. Invariably, he would walk out onstage, not having learned the new material very well, do the first two or three jokes and, when they didn't score too well, promptly resort to all his old, surefire routines.

He was tired the last few years. Not tired enough to want to quit, but the kind of tired feeling that a healthy, talented man feels after a lifetime of constant work. Sometimes before curtain time in his dressing room, he would look pitiful—old and frail. A half hour before his second show at Las Vegas, he would often say that he couldn't go on. I would urge him to try because the room was full of fans who would

284

be disappointed, and finally he would be persuaded not to let them down. Later, when he'd protest about the second show, I'd tell him that we could have one of the other stars on the Strip substitute for him, and then he'd tell me never mind, he'd manage to get by somehow. He was always a pro. I'd suggest certain cuts he could make since he was so tired which would shorten the show and allow him to finish much sooner, and he'd agree. When his entrance music would start, he would shed twenty years before my eyes as he'd straighten his shoulders, throw up his chin, and stride out on the stage like a young trouper. The applause and laughter were like adrenaline to him, and invariably he'd end up doing a show fifteen minutes to a half hour longer than necessary. And despite nightly complaining about two shows in Las Vegas, at the close of nearly every engagement, he would comment wistfully, "Gee, I wish we were playing another week."

A typical example of the magnetism a stage and live audience held for Jack happened once at Harrah's Club at Lake Tahoe when we followed a show costarring George Burns and Carol Channing. On the morning of our opening Jack awakened with a bad cold, and he called the doctor, who advised him to stay in bed and not to perform that night. George Burns had already left for home, but I persuaded Carol Channing to stay over and substitute for Jack as an addition to our featured singer, Jane Morgan, and the rest of the show we had brought with us. Just before show time Jack told me he thought it would be a good idea if he would come onstage at the end of the show just to let the press and the audience know that he wasn't seriously ill and would be there the next night to do his performance. I told him it would mean getting shaved and dressed and that I thought it was silly to get out of bed, do that, and walk all the way to the theater. In any event, I argued, Carol Channing was planning to give that message to the audience anyway. But Jack said he'd like to just say hello for a minute, and then he promised he'd get right back to bed.

When Carol took her last bows, she returned and introduced Jack. He opened with a joke about his cold and received such tumultuous applause and laughter that forty-two minutes later, by my watch, he was still talking and the audience was eating it up. Finally, I got Mary's eye at a ringside table, and she yelled up to him to quit, which he did reluctantly.

In the winter of 1971 we had a month off, and Jack took advantage of it to take one of his rare vacations, an eleven-day cruise to Puerto Vallarto and Acapulco. He booked an expensive suite on the ship and vowed that he was simply going to rest, sun, and eat, but as soon as the ship sailed, he offered his services for a big show on board and ended up spending two of his eleven days on shipboard arranging it. The following winter I received an offer for Jack to do two shows on the *Queen Elizabeth II* for a trip through the Caribbean. In addition to a suite for Jack and Mary and a room for their maid and another for me, he was to receive a fee of $15,000. But Jack decided he didn't want to go through all the bother of preparing a show at that time since Mary didn't want to go anyway.

Jack was a simple man in his food tastes, and as he got older, he began to order the same dishes at every meal. He was never fond of fancy French dishes and was basically a meat and potatoes man. He did enjoy Chinese food, but there too he had definite tastes. While others would order exotic Chinese dishes or special Cantonese or Mandarin recipes, Jack would order chop suey every time. Cornflakes was his favorite breakfast food, especially served with sliced bananas or berries. And he adored ice cream. Even though he wasn't supposed to have it because of the sugar content, he would always order it "just this one time," explaining to the waitress about his diabetes and apologizing for "cheating" a little. T-bone steaks were a favorite of his, and of all things, he loved chicken-fried steaks which were rather difficult to get at the 21 Club in New York or the Bistro in Beverly Hills. But he would be as happy as a child with a new toy when he spotted chicken-fried steak on the menu of some obscure diner at which we'd stop while touring. Our former script girl, Jeanette Eyman, wrote to me a week after Jack died that she was driving back to Los Angeles from Reno and stopped at a roadside restaurant for dinner: "There on the menu was chicken-fried steak, and I remembered how Jack always said he loved it and the only place he could get it was in restau-

rants along the highway. I suppose I was being overly sentimental, but I ordered chicken-fried steak!"

Jack was not a "dirty old man," but as he got older, he
would buy all the nudie magazines: *Playboy, Oui, Penthouse,*
and so on. When we went on trips, he would invariably stop
at the airport newsstand before take off and buy a supply,
and when we would catch him reading them, he would comment, "Isn't it terrible the things they publish nowadays? I
think they should ban these magazines from the stands."

One of his biggest jokes for nightclubs arose from the subject of pornography, when he told the audience how disgraceful some of today's sexy films were: "I went to see one
of those X-rated pictures the other night, and I couldn't believe my eyes. So I stayed to see it a second time."

The first porno picture he saw was with his friends Norman Krasna and Eddie Buzzell after the three of them had
dinner together and went to a theater across the street from
the restaurant. When *Deep Throat* opened, it caused such talk
that Jack said he would like to see it but would be embarrassed to be seen going up to the box office to buy tickets. A
friend of mine owned the theater where it was showing, and
I arranged for the manager to be watching for us one afternoon and sneak us in. We parked that day on a side street,
and as we approached the theater, Jack with his hat pulled
low to cover his face, the earlier show broke, and the audience streamed out. Who was exiting but Mel Blanc, and
when he spotted us, he yelled, "Hi, Jack, you'll love it!"

As he got older, even his own little jokes became more attuned to sex. Once while he was being driven home from the
office by his secretary, Dorothy Ohman, they waited what
seemed like an interminable time for the traffic light to
change. Jack said, "We could have an affair before this light
changes."

He liked pretty girls and would flirt with them whenever
he had the chance as he pictured himself the young romantic, almost like the character he assumed on his shows. The
last television show he taped was a Dean Martin roast, which
was done only three months before he died. Jack had a bad
cold, but he went through with the show anyway. While waiting around with his writer Hugh Wedlock, Jack was chatting
with a young blond dancer who happened to be backstage,

and he started to hold her hand as they talked. He told her he had a cold, and she recommended that he take hot tea and aspirin.

"Do you think it will do any good?" Jack asked, looking at her cleavage.

"Well, my grandfather always takes that when he has a cold," answered the girl.

Jack dropped her hand like a hot potato and decided that he'd better read his speech over.

He had the heartiest and most infectious laugh I have ever heard and he laughed many times every day at everyone's jokes and ad-libs. While trying to get additional stories and anecdotes about him, almost everyone I spoke with remembered a line they had said that had provoked Jack to falling on the floor with laughter because he was undoubtedly the best audience in the world. But as he grew older, he wasn't as sharp and didn't laugh as much, partly because he was depressed at getting older and partly because he sometimes didn't get the joke. His daughter, Joan, and her two youngest children went with Jack to see the *Ice Follies* a year or two before he died. Joan told Jack the latest joke that had been getting laughs from all her friends. Jack gave only a slight chuckle, and she couldn't understand why he didn't seem to think it was funny. She repeated the punch line and again he reacted with mild enthusiasm. During the second half of the ice show Jack suddenly started to laugh and pound his knee. When he regained his composure, he repeated the story to Joan, word for word as she had told it and then hit the punch line to emphasize the joke. It had just dawned on him!

Jack was a terrible driver, even as a young man. He was usually thinking of script ideas, opening lines, a practical joke to use on one of his friends or something else creative, and he never noticed that he was driving in the middle of the road, straddling the white line, or going the wrong direction on a one-way street. In the days of the gearshift, he could drive for miles in second gear while talking a stream to a companion or dreaming of new routines. To have a chauffeur was out of the question because he wanted to be free to pick up and go on a moment's notice. But when he reached his seventy-fifth birthday, after scraping too many fenders and getting stuck alone in his car a few times, I decided that he needed someone to drive for him. I hired a young Vietnam veteran, Eddie Villery, and made him a production assistant in our office, his principal job being the care of our star. He was a bright young man, and for the next five years he spent most of his time driving Jack, helping him in the dressing room when we played theaters and concerts out of town, and along with Jack's old friend and stand-in Ned Miller, he was always available to accompany Jack to a movie, concert, ball game, or just a Chinese dinner. Eddie had a good sense of humor, and Jack enjoyed being with him. One day when Jack, unthinkingly, started to get in the driver's side of the car, Eddie stopped him by saying, "Jack, get in the other side. Remember, *I'm* the chauffeur, you're the chauffee!*"

49

IF seventy was a traumatic age for Jack, as he approached eighty, he felt everything closing in on him, and he started to talk of dying. I would remind him that his father had lived to the age of eighty-seven, and because he was in perfect health, he would most likely outlive all of us. But the round figure of eighty represented to him the things he dreaded most: illness, the demise of his career and, ultimately, death.

After he reached seventy-five, although we didn't lie about his age, we didn't do anything to publicize it. We simply didn't talk about it. I turned down all dinners and television shows that were based on celebrating his birthdays because I reasoned that since he looked so much younger than he was, he might lose some jobs if producers or potential sponsors knew his correct age. And even though it was not a secret, when he was seventy-eight and seventy-nine, many people would guess him to be at least ten years younger. Looking great and feeling fit, however, did not compensate to him for the fact that his eightieth birthday was looming on the horizon, and he became more and more depressed about it.

When he was seventy-seven, I was directing some radio commercials in which he had to say that word "octogenarian." After he mispronounced it several times, I finally told him from the control booth, "Don't worry, Jack. In another three years, you'll be able to say it beautifully!"

As much as he hated the term, he had to laugh.

When he was seventy-eight, he said to Hugh Wedlock one day, "Hughie, I'm seventy-eight. Do you realize that soon I'll be eighty?"

"Jack," Wedlock asked, "what happened to seventy-nine?" And although he laughed at Hughie's line, he found the subject of age increasingly uncomfortable.

One day at the Hillcrest Country Club, he saw Adolph Zukor, the man who had founded Paramount Studios. Zukor was one hundred and one then but still alert, and Jack was seventy-nine. Jack went over to Zukor's table, leaned down to shake his hand, and said, "Hello, Mr. Zukor. Remember me? I'm Jack Benny."

Zukor looked up at him with a twinkle in his eye.

"Jack Benny! Are *you* still around?"

For many years sleep had been a problem for Jack, and two pills at bedtime had been a long time Benny formula. As he approached eighty, he found it more and more difficult to fall asleep, and so he increased the strength of his sleeping pills. He complained to George Burns, "I didn't sleep a wink last night. Not a minute."

"How did you sleep the night before?" Burns asked.

"Oh, the night before I slept just fine."

"Then sleep every other night," was Burns' quick advice.

Like many people when they reach their older years, Jack became very preoccupied with death, the ages of his friends who died, and the illnesses from which they died, and he read the obituary column daily—even before reading the entertainment news! He became obsessed with certain morose ideas, one of which was that if one lives long enough, one contracts every terrible disease known to mankind. He began to relate every piece of news to himself as well. If he would read in the papers of some dire illness, he immediately was reminded of similar symptoms he was having. I remember once after his eightieth birthday we were driving in the car and he was reading a newspaper. His comment concerning an item announcing the death in Switzerland of a European scientist, aged eighty-four, was: "Well, looks like I've only got another four years to go."

"How about Arthur Rubinstein, who's still going strong at eighty-seven?" was my answer, which failed to get any response.

Other than doing a political joke once in a while, Jack was unable to comprehend the politics of our country, even though he was acquainted with presidents, governors, and mayors throughout the years. Although he was basically a conservative, he maintained that he was not a member of any party but always voted for the man. As he got older, he became more confused about what was happening in Washington, reading only the headlines and much preferring to concentrate on a speech for a charity dinner or a new routine for a theatrical appearance.

During the Watergate proceedings he read the daily accounts but never quite understood it. He asked me to explain, which I did, at length, many times, but each time a new bombshell in the case exploded, he would be reminded to ask again what this Watergate business was all about.

At the peak of the energy crisis, months after the Arab oil embargo and subsequent shortage of gasoline, while the papers, radio, and television were blasting it all day long, Jack called a friend and asked, "I wish you'd explain to me what this energy crisis is that they're talking about."

It wasn't that Jack had lost interest in his fellowman that caused his seeming lack of awareness in world affairs. It was that his horizons had shrunk as he got older until they encompassed only his own world of show business and the importance of maintaining his position in that world.

Many charitable organizations wanted to honor Jack at dinners on his eightieth birthday, and our writers also wanted to use the birthday as the basis of a TV special, but Jack and I decided to keep it quiet and ease over that hurdle without any fanfare. That is, *we* decided, but Frank Sinatra decided otherwise. He said that Jack's birthday couldn't go by without a party, and he was going to throw one. Now, Sinatra was the king to millions of his fans, but to the Bennys he was king and the whole royal court, and his slightest wish was their command.

He invited twenty-four couples to his Palm Springs estate for the party, and as the day approached, Jack became more and more excited. Jack and Mary went to the Sinatra compound a week before the big party, and during that week every night was like New Year's Eve with celebrations and parties.

The first morning in the Sinatra compound Mary's breakfast arrived at their bungalow on a tray complete with a fresh rose and a small gift box. It was a lovely bracelet from Van Cleef and Arpels. The second morning was a repeat performance, only this time the small black velvet jewel box contained a Cartier watch. The third morning the tray was brought without the gift box which prompted Mary to send a brief note to Sinatra: "What happened, Frank? This morning . . . nothing?"

I arrived in Palm Springs the day before the party, and when I saw Jack, he mentioned that Norman Krasna and his wife were there from Switzerland, and it was a shame they weren't invited to the party. When I showed surprise that Norman and Earle had not been invited, Jack explained that Sinatra was handling everything and since he probably didn't know about the Krasnas, Jack couldn't tell him at the last minute to ask extra guests. I reminded Jack that Krasna was an old and close friend and I insisted that he say something to Frank, which he finally did. At five o'clock on the night of the party Sinatra phoned Norman, apologizing for calling so late, but Norman said he would have come to Jack's birthday party if he had been called only in time for dessert!

Candy Bergen wanted to send a wire of congratulations to Jack but had a difficult time getting the message through Western Union because of a joke she had with Jack for many years. When she was a little girl, she childishly called him Mr. Berny, and the name stuck. Jack, in return, called her Sandy, and eventually they made a running gag of it. When she graduated from Westlake School, he sent her a pin on which was engraved "Congratulations—Mr. Berny." Western Union was sending hundreds of congratulatory messages to Jack but didn't understand that it was a joke and tried to correct her spelling of "Jack Berny."

The guest list for the party was small and intimate and read like a Hollywood *Who's Who*. Among the invited friends were the Milton Berles, George Burns, the Billy Wilders, the

Peter Duchins, the Freddie Brissons (Rosalind Russell), Dr. Michael De Bakey, the Fred De Cordovas, Joan Benny, Nancy and Ronald Reagan, Judy and Spiro Agnew, and Frank Sinatra's mother—who made the pasta herself!

The hors d'oeuvres were plentiful, including caviar, and the drinks flowed copiously while the guests milled about Frank's lovely desert retreat, admiring the marvelous paintings and stunning collections of jade animals and Fabergé boxes.

When dinner was announced, we walked outside through a patio area to a projection-playroom in which five tables, each set for ten, had been arranged. A huge ice sculpture of a violin marked the entrance to the room. The decor was red and white in keeping with Valentine's Day, the tables covered with white linen and trimmed with red satin ribbons. White flowers surrounding large hurricane lamps made lovely centerpieces, and at each lady's place was a small gift box containing a solid gold heart and chain necklace. On the wall above the sumptuously laid buffet table was a blowup poster of Jack as a baby, complete with long white baby dress. Chasen's came all the way from Beverly Hills to cater part of the dinner, with their captains and waiters doing the honors.

Just as the main course was being served in came an ensemble of ten fiddlers brought from Los Angeles to stroll around the tables and play beautiful music, and naturally, Jack couldn't resist joining them for one number. Billy Wilder's comment about the violin group was: "Frank brought them all the way from Maxim's in Beaumont!"

After the dinner Milton Berle took over as master of ceremonies of an entertainment most of which he had spent weeks preparing with writer Buddy Arnold. Milton opened the show and then introduced the "performers" who sang hilarious lyrics to popular songs, some of which were too risqué to be printed here. Song writer Jimmy Van Heusen accompanied the singers at the piano.

To the tune of "When You Were Sweet Sixteen," Audrey Wilder sang the following parody:

> George Washington had crossed the Delaware,
> Napoleon had just met Josephine,
> James Madison and Dolley were a pair,
> Abe Lincoln wasn't born yet

When Jack was sweet,
When Jack was sweet . . . sixteen.

Tom Edison had just invented flicks,
Jim Brady dined at Luchow's with his chicks,
Ulysses Grant was in an awful fix
And Nixon wasn't born yet
To pull his tricks,
When Jack was six . . . ty-six

Governor Ronald Reagan's lyrics went to the tune of "The Sound of Music":

The sweetest sound in all the world
Is when my Nancy laughs,
The sound of staunch Republicans
Who ask for autographs.
The cheering of convention crowds
Can make my senses spin,
But the loudest sound
I ever heard
That drives me out of my skin,
Is just the sound of
Jack's vi-o-lin.

To the music of "Mother," Ruth Berle sang:

B is for the bursitis in his shoulder,
E is for his energy that's gone,
N is for neuritis since he's older,
The other N's the Nembutol he's on.
Y is for his youth that's all behind him,
Every night he prays it will come back,
Put them all together
They spell Mil . . . ton [pause]
I wish that he was young
Like
Jack!

George Burns was elected to sing the following words to "Mary";

294

He married Mary . . . Mary,
A simple name that always sparks,
Though she's a classy dame,
Her maiden name
Was Sadie Marks.
Today it's Mary . . . Mary,
And boy, how lucky can she be,
Because without Jack's fame,
Her married name
Would be Sadie . . . Marks . . . Kubelsky!

Frank Sinatra sang to the music of "Mr. Wonderful":

May I offer my congrats,
To the pussycat of all pussycats,
He's got all the charm
That most of us lack,
Mr. Wonderful—that's Jack.

When he walks out on the stage,
His charisma overshadows his age,
He's a thousand lengths
Ahead of the pack,
Mr. Wonderful—that's Jack.
This song is difficult to sing.
You will agree,
Because these lyrics that fit him,
They sure fit me,
He's been with us eighty years,
It's been SRO each time he appears,
And he's never known
A critic's attack,
Mr. Wonderful—that's Jack.

And if I only mention
Mary with restraint,
It's just because it's almost
Time for her to faint,
Now let's toast him, glass in hand,
To the sweetest birthday boy in the land,
And one year from now
I'm sure we'll be back

With our favorite son,
When he's eighty-one,
Mr. Wonderful—that's our Jack!

Then Jack Benny rose to sing his own response, "Hello, Frankie," a parody of "Hello, Dolly," in which he offered a very funny but sincere "thank you" to Sinatra for giving him "the greatest evening of my life."

It fell to Jack's oldest and closest friend, George Burns, to wind up the entertainment. He left the guests with a warm and sentimental feeling when he made a very touching speech which dampened a few eyes, and he ended with a toast to the birthday boy: "Jack, we've been friends for fifty-five years. That means we met when you were twenty-five and I was twenty-three . . . and there's not a damn thing we did then that we can't do better now. That gives you an idea of how pathetic we were when we were young! I'm sure when you'll be ninety and I'll be eighty-eight, we'll still be looking for a new opening."

After the entertainment everyone returned to the main house for coffee, after-dinner drinks, and fine cigars for the men.

Just as Jack and the others thought the party was over, around 1 A.M., Frank herded us all back to the projection room, which had been cleared of the dinner tables, and we discovered a dance band playing and a buffet table laden with a complete supper spread. At 4 A.M., as the first guests began to depart, George Burns summed up the evening beautifully when he said admiringly to Sinatra, "Frank, you sure know how to give a nice sociable!"

50

THE last year of Jack's life was not a happy one for him, although it should have been. He was doing everything he had been doing for the preceding ten years, and very successfully too. He was playing theaters, doing his one-night stands, being honored at symphony dinners, and breaking records at symphony concerts in the United States and Canada. He also did his own TV special and guested on many other programs. His income for the year was more than $1,000,000. To have such a lucrative and active ongoing career at his age was indeed a rarity. And yet he was not happy. It was because he couldn't accept being eighty years old.

His audiences, however, didn't know what he felt and how deeply he was depressed. He still looked very well, perhaps not "thirty-nine," but he could have passed for a man of sixty-five. Although he became more careless about his dress, onstage he was the meticulous, well-groomed comedian he had always been. He began to lose weight and dropped from his customary 151 pounds to 144 pounds and, later, to 138 pounds. He seemed to have lost his appetite completely and complained constantly that he was never hungry. In 1974 we were out of town for engagements almost half the year and were together for most of our meals, and he never seemed to enjoy one of them, most of the time leaving half his food untouched. Those of us close to him thought it was just nerves, but perhaps, in retrospect, it was an indication of his last, fatal illness. We would be convinced it was just a state of mind when on occasion he would manage to pack away a big meal while telling us he wasn't hungry at all. He was very fond of fruit, and at every hotel the management would usually send up a large basket of fresh fruit. At four or five in the afternoon Jack might eat an apple or banana or both, and then at six thirty, when we would go to dinner before a show, he would of course not be hungry. We explained that the fruit had filled him up, and he agreed that he wouldn't eat before meals again—but promptly forgot and then moaned about his failing appetite.

Although he was not much of a sightseer, during the last year of his life, we went to many interesting places, and most of us in the group spent our spare time visiting historic or scenic spots around the town. When we would ask Jack to join us, he would invariably say, "You go ahead. I'm not interested, and I want to practice my violin anyway."

I felt sad being with him and watching him so unhappy and nervous all the time when there was so much in his life to

297

enjoy. Every job we did became a chore to him and a giant worry, and he always predicted the worst beforehand. His only pleasure was when he walked onstage and heard the laughter and applause, and he would be sustained throughout the show and for the hour or so after when we would go out for supper and he would rehash every joke.

Any intimate twenty-eight-year association, like a marriage, has its ups and downs, and ours had its share. For the most part, we were very close through the years, and we had great respect for each other's talents and abilities. Our disagreements were generally over an idea for a television show or whether or not to play a certain engagement. I must say that he said complimentary things about me to everyone, crediting me with much more than I was entitled for the longevity of his career. In one in-depth interview for Public Television, he said the two most important influences in his career were Mary and me. And yet, when we had infrequent arguments, Jack would let his rage smolder for a long time, and in some instances, he never allowed the spark to be extinguished, especially when the "star ego" was involved.

One such unfortunate episode occurred during a period when he was playing very successfully in Las Vegas for three weeks every year at hotels like the Flamingo and the Desert Inn. His salary at the time was $50,000 a week, and had been for many years. He became very friendly with one of the owners of another Las Vegas hotel, who suggested that he play his hotel. Jack and Mary were enthusiastic about the idea. I told him that I knew the top salary at that particular hotel was $35,000 a week, and they wouldn't pay him what he had been getting, but Jack said that his friend was so anxious to have him that he was sure he'd pay whatever I asked. When the entertainment director of that hotel called, I told him that we'd be happy to make the same deal with him as we had elsewhere, and I even offered to show him the previous contracts which outlined the salary and the complimentary suite for the Bennys and their maid, plus an occasional room for me. I say "occasional" because I have never been too fond of Las Vegas, and it had been my custom to go with the show for three days at the opening to take the show through rehearsal and opening night, return for one night in the middle of the engagement to check any problems, and then go

298

up for a night or two at the closing to pay off the cast, take care of the closing tips, and arrange transportation home. Incidentally, at that time the rooms were $16 per night at that hotel.

A few days later the entertainment director called and said he was sorry but they would have to pass, not giving any reason or making a counteroffer. When I told Jack the bad news, I could see he was very hurt, but I didn't give him the "I told you so" routine and never mentioned the disappointment again. Several months later Jack called me at home one night, and he was very angry. He had been to a party at the home of his Las Vegas friend and had asked him why the deal never went through. The friend, obviously embarrassed, told him that it was my fault, that I had been too greedy and had queered the deal by asking for a room and meals for myself and wife for the entire three-week engagement. Jack was livid with rage and wouldn't let me get a word in for minutes as he exploded on the phone. I tried to reason with him, reminding him that in all the times we had been to Las Vegas, I always had too much work in our office to spend the whole time there, that I had never spent a total of more than six days during any engagement, that it was ridiculous to think that a man would not go through with paying $150,000 for the three weeks because one person was "demanding" a few hundred dollars' worth of accommodations, that I didn't have to demand free rooms for myself because if I paid for them, I would be reimbursed by Jack anyway.

But Jack didn't want to hear my reasons because he preferred to accept his friend's answer for turning him down. He didn't want to face the fact that they simply had not wanted to meet his price. For the next few weeks he was very cold and distant to me, and we spoke only on urgent business. But awhile later, as he had done other times, when he phoned me, he was very warm and friendly and told me he had a great idea and wanted to have lunch. We met, and he suggested some trip or other, and once again we were friends.

We played Las Vegas many, many times after that, and I always included the complimentary rooms in the contract, my own, too, and never had any trouble with that clause, which is routine. However, whenever that sensitive subject came up, Jack would ask me not to ask for the rooms next time because he'd rather pay for them himself since they were deductible anyway.

Years later, when I had forgotten all about the incident, we lost out on some job for which I was negotiating, and when he learned about it, he said half in jest, "You probably screwed it up like you did that Las Vegas deal."

At the time he made that remark, we were in my office with a roomful of writers, and I didn't want to embarrass him by answering, so I let it pass. He must have realized I was annoyed because a few moments later he smiled and patted my arm in a conciliatory gesture.

As recently as the summer before he died, we had been discussing his playing a one-man show in a Broadway theater for six or eight weeks. This discussion had been going on for years, practically since the time he played the Ziegfeld Theater. His idea of a one-man show was to do the same show we had been doing around the country for years, featuring a girl singer and the little girl violinist. I was against it for many reasons, the main one being that six to eight weeks would be too rigorous for a man of eighty years, especially having to do the two and one half-hour show twice on Wednesdays and Saturdays. In addition, I didn't feel he would do capacity business, and by the time he paid the costs of the show and expenses of the two months in New York he would lose money on the deal.

That last August, 1975, we played an eight-day engagement at the Candlewood Theater in New Fairfield, Connecticut, the last theater engagement of his life. The summer theater had only 775 seats, and every night he did capacity business, and he loved the audiences and the atmosphere of the place. The idea of playing New York was revived, and I asked him why he was so anxious.

"I want to show off for all my friends in New York," he said.

"Well, let's book one night at Carnegie Hall, and you can show off for three thousand of your friends," was my answer. But he wanted the long theater engagement. I was vehemently opposed to it, and the more we discussed it, the angrier he became until finally I told him that if he wanted it that badly, I would book it and then work as hard as I could to make it a success and prove myself wrong.

Actually, he was really afraid to play New York, and yet my

300

opposing his desire for that last hurrah made him angry with me. It was on his mind constantly, and he remarked to a friend shortly after Candlewood that I had screwed up New York just as I once lost him a Las Vegas deal he wanted very much. When we returned home in the fall, he went to visit George Burns who was recuperating from a heart operation, and again he brought it up, commenting that I didn't think he had any talent and I didn't have enough confidence in him to let him play a theater in New York.

Deep down, Jack never doubted that even though I may not have been infallible in every decision I made for him, my every motive was for the good of his career. Three weeks later, when George Burns asked me to represent him but only if Jack would wholeheartedly approve, Jack phoned George immediately to tell him that I was the "greatest."

A month before he died, almost as if he had a premonition of things to come, he phoned me one day while I was busy at the office. For no apparent reason, he blurted: "Irving, you know I say a lot of things I don't really mean, and I want you to know I really do love you."

51

AFTER not having starred in a motion picture in twenty-eight years, one of the two leading roles in Neil Simon's *The Sunshine Boys,* the hit play that Ray Stark was producing for MGM, was won by Jack. He was in his eightieth year when he tested for the role, and he was perfect for the part of the old vaudevillian. At one point in the test, Herb Ross, the director, asked him to do a line and then move quickly to the other side of the stage. Jack moved so fast that Ross stopped the "take" and told Jack he was too speedy.

"Remember, you're supposed to be seventy years old," cautioned Ross.

When he realized he was talking to an octogenarian, Ross, Jack, and the whole crew burst into laughter.

Jack's costar in the film was fifty-two-year old Walter Matthau, and when Jack went out to watch him do makeup tests for the role of his elderly vaudeville partner, Matthau worried whether the makeup man would be able to age him properly.

"Don't worry," said Jack seriously, "they'll make us look old enough."

Jack had a successful and what should have been a pleasant summer in the eightieth year of his life. In addition to the engagement at Candlewood Theater in Connecticut, he played four sold-out performances at the Spokane Expo, a few days at the Broadmoor Theater in Colorado Springs, and three pop symphony concerts. Arthur Fiedler conducted the Detroit Symphony for him, and he played with the Filene Symphony at Wolf Trap, near Washington, D.C., and with the Pittsburgh Symphony at Temple University in Philadelphia. But by September he was more moody than ever. In addition to having no appetite, he was complaining of stomach pains and was sure he had an ulcer or something more serious.

But in early September he was cheerful for a few days when we flew to New Orleans, where he was to play his violin with the New Orleans Symphony. In addition to the fun of playing his fiddle, he was being paid a very good fee as it was a promotion by the Maison Blanche Department Store, which presented a style show at the concert. Robert Sonfield, president of the store, took us in tow for the four days we were in New Orleans and was a wonderful host. But the bright spot of the trip for Jack was a surprise visit by his good friends golf pro Doug Saunders and his wife, Scotty. They flew to New Orleans for the concert and were house guests of Nancy and Jimmy Brennan, owners of the famous Brennan's restaurant. Scotty and Nancy, two young, attractive women, adored Jack and he was thrilled having such lovely admirers give him all that attention. He suddenly looked ten years younger, forgot about his stomach pains, and seemed like his old self again for the few days we were all together. He had such a good time that when Doug Saunders invited him to house-guest with them in Houston, Texas, in November and play in a golf tournament he was having, Jack was delighted to accept.

When we returned home, the doctor gave him every con-

302

ceivable test over a three-week period, and he ended up with a clean bill of health. We all were convinced that the pains must be psychosomatic. We pointed out to him that he should be walking on air because he was set to star in a major motion picture, was signed to star in his own special television program on NBC, was signed to play three weeks as star of the Tropicana Hotel in Las Vegas and, in addition, was lined up for forthcoming guest appearances on other television programs and could do as many symphony concerts in the next year as he had time and energy to do.

Despite the favorable results of the checkup, he complained constantly about the stomach pains, and his visits to the doctor became a daily routine. Most of us close to him became convinced that the pains were a result of getting more nervous every day about our forthcoming TV special, as well as his appearance in *The Sunshine Boys.* For many years Jack had been using cue cards for all his television appearances, and he was worried about his ability to memorize the script for the motion picture.

We signed Al Gordon, Hal Goldman, Hilliard Marks, and Hugh Wedlock as writers for the special and met with Jack to talk about the show. We all threw ideas at him and rather than try an offbeat show, we settled on a simple one that Jack had been wanting to do. In this way, I thought, we would take all the pressure off him. The title was to be *Jack Benny's Special Special,* and we were finally going to have Jack do part of his symphony concert on television as he had refined it over eighteen years. I signed Jack's friend Zubin Mehta, conductor of the Los Angeles Philharmonic, to appear in that capacity on the show, and Zubin started to line up many of his musicians for the program. Also, following the tradition of using Mr. and Mrs. Ronald Colman and then Mr. and Mrs. Jimmy Stewart, we were able to persuade Gregory Peck and his wife to appear on this program, Veronique Peck to make her acting debut. For popular music, we had Engelbert Humperdinck flying over from England. A very good show. We started to work on the script with Jack a few days before he had to go off to Dallas where he was scheduled to work at a Nieman-Marcus promotion dinner and then vacation in Houston with the Doug Saunders'.

Since I was working with the writers and on the production problems of the show, I didn't accompany him, one of the few times in years I wasn't along. Instead, Eddie Villery traveled with him, and Phil Consolo, the man who had booked the dinner, was there to pick them up at the airport the evening before the scheduled dinner. Jack rehearsed with the orchestra on the afternoon of the dinner, October 19, and Consolo phoned to tell me how well the rehearsal went and about the nice walk they had after it.

Just before the performance that evening, Jack picked up his violin to warm up and found, to his consternation, that his right hand was numb and he couldn't hold the bow. Frightened, Phil and Eddie called two doctors from the audience, who immediately diagnosed it as a stroke and ordered him to the hospital. Jack insisted that he was all right except for his right hand and he could do the show without playing the fiddle. But they looked aghast at this suggestion, especially coming from an eighty-year-old man.

The hospital in Dallas put Jack through a series of tests and after conferring with Jack's Beverly Hills doctor, Rex Kennamer, they allowed him to fly to Los Angeles the next morning, but only on condition that he go in a private hospital plane with a male nurse in attendance and be met at the Burbank airport by an ambulance to take him directly to Cedars of Lebanon Hospital.

When they arrived in Burbank and the ambulance attendants tried to put him in a stretcher, Jack objected vigorously, raising hell about having the ambulance there at all. Not only did he object, but he completely amazed the group by insisting he was hungry, and he hosted the two pilots, the male nurse, the two ambulance drivers and Eddie Villery for coffee and doughnuts at the airport coffee shop. Then he refused to lie down in the ambulance and instead rode in the front seat reading the Sunday papers all the way to the hospital.

Jack remained in the hospital for four days while they repeated all the tests they had made only the previous month. Meanwhile, the strength was coming back to his hand, and the tests were negative. Dr. Kennamer felt that he had had the slightest possible stroke that only affected his hand, and it would be completely normal in a week or two, which it was. When he left the hospital, the press was waiting for him, and

Jack humorously blamed his hospital visit on the stomach pain.

"The doctors couldn't find anything wrong with me except that I have a slight stomach pain," he announced. "Wait till I get my hospital bill! Then I'll really have a pain in the stomach!"

Jack came home on October 24, and the next day I went over to his house to visit and discuss what to do about our schedule of forthcoming appearances. The first order of business was the three-week engagement at the Tropicana Hotel in Las Vegas, which was to start November 8. Through a series of fortunate circumstances, I was able to make a deal for him to do only one show a night and two on weekends at a salary of $55,000 a week. Jack wasn't certain he'd be able to play the fiddle by opening night, but he had been wanting to do a show without playing the violin, and here was his opportunity. I told him to think about it for a few days, but when I could see he was reluctant, I canceled the date, trying to relieve him of all mental and physical pressures.

During the last five years of his life, as he would tense up before performances and regret having allowed me to book them, I had often suggested he retire, but he always resisted that idea, claiming that he didn't have enough money to quit working—and besides, what would he do with himself? He had no other interest than show business. As he got older and each engagement became more difficult, I would mention retirement more often, and he would say that someday he'd like to do nothing besides play with symphony orchestras. When we agreed to cancel the Tropicana, I felt that now should be that time to complete our commitments and then announce his retirement except for doing the symphony concerts he so dearly loved. He was delighted with this plan.

He was in good spirits for the first week he was out of the hospital, and then the stomach discomfort returned. This time it was more severe. His daily visits to the doctor brought a barrage of pills to ease the pains, but nothing seemed to help except for short periods. He would usually leave our meetings after a few minutes. However, he was able to take a lesson now and then from Gloria Chappel, his violin teacher of many years, and when he played the fiddle, he never seemed to be bothered by his stomach.

He began to come to the office less frequently until finally he stopped coming entirely, staying in bed until early afternoon and getting up only to go to the doctor or to Gloria's house for a violin lesson. I urged him to see a psychiatrist, and so did his doctors, but Jack resisted the idea. Since the tests showed nothing wrong, there was a possibility the pain was emotional, we explained to him, and he had nothing to lose by seeing a psychiatrist a few times in the hope that it might help. He would agree, but he never could bring himself to do it.

On November 17, he was to be inducted into the "Hall of Fame" at the convention of the Television Advertising Bureau at the Century Plaza Hotel in Los Angeles. When I picked him up, his stomach was bothering him, and during the cocktail hour at the hotel he told everyone about the pains and his lack of appetite. But at the dinner when he was handed his plaque, his prepared two-minute acceptance speech stretched to twenty minutes after the standing ovation and the enthusiastic response to his first line.

On the way home he seemed to have forgotten his ills as he rehashed his speech and dissected each joke. He even wanted to stop someplace for ice cream. The next morning he phoned very early to talk about the night before, and he was jubilant. But again, a few days later, the pain returned, and the doctors and the rest of us were helpless as he seemed to deteriorate before our eyes. I went ahead reluctantly with the completion of the television show without him, which was the first time I had ever done that. He couldn't get interested in anything that was happening. I went to Zubin Mehta's house to go over the music problems with him, a chore that Jack ordinarily would have loved. Later he didn't even ask what decisions we had made. Dr. Kennamer insisted that Jack would be well enough to tape our special in early January, and so I proceeded with the plans as well as I could. I lined up a photographic sitting at NBC for Mr. and Mrs. Gregory Peck and Jack, but he was unable to make it, and we did the pictures of the Pecks against photo blowups of Jack.

By then he was taking a great amount of sedatives and tranquilizers and was sleeping most of the day as we patiently waited for him to get over the persistent pain. I canceled one appearance after another, first the Santa Barbara Symphony

306

and then a guest date for the Smothers Brothers show, but he insisted that he had to accept the Louella Parsons Award from the Hollywood Women's Press Club. This was scheduled to be given to him for contributing most to the dignity and image of the entertainment industry. It was to be awarded at a luncheon at the Beverly Hills Hotel on Sunday, December 8.

The Friday before the luncheon I didn't think he was in good enough condition to speak in public, and I arranged for George Burns to stand by for just such an emergency. Jack, however, was adamant. He insisted that he had to attend since it was the first time he had been selected for that award.

"After all the news stories about my illness in Dallas, if I don't go to that luncheon with all the newspaper reporters, it'll be all over the papers again, and it will look awful."

On Saturday, December 7, after working with the writers to complete the script for our TV show, I went to Jack's home to tell him how well the show had shaped up. I found him in the best spirits he had been in weeks. He had felt better that morning, called Ned Miller, and the two went to Hillcrest for lunch and then took a long walk. I reported the news about the script, and he was delighted. We agreed to meet the following Tuesday with the writers to complete the final polish. I also reminded him that I'd pick him up at eleven thirty the next morning as we had to be at the luncheon by noon.

The next day when I arrived, he was dressed and shaved but doubled up in pain. I pleaded with him to lie down and let me call George Burns to go in his place, but he refused, straightening up and forcing himself to walk down to my car. He barely spoke on the drive to the Beverly Hills Hotel. While waiting for the luncheon to start, the photographers tried to take pictures, but he had a scowl on his face and no matter how much I encouraged him to smile, it was simply too much effort. Finally, he turned to me and whispered, "I can't make it. Please take me home and call George Burns."

My wife and I supported Jack as we walked him out to the car. His comments were few on the way home, but one I remember was: "You know, Irving, I'll bet I won't be able to make *The Sunshine Boys.*"

307

When I got him home, Mary rushed to the phone and called the doctor, and when I returned later that afternoon with the beautiful award that George had accepted in his behalf, he was sedated and asleep.

After that day the doctor ordered nurses for him around the clock, and he was sedated most of the time. I knew he would never be able to perform in the TV show, and I didn't want to hire an art director or have the sets built. I didn't book the musicians or start casting the smaller roles in the show either. But Mary insisted that the doctor said he'd be all right by taping day. And still I waited, gambling that I could always rush the sets through in time for the show. Jack had not yet seen the script, and on Wednesday morning, December 18, Mary phoned to tell me that Jack wanted me to come to the house that afternoon with the writers to go over the script. At the last minute the only writer I could find was Hugh Wedlock and the two of us went over to see Jack.

He looked fairly well, told a joke or two and was obviously delighted to see us. I didn't realize it at the time, but he had just been given a shot to relax him. But when we started to read the script, I knew immediately it would never work. It was probably the medication, but his eyes didn't seem to focus properly, and he couldn't concentrate, skipping words and sentences as he tried to read his opening monologue. He kept starting from the first line, and trying again and after a half hour, he hadn't gone four lines. As diplomatically as we could, we told him that the medication was affecting his eyes and we'd better wait for the next day to go over it, and he agreed. We put him to bed, and when Mary returned, I told her I was convinced he wouldn't be able to do the show and suggested canceling it, and she finally consented.

Two days later the doctor had another test made of the pancreas.

The next morning Mary called and asked me to come over. She told me the terrible news: Jack had terminal cancer of the pancreas, and the doctors predicted he only had from two weeks to a month to live. It seems that this is called the "hidden" cancer and often remains undetected in the various tests. Patients have sometimes died, supposedly suffering from something else, until the autopsy reveals this insidious disease.

We all were in a state of shock. Twenty-eight years of my life with him flashed before me as I thought of all the happy days we had shared, and suddenly I felt sad that our few unimportant disagreements might have caused him even a moment's displeasure. I thought of this sweet, simple man who was so beloved by all whose lives he touched. I couldn't believe I would never hear that wonderful infectious roaring laugh again or see him pound the table or his thigh as he was wont to do when something tickled him—which it often did. The world was losing someone special . . . and so was I.

I couldn't discuss it with anyone except my wife as Mary and I agreed that it must be kept quiet until the last possible moment so that he could never learn the truth.

On Christmas morning I received the phone call I had been dreading. Mary and the doctor told me that he might die that night and I should make the funeral arrangements, pick a casket and the sarcophagus. I didn't want to take the entire responsibility myself, so Don Rosenfeld, our lawyer, accompanied me on that unhappy mission. Together we spent Christmas Day at the cemetery, going over arrangements with the funeral directors, and I was determined that after the hundreds of shows I had put on for Jack, this last and most important one would go smoothly. Our last chore was selecting the sarcophagus, and we found one on the first floor of the building. I asked if that was the best they had, and the mortuary director said it was the best on the first floor, but there was a better one on the second floor.

"I think Jack would want to be in the orchestra," Don said. "I can't picture him in the balcony."

The next morning Jack was still holding on, but Dr. Kennamer said he couldn't possibly last past that day, and I told Mary we had better announce it to the world as it would be too shocking to break the news of his death without a warning. She agreed.

A few minutes after I called the wire services, the news exploded, and within the hour I began receiving calls from all over the world. I couldn't help thinking how pleased Jack would have been to know how many calls I got from the London papers and even from Australia.

That afternoon, with the news on radio and television, the friends began to arrive at the Benny home. Scores of stars, producers, and directors came by to express their grief, say good-bye, and tell their funny, sentimental stories about the man we all loved.

At 11:26 P.M. on December 26, 1974, Jack Benny passed away quietly.

Jack's opening words on radio on the Ed Sullivan program were:

"This is Jack Benny. There will be a slight pause while everyone says, 'Who cares?'"

When he died forty-three years later, millions cared . . . and cried.

INDEX

311

312

313

315

316

Ustinov, Peter, 273

Valente, Caterina, 184
Vallance, Julia, 83, 166
Van Heusen, Jimmy, 293
Variety (magazine), 29, 39, 228
Victorson, Dave, 264–65
Vidor, Charles, 83
Vigram, Herb, 184
Villery, Eddie, 289, 304

Wabash Avenue (movie), 119
Wallenstein, Alfred, 246, 250–51
Warner, Jack L., 88, 152, 191
Warwick, Dionne, 261
Wasserman, Lew, 221
Wayne, John, 261
Wayne and Schuster, 195
Webb, Clifton, 86
Webb, Jack, 262
Wedlock, Hugh, 66–67, 149, 192, 269, 287, 290, 303, 308
Weems, Ted, 62
Weiss, Sammy, 203
Welk, Lawrence, 259
Welles, Orson, 98
What's My Line? (TV show), 30
White, Ed, 267–68

White, Dr. Paul Dudley, 281
Whittaker, L. E., 160
Whittaker, Nancy, 159–60
Wilde, Arthur, 122
Wilder, Audrey, 293
Wilder, Billy, 17, 87, 95, 292
Wilkie, Wendell, 91
Will Mastin Trio, 194
Wilson, Desmond, 154
Wilson, Don, 16, 65, 75, 79, 110, 112, 122, 129, 145, 222, 259, 260
Wilson, Earl, 279
Wilson, Flip, 261
Winchell, Walter, 279
Wolf, Dave, 30–31
Wolf, Nat, 106
Wood, Gene, 198
Woods, Lyman, 28–30
Wright, Lloyd, 102
Wyman, Jane, 41, 83, 98
Wynn, Ed, 182, 230, 282–83

Yacht Club Boys, 90
Yorkin, Bud, 262
You Bet Your Life (TV show), 143

Zanuck, Darryl, 86
Zukor, Adolph, 290

319